How Organizations Manage the Future

Hannes Krämer • Matthias Wenzel
Editors

How Organizations Manage the Future

Theoretical Perspectives and Empirical Insights

Editors
Hannes Krämer
University of Duisburg-Essen
Essen, Germany

Matthias Wenzel
European University Viadrina
Frankfurt (Oder), Germany

ISBN 978-3-319-74505-3   ISBN 978-3-319-74506-0   (eBook)
https://doi.org/10.1007/978-3-319-74506-0

Library of Congress Control Number: 2018935258

© The Editor(s) (if applicable) and The Author(s) 2018
This work is subject to copyright. All rights are solely and exclusively licensed by the Publisher, whether the whole or part of the material is concerned, specifically the rights of translation, reprinting, reuse of illustrations, recitation, broadcasting, reproduction on microfilms or in any other physical way, and transmission or information storage and retrieval, electronic adaptation, computer software, or by similar or dissimilar methodology now known or hereafter developed.
The use of general descriptive names, registered names, trademarks, service marks, etc. in this publication does not imply, even in the absence of a specific statement, that such names are exempt from the relevant protective laws and regulations and therefore free for general use.
The publisher, the authors and the editors are safe to assume that the advice and information in this book are believed to be true and accurate at the date of publication. Neither the publisher nor the authors or the editors give a warranty, express or implied, with respect to the material contained herein or for any errors or omissions that may have been made. The publisher remains neutral with regard to jurisdictional claims in published maps and institutional affiliations.

Printed on acid-free paper

This Palgrave Macmillan imprint is published by the registered company Springer International Publishing AG part of Springer Nature.
The registered company address is: Gewerbestrasse 11, 6330 Cham, Switzerland

Acknowledgements

We gratefully acknowledge the intellectual support by Jochen Koch and Andreas Reckwitz as important parts of our research project on "Temporal Borders of the Present: On the Contemporary Praxis of Handling the Future" (generously funded by the Viadrina Center B/ORDERS IN MOTION), which provided us with the motivation for this edited collection. Furthermore, we thank Paula Parish for her invaluable and much-appreciated language-editing service, and we are grateful to Liz Barlow and Lucy Kidwell from Palgrave Macmillan for their support throughout the publishing process. Importantly, we are indebted to all scholars who have contributed to this edited collection, as this anthology would not exist without their thoughtful chapters and their constructive feedback.

Contents

1 Introduction: Managing the Future—Foundations
and Perspectives 1
Matthias Wenzel and Hannes Krämer

Part I Philosophical Perspectives 23

2 From Defuturization to Futurization and Back Again?
A System-Theoretical Perspective to Analyse
Decision-Making 25
Victoria von Groddeck

3 What's New? Temporality in Practice Theory
and Pragmatism 45
Anders Buch and Iben Sandal Stjerne

4 Creativity in/of Organizations for Managing Things
to Come: Lessons to Be Learnt from Philosophy 67
Günther Ortmann and Jörg Sydow

5 Organizational Futurity: Being and Knowing
in the Engagement with What Is Yet to Come 89
Seelan Naidoo

Part II Theoretical and Methodological Perspectives 111

6 Open(ing up) for the Future: Practising Open Strategy
and Open Innovation to Cope with Uncertainty 113
Maximilian Heimstädt and Georg Reischauer

7 Antenarratives in Ongoing Strategic Change: Using
the Story Index to Capture Daunting and Optimistic
Futures 133
*Tommi P. Auvinen, Pasi Sajasalo, Teppo Sintonen, Tuomo
Takala, and Marko Järvenpää*

8 What Scenarios Are You Missing? Poststructuralism
for Deconstructing and Reconstructing Organizational
Futures 153
*Ricarda Scheele, Norman M. Kearney, Jude H. Kurniawan,
and Vanessa J. Schweizer*

9 Historical Methods and the Study of How Organizations
Manage the Future 173
Yves Plourde

Part III Empirical Insights 191

10 In the Wake of Disaster: Resilient Organizing
and a New Path for the Future 193
A. Erin Bass and Ivana Milosevic

11 The Darkened Horizon: Two Modes of Organizing
Pandemics 215
Matthias Leanza

12	**Managing the Digital Transformation: Preparing Cities for the Future** *Markus Kowalski, Anja Danner-Schröder, and Gordon Müller-Seitz*	231
13	**Creating Collective Futures: How Roadmaps and Conferences Reconfigure the Institutional Field of Semiconductor Manufacturing** *Uli Meyer, Cornelius Schubert, and Arnold Windeler*	253
14	**Organizational Artifacts as Pre-presentations of Things to Come: The Case of Menu Development in Haute Cuisine** *Jochen Koch, Ninja Natalie Senf, and Wasko Rothmann*	277
15	**Solid Futures: Office Architecture and the Labour Imaginary** *David Adler*	299

Index 321

Notes on Contributors

David Adler is a research fellow in sociology at the graduate school "Self-Making: Practices of Subjectivation" at the Carl von Ossietzky University of Oldenburg, Germany, and Lecturer for Theories of Socialization at the Institute of Education Sciences at the Ruhr University Bochum, Germany. His fields of research include sociology of architecture, economic sociology, political sociology and qualitative research methods. He is the author of *Doppelte Hegemonie: Hegemonialisierung im War on Terror-Diskurs nach der Tötung bin Ladens*, Baden-Baden, 2015. He is working on a new book project on the programme and performativity of contemporary office architecture.

Tommi P. Auvinen is Lecturer in Management and Leadership at the Jyväskylä University School of Business and Economics, Finland, and Docent in Narrative Leadership Research at the University of Lapland. His teaching focuses on leadership and human resource management, and research on such leadership themes as storytelling and discursive power. Auvinen has written articles in national and international journals—including *Journal of Management Learning*, *Accounting and Business Research* and *Journal of Business Ethics*—and book chapters that are published by such esteemed institutions as Routledge and Springer.

Erin Bass is Associate Professor of Management at the University of Nebraska Omaha, USA. Her research centres on strategy, entrepreneurship and ethics. She is mainly interested in the intersection between business and society, investigating how firms acquire and develop resources and how this impacts the environments in which they operate

Anders Buch is a professor at Aalborg University Copenhagen, Denmark, at the Department for Learning and Philosophy. His empirical research area is focused on technological expert cultures, and his theoretical approach is primarily inspired by *Science & Technology Studies, Practice Theory and Pragmatism*. He has written articles and books on knowledge, learning, education, professionalism and the professional development of engineers. Since 2016 he has served as chief editor of *Nordic Journal for Working Life Studies*. Presently he is preparing an edited volume with Theodore Schatzki for Routledge: *Question of Practice in Philosophy and the Social Sciences*.

Anja Danner-Schröder is Assistant Professor (Junior Professor) in Management Studies at the Department of Business Studies and Economics at Technische Universität Kaiserslautern, Germany. Her research interests include organizational routines, high-reliability organizations, time and temporal dimensions, and the digital transformation, with a particular emphasis on practical–theoretical approaches and qualitative research methods.

Maximilian Heimstädt is a post-doctoral researcher at the Reinhard Mohn Institute of Management at Witten/Herdecke University, Germany. In his research he explores the genesis and effects of openness as an organizing principle.

Marko Järvenpää is Professor of Accounting at the University of Vaasa, Finland. He studies management accounting, like management accountants' role transformation, performance measurement, strategy and management accounting change, and sustainability and accounting, typically by conducting qualitative case and field studies, and employs interpretative theories like institutional, stakeholder and cultural theories.

Norman M. Kearney is a PhD candidate in the School of Environment, Resources and Sustainability at the University of Waterloo, Canada. Using participatory methods to integrate knowledge from multiple disciplines and perspectives, his doctoral research involves constructing scenarios for a safe and just space for humanity, which can be used not only as guides for policymakers but also as tests on the validity of dominant discourses of sustainable development. His MA in Political Economy is from Carleton University, and his BA in Philosophy and Political Science is from McMaster University.

Jochen Koch is Chaired Professor of Management and Organization and Director of the Centre for Entrepreneurship Research at the European University Viadrina in Frankfurt (Oder), Germany. His research interests include organizational creativity, organizational routines and practices, and the theory of strategic and organizational path dependence. He is the co-editor of the leading German journal *Managementforschung* (MF) and has written several books and articles in journals such as the *Academy of Management Review*, *Organization Studies* and *Strategic Management Journal*.

Markus Kowalski is a research associate and a doctoral candidate at the Chair of Strategy, Innovation and Cooperation at the Department of Business Studies and Economics, Technische Universität Kaiserslautern, Germany. His current research, teaching and consulting focus on innovation management, interorganizational networks, interfaces in innovation processes (especially open innovation), business model innovation and the digital transformation.

Hannes Krämer is professor of Communication Studies at the University of Duisburg-Essen. His research interests comprise the field of future research, practice theory, organizational sociology, social and cultural theory, border theory and boundary research. He has written a book on "The Practice of Creativity" (transcript), edited a special issue on the topic of "Mobility" (ÖZS) and several articles on methodological, social–theoretical and other questions.

Jude H. Kurniawan is a PhD candidate in the Department of Geography and Environmental Management at the University of Waterloo, Canada. For his doctoral research, Kurniawan seeks to advance methodological approaches for better anticipating hard-to-foresee scenarios for complex social systems. He contributed to scenario projects including the "Future of Urban Transport" for Singapore University of Technology and Design, "Future of Work/Technology 2050" for the Millennium Project, and he is currently working on "Canada's Low-carbon Energy Futures" for the Energy Council of Canada. Kurniawan received his Bachelor of Science degree from Northeastern University and Masters of Climate Change from the University of Waterloo.

Matthias Leanza is a lecturer (Oberassistent) in the Department of Sociology at the University of Basel, Switzerland. He has received his Diploma in Sociology from the University of Bielefeld in 2008, and holds a PhD from the University of Freiburg (2016). His book *Die Zeit der Prävention: Eine Genealogie*, published in 2017, deals with the history and present of disease prevention in Germany (and beyond).

Uli Meyer is the head of the Post-Doc Lab Reorganizing Industries at the Technische Universität (TU) München, Germany. He studied sociology, economics and computer science at the Technical University Berlin, with a dissertation (sociology) on innovation paths. Meyer was a research assistant at the

Wissenschaftszentrum Berlin für Sozialforschung (WZB) as well as the Department for Sociology at TU Berlin, where he also pursued his post-doc from 2014 to 2015. He was a visiting fellow at Stanford University, USA, as well as the University of Bologna, Italy. His research interests include organization studies, innovation studies, the impact of sociotechnical visions and the interplay between science and economy.

Ivana Milosevic is Assistant Professor of Management at the College of Charleston, USA. Her research interests include identity theory and exploration of leadership and learning processes in complex organizations. She is particularly interested in ethnographic research, with a focus on how structures enable or restrict practices.

Gordon Müller-Seitz is Chair of Strategy, Innovation and Cooperation at the Department of Business Studies and Economics at Technische Universität Kaiserslautern, Germany. His research, teaching and consulting focus on innovation management, interorganizational networks and projects, dealing with risks and uncertainties and the digital transformation. His work has been applied within multinational corporations as well as small and medium-sized enterprises and has appeared in renowned research journals and practitioner outlets.

Seelan Naidoo is a doctoral student at the University of St. Gallen (HSG), Switzerland, where he is attached to the Philosophy Department. His research interest lies at the intersection of organization studies and philosophy from which he approaches questionings of organization, organizing and the organized especially in regard to the temporality of these phenomena. He is a latecomer to academia having done time in practice as a strategist, as an executive and as a management consultant in the private, non-profit and public sectors.

Günther Ortmann was Professor of Business Administration at Helmut-Schmidt-Universität Hamburg, Germany, and is now Research Professor of Leadership at Universität Witten/Herdecke, Germany. His research areas are organization theory, in particular "organization and deconstruction" and "rules and rule following", strategic management, decision theory and management in hypermodern times. He is the co-editor of a forthcoming-themed section of *Organization Studies* on "The novel and organization studies". For more information, visit https://www.uni-wh.de/detailseiten/kontakte/guenther-ortmann-2278/f0/nc/

Yves Plourde is Assistant Professor of Strategy and International Business at HEC Montréal, Canada. His research interests lie at the intersection between international business, strategic management and organization studies. He is particularly interested in how organizations leverage their scope to achieve a global impact. He received his PhD in General Management from the Ivey Business School, Western University. His dissertation explored how Greenpeace became more effective at engaging with the future.

Georg Reischauer is a senior research associate in the Strategy and Innovation Department at WU Vienna University of Economics and Business, Austria.

Wasko Rothmann is a research fellow at the European University Viadrina, Germany. His research interests include strategic path dependence and disruptive innovation.

Pasi Sajasalo is Lecturer in Management and Leadership at the Jyväskylä University School of Business and Economics, Finland. His teaching and research interests focus on various aspects of strategy in differing contexts, such as forest industry, engineering industry, media industry and financial sector. More recently, he has focused on strategy-as-practice inspired work, including cognitive aspects of strategy, such as strategy-related sensemaking and sensegiving, in addition to networked strategy-making. His work appears in national and international journals as well as in book chapters of volumes published by national and international publishers.

Ricarda Scheele is a PhD candidate and research associate at the Center for Interdisciplinary Risk and Innovation Studies (ZIRIUS), University of Stuttgart, Germany. Her research revolves around the tensions between current quests for futures knowledge and scenarios in the context of energy and sustainability transitions and the contemporary methodological implementations of scenarios. Scheele's dissertation follows energy scenarios along their life paths—from development to their potential effects—and explores the role of plausibility as criterion for the value of scenarios in society. She is continuously interested in new methodological forms of societal engagement with sustainable futures.

Cornelius Schubert is Lecturer for Innovation Studies at the University of Siegen, Germany. He specializes in science and technology studies as well as medical and organizational sociology. He has conducted ethnographic research on human–technology interactions in surgical operations, focusing on coordination, distributed agency and improvisation in high-tech settings. He furthermore studied global innovation networks in the semiconductor industry, looking at the simultaneous creation of organizational fields and technological paths. He is a Principal Investigator (PI) in the Project "Visually Integrated Clinical Cooperation" within the Collaborative Research Centre "Media of Cooperation".

Vanessa J. Schweizer is an assistant professor in the Department of Knowledge Integration at the University of Waterloo, Canada. Her research interests include decision-making under uncertainty and the resilience of complex systems. Her scenario work centres on difficult-to-imagine futures (so-called black swan events and perfect storms). Research topics include socio-economic scenarios in the context of climate change; transition scenarios, or pathways, to sustainable development; and constellations of beliefs underlying ideologies. Her PhD is in Engineering and Public Policy from Carnegie Mellon University, and her Masters in Environmental Studies is from The Evergreen State College.

N. Natalie Senf is a research fellow at the European University Viadrina, Germany. Her research interests include aspiration levels, ambiguous feedback and creativity in haute-cuisine restaurants.

Teppo Sintonen is Lecturer of Management and Leadership at the Jyväskylä University School of Business and Economics, Finland. His research focuses on organizational change, identity, strategy and creativity, and he has specialized on narrative research methods. He has written in national and international volumes, including *Journal of Business Ethics*, *Management Learning*, *Qualitative Research* and *Journal for Critical Organization Inquiry*.

Iben S. Stjerne is a Post-doctoral fellow at the Copenhagen Business School at the Department of Strategic Management and Globalization. Her primary research focus is on the intersection between temporal–permanent organizing, practice theory and human resource management. Her research publications explore how work and employment are organized informally across firms, departments and projects. Empirically this has been investigated in primarily creative industries and more recently also in more traditional production firms with an emphasis on the interorganizational supplier–buyer relationships.

Jörg Sydow is Professor of Management at the School of Business & Economics at Freie Universität Berlin, Germany, where he is also the spokesperson of the Research Unit "Organized Creativity", sponsored by the German Research Foundation (DFG). He has served on the editorial review boards of *Organization Science*, *Organization Studies*, *Academy of Management Journal*, *Academy of Management Review*, *Journal of Management Studies* and *The Scandinavian Journal of Management*. For more information, visit http://www.wiwiss.fu-berlin.de/en/fachbereich/bwl/management/sydow/index.html.

Tuomo Takala PhD (business economics), 1991; PhD (philosophy), 2012; PhD (sociology), 2013, is Professor of Management and Leadership at the University of Jyväskylä School of Business and Economics, Finland. He has executed several administrative duties, for example, Vice Dean and Dean of the faculty. He is the editor-in-chief of EJBO (*Electronic Journal of Business Ethics and Organizational Studies*). He has conducted research on several areas including business ethics, qualitative research, responsible management, leadership studies and charisma studies. He has written numerous articles, for example, in the *Journal of Business Ethics*.

Victoria von Groddeck is a researcher at the Institute for Sociology, the Ludwig-Maximilian University of Munich, Germany. Her research focus is on organizational sociology and social theory. In her empirical research projects, she explores historic shifts in the interrelations of societal and organizational structures.

Matthias Wenzel is a post-doctoral researcher at the Chair of Management and Organization at the European University Viadrina, Germany. His research interests include strategy as practice, demand-side research in management and video methods. He has written articles in journals such as *Business Research, European Journal of Information Systems, Journal of Accounting and Organizational Change, Journal of Business Research, Long Range Planning, Organization Studies* and *Strategic Management Journal*.

Arnold Windeler is Professor of Sociology of Organizations at Technische Universität Berlin, Germany, and is a speaker of the Graduate School *Innovation Society Today: The Reflexive Creation of Novelty*, sponsored by the German Research Foundation (DFG). His research interests lie with social, organization and network theory. He has written on organizations and interfirm networks as well as on competences, and on reflexive innovation. For further information, see http://www.soz.tu-berlin.de/windeler

List of Figures

Fig. 7.1	Research setting	139
Fig. 7.2	The Story Index method	141
Fig. 8.1	A perspective for organizational researchers and practitioners examining how methodological choices shape the scenarios an organization accepts as plausible	155
Fig. 8.2	A cross-impact matrix with impact balance calculations for the Special Report on Emissions Scenarios commissioned by the Intergovernmental Panel on Climate Change. Highlighted rows specify a 'given scenario' being inspected for internal consistency. (Source: Adapted from Schweizer and Kriegler 2012)	164
Fig. 10.1	Data collection and analysis process	198
Fig. 10.2	Resilient organizing post-disaster to pursue a new future	203
Fig. 12.1	Three phases of an innovation network to manage the challenges of the future	244
Fig. 14.1	Organizational artifacts in time	282
Fig. 14.2	Data sources in relation to menu evolution	285
Fig. 14.3	Artifact dimensions	289
Fig. 14.4	Artifact dimensions and functions: potentiality and actualization	294
Fig. 15.1	Passage de l'Opéra, Paris. (Photography by Charles Marville, ca. 1866)	304

Fig. 15.2   Has the 'mothership' landed? The new Apple headquarters in Cupertino is constantly compared to a spaceship   308

Fig. 15.3   Artrium and meeting points. The Unilever headquarters for Germany, Austria and Switzerland in Hamburg by Behnisch Architekten   314

List of Tables

Table 6.1	Future-oriented practices based on openness	125
Table 10.1	Data sources	197
Table 10.2	Aggregate themes and evidence of resilient organizing and a new path for the future	200
Table 12.1	Data basis of the research study	236
Table 14.1	Data	287

1

Introduction: Managing the Future—Foundations and Perspectives

Matthias Wenzel and Hannes Krämer

Introduction

The question of how to manage the future is an inherent part of organizing. As Luhmann (2000) suggests, organizations of any kind in all areas of commercial, federal and daily life—from large corporations to public administrations to sports clubs—can be considered as structural responses to the question of how to cope with and handle the future, that is, the period that lies ahead. In turn, as Beckert (2016) highlights, these very responses drive contemporary actions and thereby trigger organizational, market and societal developments, thus pointing to a tight interplay of future and organizing. Hence, the author clarifies that 'the future matters' (p. 58).

Yet, managing the future is more than just a universal feature of organizing: in contemporary society, the temporal mode of the future is becoming more and more prevalent. Since the beginning of the post-modern period,

M. Wenzel (✉)
European University Viadrina, Frankfurt (Oder), Germany

H. Krämer
Universität Duisburg-Essen, Essen, Germany

with its observed increase in uncertainties, the future has become a problem for different social actors (Reckwitz 2016; Rosa 2005, 2016), especially for organizations (Koch et al. 2016): the post-modern insight that the future is *unknowable* has pointed out the general fallibility of controlling the future through planning techniques (Barry and Elmes 1997; March 1995; Mintzberg 1994). This, we argue, turns the processes and practices through which organizations manage the future into an interesting and relevant contemporary phenomenon that deserves more focused research attention: if conventional planning has lost its omnipotent status as the predominant mode of anticipating and enacting things to come, which alternative ways of managing the future do organizations enact, and how do they do so? As responses to these questions are under-represented in organizational literature, the aim of this short chapter—and this edited collection more broadly—is to foster a research agenda that focuses more thoroughly on how organizations manage the future.

Looking Back, but Not Forward?

Despite the relevance of managing the future, most studies that take the role of time in processes of organizing seriously focus on the temporal mode of the *past* (for comprehensive overviews see Kipping and Üsdiken 2014; Godfrey et al. 2016; Suddaby and Foster 2017; see also Plourde this volume). These studies highlight the argument that 'history matters' by pointing to the enabling and constraining character of organizational legacies. Most notably, theories and concepts like path dependence (Sydow et al. 2009; Wenzel 2015; Wenzel et al. 2017), imprinting (Marquis and Tilcsik 2013; Stinchcombe 1965), escalation of commitment (Sleesman et al. 2012; Staw 1981) and inertia (Gilbert 2005; Hannan and Freeman 1984; Tripsas and Gavetti 2000) describe and explain how organizations can be trapped by their history, thus *constraining* the scope of actions that organizations can enact in the present. In the light of unpredictable (i.e. future) events and the related need for flexible organizational responses, these works declare the stabilizing effect of past developments as a problem for organizations. Therefore, how organizations actively engage with and overcome the rigidities that the past imposes on them has become a key topic in organization research (Kipping and Üsdiken 2014). Some of the studies that have begun to explore this issue highlight the *enabling* character of the past, showing how organizations may re-interpret their history to align it with present circumstances (e.g. Gioia et al. 2002; Hjorth and Dawson 2016; Schultz and Hernes 2013), recombine past experiences to engage in innovative activities (De Massis et al. 2016; Foster et al. 2011), use their legacy as a source of sensemaking cues for the interpretation of present challenges (Ravasi and Schultz 2006) and even instrumentalize their history as a source of competitive advantage through rhetorical strategies (Suddaby et al. 2010). Yet, although these studies provide invaluable insights into the important role of history in and for organizing, they tend to accept the future as given, that is, as a context factor that organizations can at best passively sense and forecast through 'accurate' planning techniques (Hodgkinson and Wright 2002; see, however, Garud et al. 2010). Due to their focus on the temporal mode of the past, they underplay the management of the future as an important organizational phenomenon as well as its complexity in contemporary organizing.

Yet, the fact that much of the organizational literature has focused on the temporal mode of the past does not imply that the future is overlooked. Quite the contrary, in fact, as a number of streams in organization research display an affinity for things to come. However, ironically, while they highlight the importance of the future in and for organizing, they mostly trivialize the management of things to come—either by converting it into a planning problem or by considering it as a universal aspect of organizing.[1]

A first line of enquiry draws attention to the management of the future as a planning problem. For example, the renaissance of risk-related research (e.g. Bromiley et al. 2017; Martin and Helfat 2016) reflects the idea that organizational environments are ever more pluralistic and ambiguous. In response, these studies mostly suggest that organizations are required to imagine different possible futures, estimate probabilities of their occurrence and pursue actions that will most likely turn out to be optimal in the envisioned future. From this perspective, organizational survival essentially depends on planning more accurately. This leads us to classical forecasting techniques as described in the early strategic planning literature (e.g. Ansoff 1965; Chandler 1962) which have increasingly been put into question by more recent work in strategy research (e.g. Barry and Elmes 1997; Mintzberg 1994; for an exception see also Hardy and Maguire 2016). Similarly, the recent emergence of the discourse on 'big data' (Mayer-Schönberger and Cukier 2013) can be interpreted as a resurgence of 'management science' from the early days of organization and management research: ever-increasing data availability and computing power spark promises to predict the future (upcoming consumer purchases, the use of emergency brakes by autonomously driven cars in response to predicted hold-ups, etc.) based on algorithms (see Gigerenzer 2014 for a critical response). In turn, the debate on organizational foresight (e.g. Ahuja et al. 2005; Gavetti and Menon 2016; Rohrbeck et al. 2015) aims to extend beyond forecasting by arguing that organizations which mindfully engage with things to come envision the future more accurately and are, thus, better equipped to address it. This perspective on managing the future implies an interesting paradox: although this literature distinguishes itself from prediction-based techniques, its added value is still grounded in better predictions of the future (see, however, Tsoukas and Shepherd 2004a, b). Therefore, like many other contemporary concepts and streams in organization research, such as controlling and goal-setting concepts (Ordóñez et al. 2009), the 'dynamic capabilities' approach (Teece et al. 1997), neo-institutionalism (Meyer and Rowan 1977) and even parts of the entrepreneurship literature (Brinckmann and Sung 2015), it essentially turns the management of the future into a planning problem and its corresponding techniques of risk calculation: if organizations fail, they must have predicted the future inaccurately, and if organizations succeed, they must have envisioned the future correctly or at least better than others (e.g. Levine et al. 2017). Although intriguing, this line of argumentation underplays the fact that the unknowability of the future makes 'accurate' planning difficult, if not impossible. In the light of the fact that management of the future is a key concern for contemporary organizations (e.g. von Groddeck this volume), this opens up the perspective for other, perhaps even numerous ways in which organizations can manage things to come (e.g. chapters in this volume by Adler; Auvinen et al.; Bass and Milosevic; Heimstädt and Reischauer; Koch, Senf and Rothmann;

Kowalski, Danner-Schröder and Müller-Seitz; Leanza; Meyer, Schubert and Windeler; Naidoo; Ortmann and Sydow; and Scheele et al.).

A second line of enquiry points to the future as a universal feature of organizations. Most notably, process perspectives in organization research (e.g. Hernes 2014; Langley 2007, 2009; Langley et al. 2013; Sandberg et al. 2014; Tsoukas and Chia 2002; Wenzel and Koch 2018a) highlight the future as an inherent part of organizing. 'Weak' views consider processes as streams of actions and events that unfold linearly from the past to the present to the future. They conceptualize the present as a fleeting point that constantly and unavoidably moves forward (see also Orlikowski and Yates 2002). In contrast, 'strong' process views make a case for the non-linear flow of actions, arguing that the past, present and future constantly unfold in the present (see also Schultz and Hernes 2013). In both cases, the future is a universal aspect of organizing: present organizational actions either lead the organization into the future or the future is (more or less) mindfully envisioned and enacted in the present. Similarly, some scholars consider strategy-making as a whole to be inherently future-related (Drucker 1992; Sherden 1998; Teece 2014; see also Barry and Elmes 1997). This is not surprising, given that achieving and sustaining a competitive advantage is widely considered as the ultimate goal of strategy-making (Nag et al. 2007), which genuinely requires organizations to make decisions in the present through which they get or stay ahead of competitors in the future. However, if *every* strategic and organizational action is inherently related to the future, is the future *nothing*—an empty concept that does not contribute anything to strategy and organization research? Although these perspectives reinforce the idea that the future matters in and for organizations, their universal approach to the management of things to come underplays the fact that organizations perceive the future as a key temporal category that must be managed (e.g. von Groddeck this volume)—and if they consider these processes relevant, they *are* relevant, no matter to which extent any organizational action is inherently future-oriented. Thus, by considering the future as an ontological truism that automatically unfolds as part of all processes of organizing, we may overlook the specific ways in which organizations manage the future as these specific processes and practices empirically occur (see also Garud and Gehman 2012).

Although not explicitly future-related, we draw attention to a third line of enquiry that we consider particularly fruitful for gaining a more thorough understanding of how organizations manage the future: practice-based research on strategizing and organizing (e.g. Feldman and Orlikowski 2011; Golsorkhi et al. 2015; Jarzabkowski et al. 2007; Koch et al. 2016; Nicolini 2013; Vaara and Whittington 2012). Drawing on the broader 'practice turn' in the social sciences (Reckwitz 2002), this research explores the subtle and, at times, mundane streams of activities through which actors produce and re-create strategic and organizational phenomena. This focus on 'sayings and doings' (Schatzki et al. 2001) has led to a re-appreciation of strategic planning as a classical way of managing the future (Whittington and Cailluet 2008; Wolf and Floyd 2017). That is, rather than considering strategic planning as a heroic envisioning of the future that is ascribed to top managers, practice-based works indicate how all organizational actors, including middle managers and lower-level employees (Mantere 2005), produce and re-create communicative (Spee and Jarzabkowski 2011), integrative (Jarzabkowski and Balogun 2009), legitimative (Vaara et al. 2010) and other functions of strategic planning (Langley 1989, 1990) through which they envision and 'perform' organizational futures. Given the performative nature of social practices more generally (Reckwitz 2002), and strategic and organizational practices in particular (Gond et al. 2016), strategic planning procedures might even become 'rational', in that their enactment evokes the futures that they are supposed to predict (Cabantous et al. 2010; Cabantous and Gond 2011; Jarzabkowski and Kaplan 2015; see also Garud et al. 2014). Thus, a practice lens on the management of the future does not just consider the extent to which these practices produce desired or unfavourable outcomes (e.g. Mintzberg 1994), but explores the manifold ways in which such outcomes are produced and re-created (Koch et al. 2016). Although much of the practice-based literature on strategy-making has focused on formal planning procedures (Vaara and Whittington 2012), several works in this stream of research also demonstrate that organizational actors may produce and re-create the future even beyond strategic planning by enacting subtle and, at times, mundane discursive (Rouleau 2005; Rouleau and Balogun 2011; Vaara et al. 2004), bodily (Gylfe et al. 2016), material (Kaplan 2011; Knight et al. 2018), spatial (Jarzabkowski et al. 2015) and multimodal (Balogun et al. 2015; Wenzel and Koch 2018b) activities. Therefore, in choosing between various possibilities, we consider the practice perspective as a promising approach to exploring the important but under-studied management of the future (Koch et al. 2016; see also Buch and Stjerne this volume; Heimstädt and Reischauer this volume; Meyer et al. this volume).

An Overview of the Chapters in This Edited Collection

The contributions to this edited collection mark a valuable starting point for examining how organizations manage the future in greater depth. While these chapters have in common that they contribute to unpacking this phenomenon, they differ in terms of their level of abstraction, ranging from broader philosophical considerations and empirical examinations of specific processes and practices of managing the future and empirical settings to local office architecture and global pandemics. This diversity mirrors the complexity of the management of the future. Given the nascence of research on this phenomenon, this diversity also reflects the need for, firstly, reflective groundwork that helps scholars rethink the way things come to shape, and are shaped by, organizing; secondly, theoretical and methodological perspectives that unpack the management of the future; and, thirdly, empirical insights into the specific ways in which organizations imagine and enact the future. Therefore, we have structured the chapters around three themes: the first theme looks at philosophical considerations on the management of the future, the second at theoretical perspectives and methodological approaches that are useful for gaining a deeper understanding of this phenomenon and the third contains empirical insights into the ways in which managing the future occurs.

Chapter 2 by Victoria von Groddeck kicks off the section on philosophical perspectives. Her chapter develops a systems-theoretical understanding of managing the future. Specifically, this chapter draws on Niklas Luhmann's systems theory to conceptualize organizing as decision-making. As von Groddeck elucidates, this meta-theoretical perspective draws attention to the 'decisions' through which organizations relate to, and aim to influence, the future. Her subsequent analysis of the historical development of conceptions of decision-making interestingly demonstrates a recent shift from a focus on the past to the future. This observation substantiates the need for further work on the management of the future as a prevalent organizational phenomenon.

In Chap. 3, Anders Buch and Iben Stjerne elaborate on the role of the future in prominent philosophical perspectives. Their chapter focuses on Herbert Mead's pragmatism and Theodore Schatzki's version of practice theory in terms of their conceptualization of time, the future and how it unfolds in action. Based on this overview, Buch and Stjerne analyse a Danish film project that aimed to create a new movie genre, which involved major changes of institutionalized practices in the film industry. This analysis not only demonstrates that both Mead and Schatzki ascribe a fundamental role of the future to every human activity but also points to important differences: as the authors suggest, whereas Mead's pragmatist view spotlights that (ever-)new futures emerge through interaction, Schatzki's practice perspective considers things to come as both a consequential outcome and essential part of enacting social practices. Relatedly, Chap. 4 by Günther Ortmann and Jörg Sydow draws on philosophical insights to shed light on the creativity through which organizations aim to address an inherently unknowable future. In doing so, they unpack the under-appreciated ambivalence that tends to characterize creative endeavours. For example, they discuss the role of freedom and constraint in generating creative solutions for things to come. In doing so, they highlight the mutually exclusive but inter-dependent nature of providing freedom but setting constraints to spur creative outcomes.

Naidoo's contribution, Chap. 5, introduces and discusses the notion of 'organizational futurity'. This chapter relates to the ontological idea in process philosophy that organizations are in a constant state of 'becoming' (Tsoukas and Chia 2002) and, therefore, continuously face an open, unknowable future. In doing so, this chapter questions the role of organizational knowing as the central explanatory mechanism put forward by strategy and sensemaking research for gaining an understanding of how organizations manage the future. Naidoo proposes 'organizational futurity' as an alternative approach to thinking about the ways in which organizations constantly engage with things to come.

Related to the openness of the future that Naidoo addresses, Chap. 6 by Maximilian Heimstädt and Georg Reischauer kicks off the section on theoretical and methodological perspectives on the management of the future by elaborating on open innovation and open strategy as two contemporary ways in which organizations envision and enact things to come. This chapter compares and discusses prevalent practices of open innovation (crowdsourcing and corporate incubating) and open strategy (transparent and inclusive strategizing). In doing so, the authors develop an important theoretical distinction between these related practices of organizational openness: as they argue, while organizations probe the future through open innovation, they import things to come through open strategy.

In turn, Chap. 7 by Tommi Auvinen, Pasi Sajasalo, Teppo Sintonen, Tuomo Takala and Marko Järvenpää addresses a fundamental challenge of managing the future and exploring this process: capturing things to come. Specifically, they develop what they call the 'story index method'. This method draws scholars' and practitioners' attention to the narratives about strategic change that actors articulate before organizational futures are realized. In doing so, this method helps its users gain a better understanding of how actors make sense of and give sense to strategic change initiatives based on discursive images of the future, both daunting and optimistic.

Relatedly, Ricarda Scheele, Norman Kearney, Jude Kurniawan and Vanessa Schweizer introduce and discuss a reflexive method for engaging with the future: the 'cross-impact balance analysis' in Chap. 8. For this purpose, they draw, as they say, on post-structuralist insights to help scholars and practitioners engage in critical reflection about possible future scenarios. This method not only points to possible shortcomings in present imaginations of the future but also enables scholars and practitioners to reconstruct how and why actors imagine organizational futures in specific ways.

In Chap. 9, Yves Plourde, somewhat ironically, argues that to gain an understanding of how organizations manage the future, scholars should examine an organization's past. Specifically, this chapter discusses the prospects of historical methods as a means of examining the management of things to come. It does so by providing the onto-epistemological premises of historical methods that help scholars reconstruct how organizational actors make sense of, enact and organize for the future at specific points in time. To enable scholars to generate fruitful insights into the management of the future based on historical methods, the chapter also discusses key principles of using this methodological approach, using as an illustration a study of *Greenpeace* as an organization whose mission is genuinely related to the future.

Chapter 10 by Erin Bass and Ivana Milosevic kicks off the final section of the edited collection, which gathers empirical insights into the management of the future. Their chapter examines how organizations create organizational futures in response to disasters through resilient organizing. Their empirical analysis focuses on how *BP* sustained its survival after the Deep Water Horizon oil spill, a major natural disaster in the Gulf of Mexico that significantly harmed the reputation and financial stability of this organization. By reconstructing this process, Bass and Milosevic theorize how organizations prepare for, build, cultivate and commit to a new future through resilient organizing. In doing so, they highlight resilient organizing as a central driving mechanism of the process of managing the future.

Matthias Leanza's Chap. 11 reports the findings of his study on the ways in which the World Health Organization organizes its fight against future pandemics jointly with other actors on a global scale. His study explores two modes of organizing for doing so: early intervention and emergency planning. These results are based on the observation that the actors involved increasingly construct a 'darkened horizon'. That is, they have become aware that it is difficult, if not impossible, to predict and prevent pandemics before they emerge. Therefore, although the focal actors do enact early intervention, they are increasingly engaged in emergency planning to take timely counter actions once pandemics unexpectedly emerge. This observation points to early intervention and emergency planning as two complementary modes of organizing that describe and explain how the future can be managed.

In Chap. 12, Christian Kowalski, Anja Danner-Schröder and Gordon Müller-Seitz choose a smaller but nevertheless broad unit of analysis: cities. Specifically, they explore how cities manage their digital future. Their study builds on the observation that the ongoing digital transformation draws cities' attention to the open-endedness of things to come, with which they (must) engage more actively. Using empirical analysis, they reveal how cities understand, create and disseminate imaginations of their digital future through innovation networks. In doing so, this chapter not only unpacks future-related challenges of digitalization as an important contemporary phenomenon but also builds theory on how multiple actors can be collectively engaged in the management of things to come.

Relatedly, Chap. 13 by Uli Meyer, Cornelius Schubert and Arnold Windeler highlights the collective nature of managing the future. Their chapter explores how actors collectively create social and technical futures through roadmaps and conferences as field-configuring events. Using institutional and practice theory, they analyse how this process unfolded in the field of semiconductor manufacturing. Based on their analysis, they describe and explain this process as institutional work through which futures emerge and evolve in institutional fields over time.

In Chap. 14, Jochen Koch, Natalie Senf and Wasko Rothmann zoom further into the process and practice of managing the future. Their chapter focuses on the role of material artefacts in imagining and enacting things to come. They explore this issue in haute cuisine, analysing how a number of German Michelin-starred restaurants' menus evolved over time, thereby interacting with the future of these organizations. In doing so, they show that futures are inscribed into material artefacts. Based on this, they argue that although the future cannot fully rely on material representation, material artefacts may 'pre-present' things to come when they serve as a body of inscription for the future.

The final chapter, Chap. 15 by David Adler, extends the idea of a close inter-relationship between the material aspects of organizing and things to come. Specifically, this study examines the role of the future in office architecture. Based on a discourse analysis and ethnographic methodology, Adler shows how office architecture is imbued with conflicting discursive constructions of things to come, which are articulated as contradictory aspirations that have yet to be materialized and are situationally enacted. In doing so, this chapter points to the subtle performativity of managing things to come, showing how office workers are constantly driven towards the realization of future successes through office architecture.

Conclusion: Towards a Research Agenda on the Management of the Future

These chapters all provide valuable philosophical, theoretical, methodological and empirical insights into how organizations manage the future as well as examine the processes involved. However, as with any nascent topic, these insights are to be understood as a starting point for further research on this organizational phenomenon. Therefore, given the prevalence of the future in contemporary processes of organizing, we encourage future research to build on these chapters to gain a deeper and more nuanced understanding of how organizations manage the future. For example, future works may:

- extend our understanding of the management of the future by refusing pre-established meta-theoretical lenses; rather following a broader range of conceptual approaches to examine organizational futures depending on the very 'future' one is analysing. Some of the lenses that might provide useful insights into the management of the future include, but are not limited to, post-structuralist approaches like practice theory, systems theory or ANT as well as more traditional structuralist approaches.
- explore the different dimensions in which the future becomes prevalent within organizations, given that there may be practices, discourses, narratives, media or artefacts that produce and make salient different futures. Future research could focus on an in-depth analysis of such elements to extend our understanding of the interplay and performance of those for managing the future.
- examine the various roles that decision-making as well as fear and risk calculations play in producing and re-creating the (imagined) future, and specify the different forms of organizational futures that these tools and techniques (re-)produce by analysing futurity and varying forms of openness.
- deepen our understanding of the relationship between the future, the past and the present based on historical and future-oriented methods.

- study the power relations within the management of the future to understand asymmetry in the production of a hegemonic future and 'contests' between different futures by analysing the manifold artefacts, practices, hierarchies, innovation networks, events and other concepts that may be relevant in these processes.

These are just some of the research opportunities that a focus on the management of the future provides. We hope that this edited collection inspires future research to take the future in and for organizing more seriously.

Note

1. The following overview is not intended to be a full-blown review of future-related organization research. Rather, we provide illustrative examples for a synthesis of general trends in this literature.

References

Adler, David. this volume. Solid Futures: Office Architecture and the Labor Imaginary. In *How Organizations Manage the Future: Theoretical Perspectives and Empirical Insights*, ed. Hannes Krämer and Matthias Wenzel. Basingstoke: Palgrave Macmillan.

Ahuja, Gautam, Russell W. Coff, and Peggy M. Lee. 2005. Managerial Foresight and Attempted Rent Appropriation: Insider Trading on Knowledge of Imminent Breakthroughs. *Strategic Management Journal* 26 (9): 791–808.

Ansoff, H. Igor. 1965. *Corporate Strategy: An Analytic Approach to Business Policy for Growth and Expansion*. New York: McGraw-Hill.

Auvinen, Tommi P., Pasi Sajasalo, Teppo Sintonen, Tuomo Takala, and Marko Järvenpää. this volume. Antenarratives in Ongoing Strategic Change: Using the Story Index to Capture Daunting and Optimistic Futures. In *How Organizations Manage the Future: Theoretical Perspectives and Empirical Insights*, ed. Hannes Krämer and Matthias Wenzel. Basingstoke: Palgrave Macmillan.

Balogun, Julia, Katie Best, and K. Lê Jane. 2015. Selling the Object of Strategy: How Frontline Workers Realize Strategy Through Their Daily Work. *Organization Studies* 36 (10): 1285–1313.
Barry, David, and Michael Elmes. 1997. Strategy Retold: Toward a Narrative View of Strategic Discourse. *Academy of Management Review* 22 (2): 429–452.
Bass, A. Erin, and Ivana Milosevic. this volume. In the Wake of Disaster: Resilient Organizing and a New Path for the Future. In *How Organizations Manage the Future: Theoretical Perspectives and Empirical Insights*, ed. Hannes Krämer and Matthias Wenzel. Basingstoke: Palgrave Macmillan.
Beckert, Jens. 2016. *Imagined Futures: Expectations and Capitalist Dynamics*. Cambridge, MA: Harvard University Press.
Brinckmann, Jan, and Min K. Sung. 2015. Why We Plan: The Impact of Nascent Entrepreneurs' Cognitive Characteristics and Human Capital on Business Planning. *Strategic Entrepreneurship Journal* 9 (2): 153–166.
Bromiley, Philip, Devaki Rau, and Yu. Zhang. 2017. Is R&D Risky? *Strategic Management Journal* 38 (4): 876–891.
Buch, Anders, and Iben S. Stjerne. this volume. What's New? Temporality in Practice Theory and Pragmatism. In *How Organizations Manage the Future: Theoretical Perspectives and Empirical Insights*, ed. Hannes Krämer and Matthias Wenzel. Basingstoke: Palgrave Macmillan.
Cabantous, Laure, and Jean-Pascal Gond. 2011. Rational Decision-Making as Performative Praxis: Explaining Rationality's Éternel Retour. *Organization Science* 22 (3): 573–586.
Cabantous, Laure, Jean-Pascal Gond, and Michael Johnson-Cramer. 2010. Decision Theory as Practice: Crafting Rationality in Organizations. *Organization Studies* 31 (11): 1531–1566.
Chandler, Alfred D. 1962. *Strategy and Structure: Chapters in the History of the American Industrial Enterprise*. Cambridge, MA: MIT Press.
De, Massis, Federico Frattini Alfredo, Josip Kotlar, Antonio Messeni Petruzzelli, and Mike Wright. 2016. Innovation Through Tradition: Lessons from Innovative Family Businesses and Directions for Future Research. *Academy of Management Perspectives* 30 (1): 93–116.
Drucker, Peter F. 1992. *Managing for the Future*. London: Routledge.
Feldman, Martha S., and Wanda J. Orlikowski. 2011. Theorizing Practice and Practicing Theory. *Organization Science* 22 (5): 1240–1253.
Foster, William M., Roy Suddaby, Alison Minkus, and Elden Wiebe. 2011. History as Social Memory Assets: The Example of Tim Hortons. *Management and Organizational History* 6 (1): 101–120.

Garud, Raghu, and Joel Gehman. 2012. Metatheoretical Perspectives on Sustainability Journeys: Evolutionary, Relational, and Durational. *Research Policy* 41 (6): 980–995.

Garud, Raghu, Arun Kumaraswamy, and Peter Karnøe. 2010. Path Dependence or Path Creation? *Journal of Management Studies* 47 (4): 760–774.

Garud, Raghu, Henri A. Schildt, and Theresa K. Lant. 2014. Organizational Storytelling, Future Expectations, and the Paradox of Legitimacy. *Organization Science* 25 (5): 1479–1492.

Gavetti, Giovanni, and Anoop Menon. 2016. Evolution Cum Agency: Toward a Model of Strategic Foresight. *Strategy Science* 1 (3): 207–233.

Gigerenzer, Gerd. 2014. *Risk Savvy: How to Make Good Decisions*. New York: Penguin.

Gilbert, Clark. 2005. Unbundling the Structure of Inertia: Resource Versus Routine Rigidity. *Academy of Management Journal* 48 (5): 741–763.

Gioia, Dennis A., Kevin G. Corley, and Tommaso Fabbri. 2002. Revising the Past (While Thinking in the Future Perfect Tense). *Journal of Organizational Change Management* 15 (6): 622–634.

Godfrey, Paul C., John Hassard, Ellen S. O'Connor, Michael Rowlinson, and Martin Ruef. 2016. What Is Organizational History? Toward a Creative Synthesis of History and Organization Studies. *Academy of Management Review* 41 (4): 590–608.

Golsorkhi, Damon, Linda Rouleau, David Seidl, and Eero Vaara. 2015. Introduction: What Is Strategy as Practice? In *Cambridge Handbook on Strategy as Practice*, ed. Damon Golsorkhi, Linda Rouleau, David Seidl, and Eero Vaara, 1–29. Cambridge, UK: Cambridge University Press.

Gond, Jean-Pascal, Laure Cabantous, Nancy Harding, and Mark Learmonth. 2016. What Do We Mean by Performativity in Organizational and Management Theory? The Uses and Abuses of Performativity. *International Journal of Management Reviews* 18 (4): 440–463.

Gylfe, Philip, Henrika Franck, Curtis Lebaron, and Saku Mantere. 2016. Video Methods in Strategy Research: Focusing on Embodied Cognition. *Strategic Management Journal* 37 (1): 133–148.

Hannan, Michael T., and John Freeman. 1984. Structural Inertia and Organizational Change. *American Sociological Review* 49 (2): 149–164.

Hardy, Cynthia, and Steve Maguire. 2016. Organizing Risk: Discourse, Power, and "Riskification". *Academy of Management Review* 41 (1): 80–108.

Heimstädt, Maximilian, and Georg Reischauer. this volume. Open(ing) Up for the Future: Practising Open Strategy and Open Innovation to Cope with

Uncertainty. In *How Organizations Manage the Future: Theoretical Perspectives and Empirical Insights*, ed. Hannes Krämer and Matthias Wenzel. Basingstoke: Palgrave Macmillan.

Hernes, Tor. 2014. *A Process Theory of Organization*. Oxford: Oxford University Press.

Hjorth, Daniel, and Alexandra Dawson. 2016. The Burden of History in the Family Business Organization. *Organization Studies* 37 (8): 1089–1111.

Hodgkinson, Gerard P., and George Wright. 2002. Confronting Strategic Inertia in a Top Management Team: Learning from Failure. *Organization Studies* 23 (6): 949–977.

Jarzabkowski, Paula, and Julia Balogun. 2009. The Practice and Process of Delivering Integration Through Strategic Planning. *Journal of Management Studies* 46 (8): 1255–1288.

Jarzabkowski, Paula, and Sarah Kaplan. 2015. Strategy Tools-in-Use: A Framework for Understanding 'Technologies of Rationality' in Practice. *Strategic Management Journal* 36 (4): 537–558.

Jarzabkowski, Paula, Julia Balogun, and David Seidl. 2007. Strategizing: The Challenges of a Practice Perspective. *Human Relations* 60 (1): 5–27.

Jarzabkowski, Paula, Gary Burke, and Paul Spee. 2015. Constructing Spaces for Strategic Work: A Multimodal Perspective. *British Journal of Management* 26 (S1): S26–S47.

Kaplan, Sarah. 2011. Strategy and PowerPoint: An Inquiry into the Epistemic Culture and Machinery of Strategy Making. *Organization Science* 22 (2): 320–346.

Kipping, Matthias, and Behlül Üsdiken. 2014. History in Organization and Management Theory: More than Meets the Eye. *The Academy of Management Annals* 8 (1): 535–588.

Knight, Eric, Sotirios Paroutis, and Loizos Heracleous. 2018. The Power of PowerPoint. *Strategic Management Journal* 39(3).

Koch, Jochen, Hannes Krämer, Andreas Reckwitz, and Matthias Wenzel. 2016. Zum Umgang mit Zukunft in Organisationen – eine praxistheoretische Perspektive. *Managementforschung* 26: 161–184.

Koch, Jochen, N. Natalie Senf, and Wasko Rothmann. this volume. Organizational Artifacts as Pre-presentations of Things to Come: The Case of Menu Development in Haute Cuisine. In *How Organizations Manage the Future: Theoretical Perspectives and Empirical Insights*, ed. Hannes Krämer and Matthias Wenzel. Basingstoke: Palgrave Macmillan.

Kowalski, Markus, Anja Danner-Schröder, and Gordon Müller-Seitz. this volume. Managing the Digital Transformation: Preparing Cities for the Future. In *How Organizations Manage the Future: Theoretical Perspectives and Empirical Insights*, ed. Hannes Krämer and Matthias Wenzel. Basingstoke: Palgrave Macmillan.

Langley, Ann. 1989. In Search of Rationality: The Purposes Behind the Use of Formal Analysis in Organizations. *Administrative Science Quarterly* 34 (4): 598–631.

———. 1990. Patterns in the Use of Formal Analysis in Strategic Decisions. *Organization Studies* 11 (1): 17–45.

———. 2007. Process Thinking in Strategic Organization. *Strategic Organization* 5 (3): 271–282.

———. 2009. Studying Processes in and Around Organizations. In *SAGE Handbook of Organizational Research Methods*, ed. David A. Buchanan and Alan Bryman, 409–429. London: Sage.

Langley, Ann, Clive Smallman, Haridimos Tsoukas, and Andrew H. van de Ven. 2013. Process Studies of Change in Organization and Management: Unveiling Temporality, Activity, and Flow. *Academy of Management Journal* 56 (1): 1–13.

Leanza, Matthias. this volume. The Darkened Horizon: Two Modes of Organizing Pandemics. In *How Organizations Manage the Future: Theoretical Perspectives and Empirical Insights*, ed. Hannes Krämer and Matthias Wenzel. Basingstoke: Palgrave Macmillan.

Levine, Sheen S., Mark Bernard, and Rosemarie Nagel. 2017. Strategic Intelligence: The Cognitive Capability to Anticipate Competitive Behavior. *Strategic Management Journal* 38 (12): 2390–2423.

Luhmann, Niklas. 2000. *Organisation und Entscheidung*. Opladen: Westdeutscher Verlag.

Mantere, Saku. 2005. Strategic Practices as Enablers and Disablers of Championing Activity. *Strategic Organization* 3 (2): 157–184.

March, James G. 1995. The Future, Disposable Organizations and the Rigidities of Imagination. *Organization* 2 (3–4): 427–440.

Marquis, Christopher, and András Tilcsik. 2013. Imprinting: Toward a Multilevel Theory. *The Academy of Management Annals* 7 (1): 195–245.

Martin, Jeffrey A., and Constance E. Helfat. 2016. Dynamic Managerial Capabilities: Review and Assessment of Managerial Impact on Strategic Change. *Journal of Management* 41 (5): 1281–1312.

Mayer-Schönberger, Victor, and Kenneth Cukier. 2013. *Big Data*. Boston: Houghton Mifflin Harcourt.

Meyer, John W., and Brian Rowan. 1977. Institutionalized Organizations: Formal Structure as Myth and Ceremony. *American Journal of Sociology* 83 (2): 340–363.
Meyer, Uli, Cornelius Schubert, and Arnold Windeler. this volume. Creating Collective Futures: How Roadmaps and Conferences Re-configure the Institutional Field of Semiconductor Manufacturing. In *How Organizations Manage the Future: Theoretical Perspectives and Empirical Insights*, ed. Hannes Krämer and Matthias Wenzel. Basingstoke: Palgrave Macmillan.
Mintzberg, Henry. 1994. *The Rise and Fall of Strategic Planning: Reconceiving Roles of Planning, Plans, Planners*. New York: Free Press.
Nag, Rajiv, Donald C. Hambrick, and Ming-Jer Chen. 2007. What Is Strategic Management, Really? Inductive Derivation of a Consensus Definition of the Field. *Strategic Management Journal* 28 (9): 935–955.
Naidoo, Seelan. this volume. Organizational Futurity: Being and Knowing in the Engagement with What Is Yet to Come. In *How Organizations Manage the Future: Theoretical Perspectives and Empirical Insights*, ed. Hannes Krämer and Matthias Wenzel. Basingstoke: Palgrave Macmillan.
Nicolini, Davide. 2013. *Practice Theory, Work and Organization: An Introduction*. Oxford: Oxford University Press.
Ordóñez, Lisa D., Maurice E. Schweitzer, Adam D. Galinsky, and Max H. Bazerman. 2009. Goals Gone Wild: The Systematic Side Effects of Overprescribing Goal Setting. *Academy of Management Perspectives* 23 (1): 6–16.
Orlikowski, Wanda J., and JoAnne Yates. 2002. It's About Time: Temporal Structuring in Organizations. *Organization Science* 13 (6): 684–700.
Ortmann, Günther, and Jörg Sydow. this volume. Creativity in/of Organizations for Managing Things to Come: Lessons to Be Learnt from Philosophy. In *How Organizations Manage the Future: Theoretical Perspectives and Empirical Insights*, ed. Hannes Krämer and Matthias Wenzel. Basingstoke: Palgrave Macmillan.
Plourde, Yves. this volume. Historical Methods and the Study of How Organizations Manage the Future. In *How Organizations Manage the Future: Theoretical Perspectives and Empirical Insights*, ed. Hannes Krämer and Matthias Wenzel. Basingstoke: Palgrave Macmillan.
Ravasi, Davide, and Majken Schultz. 2006. Responding to Organizational Identity Threats: Exploring the Role of Organizational Culture. *Academy of Management Journal* 49 (3): 433–458.

Reckwitz, Andreas. 2002. Toward a Theory of Social Practices: A Development in Culturalist Theorizing. *European Journal of Social Theory* 5 (2): 243–263.
———. 2016. Zukunftspraktiken. Die Zeitlichkeit des Sozialen und die Krise der modernen Rationalisierung der Zukunft. In *Kreativität und soziale Praxis. Studien zur Sozial- und Gesellschaftstheorie*, ed. Andreas Reckwitz, 115–135. Bielefeld: transcript.
Rohrbeck, René, Cinzia Battistella, and Eelko Huizingh. 2015. Corporate Foresight: An Emerging Field with a Rich Tradition. *Technological Forecasting and Social Change* 101: 1–9.
Rosa, Hartmut. 2005. *Beschleunigung: Die Veränderung der Temporalstrukturen in der Moderne*. Frankfurt a.M.: Suhrkamp.
———. 2016. *Resonanz: Eine Soziologie der Weltbeziehung*. Frankfurt a.M.: Suhrkamp.
Rouleau, Linda. 2005. Micro-practices of Strategic Sensemaking and Sensegiving: How Middle Managers Interpret and Sell Change Every Day. *Journal of Management Studies* 42 (7): 1413–1441.
Rouleau, Linda, and Julia Balogun. 2011. Middle Managers, Strategic Sensemaking, and Discursive Competence. *Journal of Management Studies* 48 (5): 953–983.
Sandberg, Jörgen, Bernadette Loacker, and Mats Alvesson. 2014. Conceptions of Process in Organization and Management: The Case of Identity Studies. In *The Emergence of Novelty in Organizations*, ed. Haridimos Tsoukas, Ann Langley, Barbara Simpson, and Raghu Garud, 318–344. Oxford: Oxford University Press.
Schatzki, Theodore R., Karin Knorr Cetina, and Eike von Savigny. 2001. *The Practice Turn in Contemporary Theory*. London: Routledge.
Scheele, Ricarda, Norman M. Kearney, Jude H. Kurniawan, and Vanessa J. Schweizer. this volume. What Scenarios Are You Missing? Poststructuralism for Deconstructing and Reconstructing Organizational Futures. In *How Organizations Manage the Future: Theoretical Perspectives and Empirical Insights*, ed. Hannes Krämer and Matthias Wenzel. Basingstoke: Palgrave Macmillan.
Schultz, Majken, and Tor Hernes. 2013. A Temporal Perspective on Organizational Identity. *Organization Science* 24 (1): 1–21.
Sherden, William A. 1998. *The Fortune Sellers: The Big Business of Buying and Selling Predictions*. New York: Wiley.
Sleesman, Dustin J., Donald E. Conlon, Gerry McNamara, and Jonathan E. Miles. 2012. Cleaning Up the Big Muddy: A Meta-Analytic Review of the

Determinants of Escalation of Commitment. *Academy of Management Journal* 55 (3): 541–562.

Spee, A. Paul, and Paula Jarzabkowski. 2011. Strategic Planning as Communicative Process. *Organization Studies* 32 (9): 1217–1245.

Staw, Barry M. 1981. The Escalation of Commitment to a Course of Action. *Academy of Management Review* 6 (4): 577–587.

Stinchcombe, Arthur L. 1965. Social Structure and Organizations. In *Handbook of Organizations*, ed. James G. March, 142–193. Chicago: Rand McNally.

Suddaby, Roy, and William M. Foster. 2017. History and Organizational Change. *Journal of Management* 43 (1): 19–38.

Suddaby, Roy, William M. Foster, and Chris Quinn Trank. 2010. Rhetorical History as a Source of Competitive Advantage. *Advances in Strategic Management* 27: 147–173.

Sydow, Jörg, Georg Schreyögg, and Jochen Koch. 2009. Organizational Path Dependence: Opening the Black Box. *Academy of Management Review* 34 (4): 689–709.

Teece, David J. 2014. The Foundations of Enterprise Performance: Dynamic and Ordinary Capabilities in an (Economic) Theory of Firms. *Academy of Management Perspectives* 28 (4): 328–352.

Teece, David J., Gary Pisano, and Amy Shuen. 1997. Dynamic Capabilities and Strategic Management. *Strategic Management Journal* 18 (7): 509–533.

Tripsas, Mary, and Giovanni Gavetti. 2000. Capabilities, Cognition, and Inertia: Evidence from Digital Imaging. *Strategic Management Journal* 21 (10/11): 1147–1161.

Tsoukas, Haridimos, and Robert Chia. 2002. On Organizational Becoming: Rethinking Organizational Change. *Organization Science* 13 (5): 567–582.

Tsoukas, Haridimos, and Jill Shepherd. 2004a. Coping with the Future: Developing Organizational Insightfulness. *Futures* 36 (2): 137–144.

———. 2004b. *Managing the Future: Foresight in the Knowledge Economy*. Malden: Blackwell.

Vaara, Eero, and Richard Whittington. 2012. Strategy-as-Practice: Taking Social Practices Seriously. *Academy of Management Annals* 6 (1): 285–336.

Vaara, Eero, Birgit Kleymann, and Hannu Seristö. 2004. Strategies as Discursive Constructions: The Case of Airline Alliances. *Journal of Management Studies* 41 (1): 1–35.

Vaara, Eero, Virpi Sorsa, and Pekka Pälli. 2010. On the Force Potential of Strategy Texts: A Critical Discourse Analysis of a Strategic Plan and Its Power Effects in a City Organization. *Organization* 17 (6): 685–702.

von Groddeck, Victoria. this volume. From Defuturization to Futurization and Back Again? A System-Theoretical Perspective to Analyze Decision-Making. In *How Organizations Manage the Future: Theoretical Perspectives and Empirical Insights*, ed. Hannes Krämer and Matthias Wenzel. Basingstoke: Palgrave Macmillan.

Wenzel, Matthias. 2015. Path Dependence and the Stabilization of Strategic Premises: How the Funeral Industry Buries Itself. *Business Research* 8 (2): 265–299.

Wenzel, Matthias, and Jochen Koch. 2018a. From Entity to Process: Toward More Process-Based Theorizing in the Field of Organizational Change. *Journal of Accounting and Organizational Change*.

———. 2018b. Strategy as Staged Performance: A Critical Discursive Perspective on Keynote Speeches as a Genre of Strategic Communication. *Strategic Management Journal* 39 (3).

Wenzel, Matthias, Heinz-Theo Wagner, and Jochen Koch. 2017. The Funeral Industry and the Internet: On the Historical Emergence and Destabilization of Strategic Paths. *European Journal of Information Systems* 26 (4): 361–378.

Whittington, Richard, and Ludovic Cailluet. 2008. The Crafts of Strategy: Special Issue Introduction by the Guest Editors. *Long Range Planning* 41 (3): 241–247.

Wolf, Carola, and Steven W. Floyd. 2017. Strategic Planning Research: Toward a Theory-Driven Agenda. *Journal of Management* 43 (6): 1754–1788.

Part I

Philosophical Perspectives

2

From Defuturization to Futurization and Back Again? A System-Theoretical Perspective to Analyse Decision-Making

Victoria von Groddeck

Introduction

The idea of coping with an unknown future is not a post-modern, contemporary problem; it was the initial 'trigger' for the emergence of a modern world that we have experienced for nearly three centuries. The prospect that neither God nor other transcendental forces determine the fate of society but rather the actions of societal members is tightly coupled with the idea of an open future (Koselleck 2004; Luhmann 1976). During this period of modernity, it seems that the organization in particular became the expert in dealing with an open future. The idea that society is not subject to an uncontrollable fate but rather a complex endeavour that can be managed and influenced is related to the idea that an organization is able to realize future ends in a legitimate and, moreover, a rational, efficient manner. For example, Durkheim (1984) saw social-professional organizations as a substitute for lost morals. The more

V. von Groddeck (✉)
Institute for Sociology, Ludwig-Maximilians-Universität (LMU),
Munich, Germany

prominent example is, of course, Max Weber (1958), who defined bureaucracy as the legitimate form of legal-rational authority. Organizations, at least in their (self)description, seem to be societal places where not only their own but also the future of modern society is decided. Planning and control instruments are developed with the promise to both enhance efficiency and determine the future. 'Scientific management' is the classic keyword. The idea of causal and rational control and of social and organizational engineering decomposes itself in the face of increasing societal dynamics and complexity in the course of modernity. Today, nobody in an organization would believe that rational control and planning can guarantee the realization of planned ends in the future. It is difficult to believe in the concept of rational planning, since the environment and its dynamics seem to be too opaque. Nonetheless, it seems that it is exactly the distrust in classical ideas of planning that enhances the interest in tools and instruments that allows organization to cope with an open and unclear future (Buchanan and O'Connell 2006; Scott 2004). The experience of a complex world does not lead to a decreasing interest in the question of how to organize for the future. From basic ideas of future determination by planning, more sophisticated instruments of strategic planning were developed and continuously refined; for example, forecasting instruments were replaced by scenario-planning and complemented by creativity or trend-research techniques (e.g. Liebl and Schwarz 2010). The future orientation of organizations seems to be unbroken, but the methods of dealing with an unknown future might have changed.

As system theory is a general sociological theory that focuses on the question of how systems emerge, gain stability and change, the question of temporality is at its core. From this it follows that this theoretical perspective provides a productive framework for analysing changes in how organizations or organizational practices relate to time. It therefore bridges debates on how to perceive organizations as a procedural and temporal engagement on the one hand (Hernes 2007; Tsoukas and Chia 2002), and attempts to interpret new temporal forms of organizing (Bakker et al. 2016) on the other. Furthermore, it is a perception that combines process-theoretical thinking but also takes decision-making as its focus to interpret organizing. It therefore also contributes to the line of academic thinking which argues for a revitalization of decision as the basic notion for organizational research (Ahrne et al. 2016; Apelt et al. 2017), as this enables organization research to both point out its own research focus and show how organizing also affects other social fields.

Therefore, the aim of this chapter is twofold:

1. To introduce system-theoretical thinking in general (Luhmann 1976, 1995), with a focus on organization and organizing (Nassehi 2005; von Groddeck et al. 2016). The aim is to provide a framework for empirical research both to analyse organizations as a procedural endeavour in general and to analyse in particular how organizations produce and organize (their) future by decision-making.
2. To illustrate the ability of this theoretical lens through an analysis of the discourse of decision-making, showing how changes in relating to time dimensions correspond with new forms of decision-making.

Introducing System-Theoretical Thinking

Structure and Time

Niklas Luhmann developed his system theory as a critique of theories that presuppose stable structures to explain social action and order. The aim was to build a theory that can explain order as a *process of structuration*. System theory is therefore a perspective that stands in sharp contrast to every theoretical perspective that explains action from the deduction of complex structures. System theory tries to explain the way in which reality structures itself through its own connecting operations: Luhmann is interested in the autopoiesis of systems (Luhmann 2005a). The basic operations that constitute systems are communications. Communications, as basic elements, are events that do not last. They vanish as they have occurred. Luhmann's basic research aim therefore is to explain both the connectivity between these fading events and that its form is neither determined nor arbitrary. His research interest is to clarify how and under what circumstances communications interconnect. He therefore redefined structure as a communicative element that enables the connection of communicative elements: 'Therefore we will constrain the concept of structure in another way: not as a special type of stability but by its function of enabling the autopoietic reproduction of the system from one event of the other' (Luhmann 1995, p. 286). Structures limit the space of possible connections. Structures are expectations that make connectivity more probable by establishing constraints that limit the scope of possible connections and thereby make connectivity more probable. Every communication is both a new event at the present point in time and a connection to a previous event. Events, therefore, do not just occur; they always occur in a structuralized form: 'The selection of constraints works as a constraint on selections, *and this consolidates the structure*' (Luhmann 1995, p. 284). Structures do not eliminate contingency but make it 'manageable', which is important, as structures never establish clear-cut determination but allow a combination of determinacy and indeterminacy. This is a prerequisite for autopoietic operations; otherwise, a system would stop operating—either out of full determination or out of entropy.

Structures are not elements that last in time, they occur only in an operative, present-based form: '(…) structures exist only in a present; they extend through time only in the temporal horizon of the present, integrating present's future with the present past' (Luhmann 1995, p. 293). Thus, *structures perceived in this sense make it possible to observe how past, present and future are constructed and how constructions of time constrain the scope of possible connectivity within the system.*

The discussion so far shows that system theory focuses on the present. Future and past have become dimensions that are dependent on the present: 'In fact, if we have an almost infinite historical past, structured and limited only by our actual interests, and if we have an open future, the present becomes the turning point, which switches the process of time from past into future' (Luhmann 1976, p. 133). Luhmann's definition of time rejects an objective idea of time, which perceives past, present and future as modalities in which meaning can transgress over time. For Luhmann, time is 'the interpretation of reality with regard to the difference between past and future' (Luhmann 1976, p. 135). In this conception, past and future are only horizons of the present and can never be touched: 'The future cannot begin. Indeed, the essential characteristic of a horizon is that we can never touch it, never get at it, never surpass it, but that despite that, it contributes to the definition of the situation. Any movement and any operation of thought only shifts the guiding horizon but never attains it' (Luhmann 1976, p. 140). This means that temporal forms can be perceived only as forms that are based in the present.

To summarize, system theory is a theory which basically tries to answer the question of how the continuation or discontinuation of connectivity is made possible based on the operations of social practice itself, in *the present moment of practice*. The focus on the present directs our observation to the present construction of structures in general, as they integrate time in the present and thereby mirror certain pictures of past and future. This leads to an analysis of how systems, for example, organizations, decrease the scope of future possibilities in the present or how the openness of the future is increased, always dependent on the present structure that limits the scope of what seems to be a suitable future connection. Luhmann speaks of 'defuturization' and 'futurization' (Luhmann 1976, p. 141). In the following, I will show how the notions of defuturization and futurization can be used as a theoretical lens to analyse how organizations relate to both past and future to make sense of the present. Forms of futurization and defuturization can differ, and call for sensible empirical analysis.

Organization, Organizing and the Temporal Dimension of Decision-Making

The general principles of the autopoiesis of systems and their specific usage of time can be transferred to the realm of organization and organizing. Luhmann viewed an organization as a social system that emerges by connecting specific forms of communication: decisions. Perceiving decisions as the basic elements of organizations connects Luhmann's perspective to mainstream organizational theory and sociology (e.g. Cyert and March 1963; Lindblom 1959; March and Simon 1959; Simon 1959, 1961) with their ambition to deconstruct the relation between decisions and outcome as indirect, complex and not causally determined (Brunsson 1982; Cohen et al. 1990; Simon 1959).

By viewing decisions as the basic element of organizational autopoiesis, Luhmann, on the one hand, connected with this line of research while, on the other hand, choosing a more radical perspective. He was interested in how organizations emerge through the connectivity of decisions. The single decision, the decision-maker, or the outcome of decisions are not the starting point; instead, linking decisions make the organization (for this line of thinking, see Andersen 2003; Apelt et al. 2017; Blaschke et al. 2012; Esposito 2013; Knudsen 2005; Luhmann 1964, 2000; Nassehi 2005; Schoeneborn et al. 2014). In this sense, organization is not a stable entity or a formal structural complex, but, as outlined above, a form of practice that reproduces itself through linking decisions. Luhmann described decision-making as a paradox. For him, only principally undecidable questions can be decided (von Foerster 1992; Åkerstrøm Andersen 2003; Luhmann 2005b). This means that decisions must be made in situations in which you do not know which alternative is preferable. Decisions are necessary only if the alternatives at stake are equivalent; otherwise you just calculate the right solution or you just keep acting. The fact that decisions decide undecidable issues suggests that decisions are relatively unstable. After the decision is made, the contingency of the two alternatives is fixed rather than eliminated. The decision can be easily criticized, corrected or improved, as it always conveys the fact that there had been another alternative, and it is this critique, correction or improvement that calls for new decisions and thereby stabilizes the organizational autopoiesis: 'Decision communication functions to absorb uncertainty in the organization, and fixes and attunes expectations. However, new uncertainty is simultaneously produced. It becomes apparent that the decision could have been made differently. Furthermore, new decisions are potentialized when a decision is made. This means that a decision produces new possible connections for future communication' (Andersen and Pors 2017, p. 121).

Here again, connectivity is also guaranteed by structures which, in the case of organizations themselves, are a matter of decision and function as specific premises for subsequent decisions. The paradox of decision cannot be solved but only postponed into the future. Organization from this perspective can never be perceived as a stable or substantial entity, but only as an operative process or an ongoing practice. Luhmann's theory of organization is therefore a theory of *organizing* and belongs to organizational theories that argue for a process-theoretical conception (Hernes 2007; Tsoukas and Chia 2002). The process of organizing, in this line of thinking, is fuelled by the paradoxical character of decisions. As the paradox of decision can only be postponed by decisions in a present, it produces the need for further decisions in a future present. This keeps the structuration of organizations going.

As noted above, all operations of a system take place in the present. Time is a form of interpretation of reality that distinguishes past and future in the present. For organizations, this is true in an acuminate way:

> (…) decision making actualizes an (…) reverse relationship between past and future. From each present the past is observed as *no longer changeable*, while the future is observed as *still changeable*. Analogously, a decision *cannot be determined by the past*. It constructs the alternativity of its alternative from the perspective of 'what might be'; and it constructs it in the present time. However, with regard to future present times, the decision proceeds from the assumption *that it will make a difference whether and how a decision is taken*. In other words, there is no commitment to the (no longer changeable) past, but commitment to the (still changeable) future. (Luhmann 2005b, pp. 88–89)

Organizations are, like every other social system, present-based; however, they also seem to be significantly *future-oriented*. The motivation for decision-making is tightly coupled with the idea that the decision affects the future. This is only possible if the organization develops a memory of both the future and the past, which serves as a structure that functions as a decision premise. This memory is the structural blind spot of the decision, because without a reliance on memory, the distinction of an unchangeable past and a changeable future cannot be made in the present.

Thus, the theoretical perspective as outlined leads to the analytical question of how decisions open up particular pictures of past and future, and how these constructions are used to decide in the present. As outlined above, the idea of futurization and defuturization provides a heuristic to observe how the construction of time dimensions influence the scope of what seems possible in a particular present practice. The construction of time dimension is an empirical question and it therefore directs the focus of the analysis to the question how these constructions are commonly drawn and how these constructions change.

Illustration: The Change of Decision Semantics

At this point, I want to briefly illustrate how this theoretical perspective can be used for empirical analysis in the realm of organizing. Albeit this framework can serve as an observation lens for every organizational practice, I want to show in the following how the semantic discourse of decision-making can be analysed from this theoretical stance. The underlying methodological idea is that semantics build a reservoir of ambiguous but condensed meaning that goes beyond single practice contexts. The use of language, semantics and concepts builds a reservoir of meanings that establish social expectations of different forms of practice that are considered acceptable and legitimate (Koselleck 1982, p. 410) but do not lead causally to certain forms of practice. They open a space where specific forms of practice are more expectable and plausible compared to others: semantics serve as structures. In this case, I assume that the management-philosophical discourse on decision-making and the semantics that are used in there offer an access to beliefs and semantics, which play a significant role in organizational decision-making at a particular point in time. Semantics can be perceived as structures that build a reservoir of decision premises that can be actualized in a present decision situation. Thus, to understand what it means to organize for the future, the task must be to analyse how these semantic structures serve to defuturize or futurize the present. Moreover, as outlined above, every decision also creates its own temporality and marks a distinction between past and future. Hence, the aim is to analyse the temporal semantics connected with the semantics of deciding within these texts.

By analysing semantics, I follow an analytical strategy that focuses on the exploration of historical shifts of semantics to understand present phenomena and challenges in organizations (Andersen 2011; Henkel

2013; Luhmann 2004; Rennison 2007; Atzeni and von Groddeck 2015). I studied articles on decision-making in *Harvard Business Review* (HBR) and *California Management Review* (CMR). I chose these journals as they serve as an exemplified source of mainstream management thought over a long period of time: HBR was first published in 1922, CMR in 1958. The discourse of decision-making in HBR and CMR is therefore used as a source to analyse how common the descriptions are of the construction of time dimensions and the need for specific forms of deciding at a certain point in time. I selected all articles containing the keyword 'decision' and analysed these articles according to Koselleck's approach to discourse analysis (Åkerstrøm 2003). First, I traced the meaning of individual decision concepts by comparing it with counter-concepts in the particular article. Second, I analysed how future and past are constructed within these individual concepts of decision and how this leads to forms of futurization or defuturization. Third, I compared the articles to trace analogies. Approximately 60 articles were analysed.

The reconstruction of the change in semantics of decision-making that follows serves two aims. First, it illustrates how a system-theoretical approach can be used for empirical research in the realm of organization research by reconstructing the relation of time dimensions and forms of decision-making. It thereby introduces an approach which combines a process-theoretical perspective with an organization theory that views decision as the central operating mode. Second, it reveals that futurization of the present has increased over a very long period, whereas in the present both an extreme increase of futurization and an extreme increase of defuturization can be observed. Although the increase of futurization in general might not be all that surprising, the last finding in particular shows to what extent the system-theoretical framework contributes to current research debates on 'future organizing'. It provides a sociological reinterpretation that shows that attempts to prepare for the future, like, for example, the building of dynamic capabilities (e.g. Teece et al. 1997) or scenario-planning and trend-research (e.g. Liebl and Schwarz 2010), do not only lead to a sophisticated future orientation but also at the same time to a concentration on the present. The aim of this chapter is therefore not so much to connect to certain research debates in organization or management research but to show how the proposed theoretical framework can be used for empirical analysis that provides insights into general shifts of sense-making in organization. It might, however, shed light on blind spots while creating new ones.

Coping with the Contingent Past: The Knowledge-Based Decision

A first glance into the very first publication of HBR reveals that the semantic concept of decision-making was already present at this time. The purpose of the article by Donham (1922) is the promotion of a 'proper theory of business' when it comes to important decisions:

> Unless we admit that *rules of thumb*, the *limited experience* of the executives in each individual business, and the *general sentiment of the street*, are the sole possible guides for executive *decisions of major importance*, it is pertinent to inquire how the representative practises of business men generally may be made available as a broader foundation for such decisions, and how a *proper theory of business*, to meet the need, must develop to such a point that the executive, who will make the necessary effort, *may learn effectively from the experience of others in the past what to avoid and how to act under the conditions of the present*. Otherwise, business will continue *unsystematic, haphazard, and for many men a pathetic gamble (…)*. (1922, p. 1)

We learn from this citation how the idea of a rational organization that can be efficiently planned is produced by a certain temporal distinction. In the first part of the citation, Donham states that until now, 'business men' made 'decisions of major importance' based on 'rules of thumb', 'limited experience' and the 'sentiment of the street'. The reference to decision-making and the question of what to do to improve the business are clearly in the past. The critique by Donham is not that the wrong temporal orientation of decision-making is being used, but that the manner in which information is drawn from the past is wrong. To cope with present problems and questions, 'business men' cannot rely on a limited perspective; they need to ground their decision in a 'proper theory of business'. Thus, the future here is not the problematic reference. It is just the continuance based on the decision taken in the present. The future here is a continued present; the distinctive dimension is the past. The past is seen as a reservoir of knowledge which can be used in the right way when theory is applied. The construction of time produces the need for decision-making in the present by distinguishing a contingent past as a reservoir of knowledge and an unproblematic future as the continuance of the present. The decision ends the uncertainty produced by the past and produces a clear future. The effect of this form of decision is 'defuturization' (Luhmann 1976, p. 141), as it works with a picture of an unproblematic future when the right decision is made. This form of decision-making transforms the open future into a fixed form. In organization theory, this form of decision-making was described using the well-known notion of 'uncertainty absorption' (March and Simon 1959).

Coping with a Fast-Changing World: The Decision for Long-Term Success

As we have seen in the previous section, reality was already described as dynamic and rather complex, but after the Second World War, the perception of a changing environment became increasingly dominant. This is again reflected in organization theory. Scott marked this transformation as the 'entry of open system models' (Scott 2004, p. 4). A citation from Schultz's (1952) article on 'Decision-making: A Case Study in Industrial Relations' might illustrate the transformation:

> Every organization needs *flexibility* in meeting *new problems* if it is to be *successful in the long run*. Thus, the *restricting forces within a situation* take on great significance. For preventive as well as restorative reasons, analysis of how a confining environment develops and understanding of the nature of such an environment become universally important. (p. 105)

Rather than referring to an uncertain and turbulent past from which an executive must draw theory-based conclusion, this citation refers to the uncertain development of the environment. To cope with 'new problems' that seem to pop up regularly, the environment must be analysed. Therefore, what we see here is still a form of decision that should be made based on knowledge. The knowledge cannot be drawn solely from the past; instead, it must be combined with an analysis of the dynamics of the present. This indicates a change in the construction of temporal dimension. Whereas in the previous section, drawing conclusions from the past was the problem, the problematic horizon now becomes the present and the future. If problems are not solved adequately in the present, the future present is in danger.

The future loses its unproblematic status and comes into focus. Decisions become decisions about plans as a vehicle to condition the future. With the emergence of planning semantics, it becomes clearer that aligning the organization to keep the future unproblematic requires additional effort. Thus far, we can see that trust in the past as a reservoir for the right knowledge is minimized. The idea that decisions in the present fix the future of an organization is still common, although it is starting to change. The past is still the reservoir for knowledge; however, the methods and techniques must capture the changing dynamics of the environment rather than underlying forces of a certain business field. The future can be fixed if the right decision is made in the present. However, a semantic shift can be observed. The future is no longer a future present but becomes a present future. The future is postponed, and it is described as 'a long-range' horizon, which still promises success but the belief that the promise is kept is related to the premise that the dynamics of the past and present environment must be understood and managed in the right way. Not surprisingly, concepts like 'long range planning' and 'forecasting' emerge during this period (e.g. Wrapp 1957; Ackoff 1970). The dominance still lies in techniques of defuturization, but there are hints—like the idea that ideas matter—that this dominance is slowly changing.

Coping with the Contingent Future: The Strategic Decision

A notable change in the semantics of decision-making can be illustrated by the following citation from the article 'Scenarios. Uncharted waters ahead' by Pierre Wack in 1985. In the article, he explicitly questioned the technique of producing a certain picture of the future by interpreting and analysing the past:

Forecasts are not always wrong; more often than not, they can be reasonably accurate. And that is what makes them so dangerous. They are usually constructed on the assumption that *tomorrow's world will be much like today's*. They often work because the world does not always change. But sooner or later forecasts will fail when they are needed most: in *anticipating major shifts in the business environment* that make whole *strategies* obsolete. (…) My thesis (…) is this: the way to solve this problem is not to look for better forecasts by perfecting techniques or hiring more or better forecasters. Too many forces work against the possibility of getting the right forecast. *The future is no longer stable*; it has become a *moving target*. No single 'right' projection can be deduced from *past behavior*. The better approach, I believe, is to *accept uncertainty*, try to understand it, and make it part of our reasoning. Uncertainty today is not just occasional, temporary deviation from a reasonable predictability; it is a basic structural feature of the business environment. *The method used to think about and plan for the future must be made appropriate to a changed business development.* (p. 73)

Here, a new understanding of the future has emerged which is mirrored in a change of semantics: the uncertainty of the future cannot be transformed into certainty by applying adequate planning techniques in the present. On the contrary, the aim is not to reduce uncertainty but to 'accept uncertainty', to accept that 'tomorrow's world' will not be 'much like today's'. The future is not stable anymore; it is a 'moving target'. The past here is described as 'past behaviour' that holds relevant information only in a world without 'major shifts'. However, in times where uncertainty is the 'basic structural feature of the business environment', the past becomes a horizon that will not continue. The orientation of the present decision must be to understand and analyse a future that holds various possible outcomes. The future turns from being a future present into a future future, since we can no longer anticipate what the future will bring. Here, the paradoxical character of decision-making becomes explicit. In the present, the task is to prepare and plan for something that must be treated as not plannable. Decision-making is no longer described in terms of planning semantics. Semantics like the 'strategic decision' and 'risk' emerge accompanied by techniques like 'scenario thinking' (Åkerstrøm Andersen and Grønbæk Pors 2017). Thus, the strategic decision is a decision that operates on the futurization of the present.

Praising Both the Future of the Future and the Feeling for the Present: The Sensual Decision

In recent years, starting around the turn of the millennium, an additional semantic shift could be observed. What we see at this stage is a new semantic conception of decision-making, which, in part, is an escalation of the strategic decision. An organization must prepare for the totally unexpectable future. This cannot be done by 'planning' or 'rational analysing', but by 'sensing' in the present how to adapt an organization to an unknown future. This semantic shift can be illustrated by an extract from an article which discusses the use of 'dynamic capabilities' (Teece et al. 1997) by organizations as one possible mode of coping with a fast-moving world:

> Building better sensing and dynamic capabilities throughout the organization is a powerful way to manage stormy waters with fast-moving currents. (…) Ideally, *sensing and adaptation systems* are less-tailored to the firm's current capabilities and more to future trends and uncertainties. Even in the best case, much will be missed in fast-changing environments. This means that strategic leaders, rather than systems, will be the last line of defence when unexpected scenarios materialize. The contingent nature of dynamic capabilities as well as the crucial role of leaders both merit greater attention in how organizations can and should adapt when facing deeply uncertain futures. (Day and Shoemaker 2016, p. 75)

One of the ideas expressed in this extract is that an organization can build contingent capabilities in the present, enabling the organization to dynamically adapt to 'stormy waters' and 'sense' the potential of the future. As it is all about adapting to and sensing a future which is completely unknown, the capabilities must in themselves be dynamic. The futurization of the present is actually a futurization of the future. However, as far as the present is concerned, it is clear that even when an organization can build dynamic capabilities, 'much will be missed in fast-changing environments'. Thus, the sensual capacity of the leader in the very present builds 'the last line of defence'. Hence, what we see in the moment is actually the disappearance of the explicit semantic of decision-making.

The decision emerges as a description of the need for action in the present by envisaging a future which is completely different from the present. As adaption to this horizon is nearly impossible, much relies on the very present senses of the leader, who seems to be the only one to be able to integrate this futurized future into the present and thereby defuturize it. It seems that the distinction between the present and an immensely futurized future produces a new form of decision-making in the present rather than the distinction of past and future. It is a form of decision that reactivates defuturization by futurization of the future.

Conclusion

What happens when organizations organize the future? From a system-theoretical point of view, this task has always been done in the very present by making decisions. Decisions are operations that build their own temporality. Decisions can only be made when they construct a picture of the past and a picture for the future. Decisions select and actualize a memory of both future and past. The assumption of this chapter is that the actual selection and actualization of certain memories in the actual operations of decision-making is connected to semantics of decision-making that mirror specific time conceptions. These semantics work as premises for the process of decision-making in organizations, not because they transport a concrete memory but because they transport modalities of how the scope of future and past is constrained. The analytical question, therefore, is to explore whether the memories of the time dimensions are closed or open. Regarding the future, this means analysing whether the future in the present is futurized (opened) or defuturized (closed). Thus, to understand how the idea of organizing has changed in modern society, the analysis of semantic changes might be a suitable starting point.

The analysis of a history of decision-making conducted in this study, which used material from the HBR and the CMR, as an influential reservoir of western ideologies of good management and deciding, revealed a shift from past orientation to future orientation. The first form of the semantic concept of decision is the *knowledge-based decision*. Here, the need for decision arises by pointing to a past that bears the relevant information for decision-making when the right theory is applied. The decision produces the favoured future. The effect of the decision is the defuturization of the future in the present through relying on the past. This semantic form was slowly destabilized by a semantic form, which I called the *decision for long-term success*. The decision should be made based on knowledge, but the knowledge cannot be drawn solely from the past but must be combined with an analysis of the dynamics of the present. This indicates a change in the construction of temporal dimension. The future becomes a problematic horizon. Decisions become decisions about plans to condition the future. This semantic conception still defuturizes the future, although it is decreasing. Thus, the semantic concept of the *strategic decision* manifests the shift from the defuturizing of the present to futurization. Here, the semantic of decision becomes explicitly paradoxical: it is about preparing for something that must be treated as something for which we cannot prepare. On the other hand, since the turn of the millennium, the semantic conception of decision-making can be observed through further increase in the futurization of the present and a new increase of defuturization by emphasizing the sensual perception of the complex present. Decisions are described as *sensual decisions*.

In sum, the aim of the study was to show how the transformation of the concept of decision can be analysed from a system-theoretical framework. The focus point was to show how the meaning of decisions is directly intertwined with the construction of time dimensions. Depending on how the time dimensions are constructed, different strategies of futurization and defuturization (and their combination) are used to legitimate a specific form of decision. In the illustration of the analysis of decision semantics, the purpose was to show how decision semantics have changed, as this provides a hint of how these semantic concepts of decision might influence organizational practice. This is, of course, an abstract and theoretical approach. The results that are indicated here might therefore serve as a general sociological reflection of applied management techniques and, indeed, call for more in-depth research. Nonetheless, the aim of the study was to indicate the fruitfulness of this perspective as it encompasses both a fundamental temporal theory and a diagnostic framework in order to distinguish modes of organizing for the future.

References

Ackoff, Russell L. 1970. A Concept of Corporate Planning. *Long Range Planning* 3: 2–8.
Ahrne, Göran, Nils Brunsson, and David Seidl. 2016. Resurrecting Organization by Going Beyond Organizations. *European Management Journal* 34: 93–101.
Åkerstrøm Andersen, Niels. 2003. *Discursive Analytical Strategies: Understanding Foucault, Koselleck, Laclau, Luhmann*. Bristol: Policy Press.
———. 2011. Conceptual History and the Diagnostics of the Present. *Management & Organizational History* 6: 248–267.
Åkerstrøm Andersen, Niels, and Justine Grønbæk Pors. 2017. On the History of the Form of Administrative Decisions: How Decisions Begin to Desire Uncertainty. *Management & Organizational History* 12: 119–141.
Apelt, Maja, Cristina Besio, Giancarlo Corsi, Victoria v Groddeck, Michael Grothe-Hammer, and Veronika Tacke. 2017. Resurrecting Organization Without Renouncing Society: A Response to Ahrne, Brunsson and Seidl. *European Management Journal* 35: 8–14.
Atzeni, Gina, and Victoria von Groddeck. 2015. Normality, Crisis and Recovery of Narrating Medical Professionalism. *Tamara Journal for Critical Organization Inquiry* 13: 25–40.
Bakker, Rene M., Robert DeFillippi, Andreas Schwab, and Jörg Sydow. 2016. Temporary Organizing: Promises, Processes, Problems. *Organization Studies* 37: 1703–1719.
Blaschke, Steffen, Dennis Schoeneborn, and David Seidl. 2012. Organizations as Networks of Communication Episodes: Turning the Network Perspective Inside Out. *Organization Studies* 33: 879–906.
Brunsson, Nils. 1982. The Irrationality of Action and Action Rationality: Decisions, Ideologies and Organizational Actions. *Journal of Management Studies* 19: 29–44.
Buchanan, Leigh, and Andrew O'Connell. 2006. A Brief History of Decision Making. *Harvard Business Review* 84: 32–41.
Cohen, Michael D., James G. March, and Johann P. Olson. 1990. A Garbage Can Model Organizational Choice. In *Decisions and Organizations*, ed. James G. March, 294–334. Oxford: Blackwell.
Cyert, Richard M., and G. James. 1963. *A Behavioral Theory of the Firm*. Englewood Cliffs: Prentice-Hall.
Day, George, and Paul Schoemaker. 2016. Adapting to Fast-Changing Markets and Technologies. *California Management Review* 58: 59–77.

Donham, Wallace B. 1922. Essential Groundwork for a Broad Executive Theory. *Harvard Business Review* 1: 1–10.

Durkheim, Emile. 1984. Preface to the Second Edition. In *The Division of Labour in Society*, ed. Emile Durkheim, xxxi–xlix. New York: The Free Press.

Esposito, Elena. 2013. The Structures of Uncertainty: Performativity and Unpredictability in Economic Operations. *Economy and Society* 42: 102–129.

Henkel, Anna. 2013. Geneaology of the Pharmacon: New Conditions for the Social Management of the Extraordinary. *Management & Organizational History* 8: 262–276.

Hernes, Tor. 2007. *Understanding Organization as Process: Theory for a Tangeld World*. London: Routledge.

Knudsen, Morten. 2005. Displacing the Paradox of Decision Making. In *Niklas Luhmann and Organization Studies*, ed. David Seidl and Kai Helge Becker, 107–126. Malmö: Liber andCopenhagen Business School Press.

Koselleck, Reinhard. 1982. Begriffsgeschichte and Social History. *Economy and Society* 11 (4): 409–427.

———. 2004. *Futures Past: On the Semantics of Historical Time*. New York: Columbia University Press.

Liebl, Franz, and Jan O. Schwarz. 2010. Normality of the Future: Trend Diagnosis for Strategic Foresight. *Futures* 42 (4): 313–327.

Lindblom, Charles E. 1959. The Science of 'Mudling Through'. *Public Administration Review* 19: 79–80.

Luhmann, Niklas. 1964. *Funktionen und Folgen formaler Organisation*. Berlin: Duncker and Humblot.

———. 1976. The Future Cannot Begin: Temporal Structure in Modern Society. *Social Research. An International Quarterly of the Social Sciences* 43: 130–152.

———. 1995. *Social Systems*. Stanford: Stanford University Press.

———. 2000. *Organisation und Entscheidung*. Wiesbaden: Westdeutscher Verlag.

———. 2004. *Gesellschaftsstruktur und Semantik 1: Studien zur Wissenssoziologie der modernen Gesellschaft*. Frankfurt am Main: Suhrkamp.

———. 2005a. The Concept of Autopoiesis. In *Niklas Luhmann and Organization Studies*, ed. David Seidl and Kai Helge Becker, 54–63. Malmö: Liber & Copenhagen Business School Press.

———. 2005b. The Paradox of Decision Making. In *Niklas Luhmann and Organization Studies*, ed. David Seidl and Kai Helge Becker, 85–106. Malmö: Liber & Copenhagen Business School Press.

March, James G., and Herbert A. Simon. 1959. *Organizations*. New York/London/Sydney: Wiley.
Nassehi, Armin. 2005. Organizations as Decision Machines: Niklas Luhmann's Theory of Organized Social Systems. In *Contemporary Organization Theory*, ed. Campell Jones and Rolland Munro, 178–191. Oxford: Blackwell.
Rennison, Betina. 2007. Historical Discourses of Public Management in Denmark: Past Emergence and Present Challenge. *Management & Organizational History* 2: 2–26.
Schoeneborn, Dennis, Steffen Blaschke, Francois Cooren, Robert D. McPhee, David Seidl, and James R. Taylor. 2014. The Three Schools of CCO Thinking: Interactive Dialogue and Systematic Comparison. *Management Communication Quarterly* 28 (2): 285–316.
Schultz, George P. 1952. Decision Making: A Case Study in Industrial Relations. *Harvard Business Review* 30: 105–113.
Scott, W. Richard. 2004. Reflections on a Half-Century of Organizational Sociology. *Annual Review of Sociology* 30: 1–21.
Simon, Herbert. 1959. Theories of Decision-Making in Economics and Behavioral Science. *The American Economic Review* XLIX (3): 253–283.
———. 1961. *Administrative Behavior. A Study of Decision-Making in Administrative Organization*. 2nd ed. New York: The Macmillan Company.
Teece, David, Gary Pisano, and Amy Shuen. 1997. Dynamic Capabilities and Strategic Management. *Strategic Management Journal* 18: 509–533.
Tsoukas, Haridimos, and Robert Chia. 2002. On Organizational Becoming: Rethinking Organizational Change. *Organization Science* 13: 567–582.
von Foerster, Heinz. 1992. Ethics and Second-Order Cybernetics. *Cybernatics & Human Knowing* 1: 9–19.
von Groddeck, Victoria, Jasmin Siri, and Katharina Mayr. 2016. Die Entscheidungsvergessenheit der Organisationsforschung. Ein Plädoyer für eine operative Entscheidungsforschung. *Soziale Systeme* 20: 167–192.
Wack, Pierre. 1985. Scenarios. Uncharted Waters Ahead. *Harvard Business Review* 63: 73–89.
Weber, Max. 1958. The Three Types of Legitimate Rule. *Berkeley Publications in Society and Institutions* 4: 1–11.
Wrapp, H. Edward. 1957. Organization for Long-Range Planing. *Harvard Business Review* 35: 37–47.

0# 3

What's New? Temporality in Practice Theory and Pragmatism

Anders Buch and Iben Sandal Stjerne

Introduction

Quite a lot of resources are used and efforts are made to envision, predict and foretell organizational futures and forthcoming social orders. In the past, preparing for and anticipating social futures has preoccupied leaders and organizers, and, in contemporary organizational life, methods of telling and forecasting forthcoming social orders have been turned into a commodity that organizations pursue to be better prepared for future challenges (Urry 2016). In a competitive market, organizations see a need to innovate in order to stay abreast with current technological, financial and organizational trends, and, preferably, to become trendsetters. In the so-called creative industries, the need to 'know' or 'invent' the future is particularly pertinent (Becker 1982). Creative industries thus provide

---

A. Buch (✉)
Aalborg University, Copenhagen, Denmark

I. S. Stjerne
Department of Strategic Management and Globalization, Copenhagen Business School, Frederiksberg, Denmark

© The Author(s) 2018
H. Krämer, M. Wenzel (eds.), *How Organizations Manage the Future*,
https://doi.org/10.1007/978-3-319-74506-0_3

interesting cases for understanding the role of novelty in organizing for the future. Creative projects need to find the right balance between past and future in order to be successful. New unfamiliar practices are required that build future practices and accessibility and familiarity from past practices that allow for identification (Jones et al. 2012; Becker 1982; Lampel et al. 2000; Wijnberg and Gemser 2000).

Developing a successful project taps into a limited timespace of opportunity. Creative organizations operate with materializing visions while drawing on experience and linking to references from the past (Stjerne and Svejenova 2016). Creativity is obviously directed towards social futures, and novelty, originality, change and transformation of the current states of affairs are components of creative processes. However, what is more precisely meant by creativity has varied over time and is still subject to disputes within philosophy and the social sciences over the nature of human activity (Joas 1996). We will not engage in this broad discussion. Our focus is narrower, as we are interested in the conceptions of novelty in accounts of social futures.

In the social sciences, generally, social futures have traditionally been conceptualized along two different models of human action: the individualistic model and the structuralist model. In the individualistic model, human action is construed around modernist ideas about the autonomous, rational individual who interacts with other individuals in order to pursue goals. In this perspective, social futures derive from, and are caused by, individuals in processes of aggregation. Alternatively, more structuralist (or holistic) models stress the *sui generis* nature of the social. In this perspective, social futures find their form in processes of structural interplay and self-correction that produce novelties. The battles between the individualist and structuralist models of human action have raged in the social sciences for decades, but alternatives that seek to avoid the voluntarism of individualism and the determinism of structuralism have also been sought (Sawyer 2005).

In contemporary organization studies, more specifically, Garud et al. (2016) describe how the discussion on the notion of novelty and emergence in organizational activity has crystallized into different perspectives or 'lenses'. These lenses have underlying assumptions about space and time, and on whether emergence is seen as an externalized or endogenous feature of organizational contexts. One perspective presumes that emergence appears over linear time as a result of complex interactions among atomistic micro-agents in specific systems or contexts. In this *complexity* perspective on organizational activity, time becomes an exogenous tracking device for the detection of 'new' phenomena. Another perspective sees emergence as the result of the unfolding of *networks*. In this perspective, actors are not seen as atoms within a context; rather, agency is distributed among actors and their environments, and contexts are the product of how actors are related to one another. Still, assumptions about time are similar to those of the complexity perspective: time is exogenous as a background for the unfolding of 'new' phenomena. In opposition to these perspectives, a third *processual* perspective on emergence endogenizes experienced time in its account. In this perspective, past, present and future are intertwined in producing experience as the basis of organizational activity.

By stressing the inherently *temporal* nature of human activity, various philosophical approaches (e.g. Bergson, Whitehead, Mead, Heidegger and Ricoeur) have contributed to theorizing social futures in ways that try to accommodate the creativity of human action (Joas 1996; Garud et al. 2016; Dawson and Sykes 2016). In organization studies, these approaches have recently been adopted as the departure for empirical studies of organizations that stress a processual character of human activity (e.g. Garud et al. 2016; Langley and Tsoukas 2017).

In this chapter, we follow this trend in philosophy and organization studies as we set out to discuss two temporal approaches to social order that accentuate the role of novelty and change in accounts of social organization, activity and human action, namely, the pragmatist approach of George Herbert Mead and the practice theoretical approach of Theodore R. Schatzki. The ambition of both approaches is to theorize social life and social order to explain how change and stasis come about as human activity unfolds in time and space—and to avoid both individualist and structuralist conceptions of human action. Furthermore, both approaches are preoccupied with understanding the nature of the determination of (social) events as the future turns into present states of affairs. It should be noted that the temporal approaches outlined by Mead and Schatzki are not preoccupied with the so-called objective time, that is, chronological quantified clock time, successive time or *Chronos*. Rather, they discuss how temporality unfolds and structures human experience in the categories of past, present and future to allow people to engage in activity. In this perspective, time is related to human conduct as it is organized and unfolds in social settings. It relates to what has traditionally been called *Kairos*, that is, the right or opportune moment (for action).

To guide our discussion, we set out to outline Mead's and Schatzki's conceptions of temporality. We will investigate how they, respectively, conceive of novelty in their theoretical accounts. With this in mind, we introduce an empirical case from an organizational setting in the creative industry: the production of the film *Antboy*. To illustrate the points about novelty, we will discuss this case using the conceptual resources put at our disposal by the two approaches to better understand how organizing for the future can in fact accommodate the processes of creativity that bring about novelty. We also briefly point to some differences between the two perspectives.

Mead and the Philosophy of the Present

George Herbert Mead is probably known to most social scientists for his seminal work on intersubjectivity in social psychology. But as a prominent figure in classical American pragmatism, he was also thoroughly engaged in metaphysical discussions as an advocate for new approaches in scientific inquiry. When reading his reflections on time, as outlined primarily in *The Philosophy of the Present* (originally published in 1932), they seem, at first sight, to have little importance for organizational studies, as they mainly address issues within the natural sciences, with thorough discussions on the importance of Einstein's theory of relativity and, at that time, new advances in quantum mechanics. But Mead's ambition was to develop a general theory of time, which situates the experiencing subject in a temporal context that spans past, present and future. Although most of Mead's discussions revolve around the observing and experimenting scientist, the discussions are in no way confined to the scientific domain. Their implications have general relevance for social life as it unfolds in organizational settings.

The fundamental idea in Mead's philosophy of time can be extracted from the title of his treatise: *The Philosophy of the Present*. His point is that the present has ontological priority. It is always in the present that the experiencing subject is envisioning the future through plans, projects, aspirations and so on. Similarly, the past is only accessible from the present as memories, inscriptions and monuments. Therefore, it is in the present that we have access to reality, whether this reality is past, present or future. Our experience of reality is confined to the present as we always only exist in the present. However, this does not mean that the present is unison. For Mead, the 'now' is always differentiated or 'stretched' in human existence. Although living and acting in the present, humans always seek to anticipate their actions by reaching out to projected futures. Likewise, living in the present, people receive and recall the past in their present activities. The present, stretching out to the past and the future, is not an occurrence that extends the experiencing subject into a determined past and future; on the contrary, it is an active process of the reconstruction (cf. Dewey 1920) of thought in the present. The present is the locus that gives meaning to and constantly (re)describes both the past and the future. The past is reinterpreted in the light of new experiences, and the future is anticipated in the light of past experiences. In this sense, the present is the locus where both the past and the future can be—and necessarily must be—represented and re-represented. But Mead's point is not only an epistemological one. Not only do we come to *know* and interpret the past in new ways as time proceeds, but the past is literally changing as time proceeds:

> The pasts that we are involved in are both irrevocable and revocable. It is idle, at least for the purposes of experience, to have recourse to a 'real' past within which we are making constant discoveries; for that past must be set over against a present within which the emergent appears, and the past, which must then be looked at from the standpoint of the emergent, becomes a different past. [...] It is idle to insist upon universal or eternal characters by which past events may be identified irrespective of any emergent, for these are either beyond our formulation or they become so empty that they serve no purpose in identification. (Mead 1932/2002, p. 36)

Like Dewey's, Mead's ontology is relational in the sense that the knowing subject and the known object are related in the act of coming to know. So, even though the past event is irrevocably gone and cannot be encountered anew, its meaning can—and does—change over time, as the subjects' experiences change. The past is constituted as a relationship between subject and object. This constant constitutional reconstruction means that even though human action is always bound by the present, the human self is also always reflectively transcending the present in creative and novel ways.

Mead's philosophy—as classical American pragmatist in general—was immensely influenced by Darwinian evolutionary thinking (e.g. Joas 1997, p. 169). Mechanistic determinism as well as teleological determinism was rejected. Instead, Mead sees the future as 'incurable contingent' (Mead 1972, p. 313 ff.) and open—ripe for novelty and emergence. The pragmatists were arguing against the Cartesian 'spectators' view of knowledge that separates the human individual (res cogitans) from the world (res extensa). The pragmatists saw the human individual as a social and biological organism that—in cooperation with other individuals—adapts to its physical environment to survive. As a biological organism, humans are not separated from the environment/world, but rather are already a part of it. Thus, there is no epistemological 'gap' to bridge—as biological organisms, humans are already, in the ontological sense, in and part of the world. This Darwinian conception of humans' place in the world has profound consequences for the way we should understand time. It installs novelty and emergence as a fundamental evolutionary premise in being. Laplacian mechanistic determinism is rejected and so is Aristotelian teleological determinism. The Darwinian evolutionary idea is that although something is caused by past events, it is not determined in all its future consequences. Novelty and emergence prevail in human activity.

This Darwinian insight is crucial to Mead's temporal account. Novelty and emergence play a role in the process of experiencing the world. As we engage with the world, we are faced with unexpected and unanticipated events that prompt us to reflect upon what we see and hear. Being confronted with unexpected events, in the present, can thus lead us to reconstruct the past. When new information is provided, this might lead to reflective processes that can result in a constitutional reconstruction of the past in the ontological sense outlined above. Here the new is something external, produced in the environment that impacts the experiencing organism. But the new also has another, internal component. Experience is not a passive process where the organism's 'me' is exposed to the environment; rather, experience is an active process propelled by the 'I'. In Mead's philosophy, the 'I' is a source of activity and creativity, an active and unpredictable component of the self (Mead 1934/1972, p. 197 ff.). In our experience of the world, in the present, the 'I' is the component that stretches the experience into the future, driven by the organism's problems and aspirations. Furthermore, the organism's problems and aspirations are provisional, and often change over time. Novelty seems to be built into the way we exist and engage with the world, as a biological organism in relation to its environment. Also, in evolution, emergence plays a crucial role. When an organism adapts to the environment, or constructs niches for its survival, something fundamentally new emerges from the interaction between organism and environment. These new phenomena will, in time, form a new basis for the interplay be*tween organism and environment.*

Schatzki's Event Ontology

Schatzki's account takes its point of departure in Heidegger's phenomenological considerations on time and human activity. As outlined in *Sein und Zeit*, and further developed and modified in Heidegger's later work, *Dasein* (translated as 'being there' or 'presence'—and roughly denoting human-being-in-the-world) is thrown into the world. Here, the world shows up in the 'clearing' as what exists. When *Dasein* steps into the clearing, entities show up as being there. It is through *Dasein*'s stepping into the clearing that the world is opened. The event denotes the quality of the happening of *Dasein*'s stepping into the clearing. Time and space are essential features of the clearing and thus become fundamental for *Dasein*'s ways of opening the world as a happening. In this sense, the human being is futurity, in that it takes over being the clearing (*Da*). This Heideggerian insight becomes crucial, as Schatzki characterizes human activity as fundamentally temporal.

For Schatzki, human activity is event-like. Like non-human, non-intentional events—for example, earthquakes or thunderstorms—human activity also has event-character. It is an event in the sense that it happens, befalls or takes place, just like non-intentional events. However, whereas non-human events are mere occurrences, activities are characterized by their intentional, temporal and spatial nature. Human activity, like mere occurrences, happens in objective time and space, but human activity differs from mere occurrences in that they unfold timespace in their happening. Human temporality unfolds the activity-event in three dimensions, which happens simultaneously, together: past, present and future. In this perspective, past, present and future do not form a succession in time; rather, past, present and future are dimensions of an event that happens at one stroke.

The structure of the activity-event must be understood in relation to *Dasein*'s thrownness. When we act, in the present, we are already in the world; in a specific situation, we act responsively and reflectively to the entities we find ourselves among. From the past, we draw forward aspects of situations that inform or motivate our actions, and we project (desired) ways of being into the future as objectives and ends in view. When we act, we are thus temporally stretched in between our motivating reason (which might be rational or not) and the goals and ends that we project into the future:

> The event of activity has a structure quite unlike that of other events. It is a temporal event in the sense of the temporality of activity. More specifically, it has three temporal dimensions, namely, coming toward that for the sake of which one acts (the future), coming or departing from that to or in the light of which one reacts (the past), and acting itself (the present). I summarily abridged this structure as teleologically acting motivatedly. Activity is a teleological event. (Schatzki 2010, p. 170)

As a temporal phenomenon, activity is indeterminate. Activity is not fixed prior to its happening in time. Rather, it is fixed by the fact that the activity is happening as an event, that is, it is the unfolding of past, present and future that is determining the event as it happens. The activity finds its determination as it is performed by people who act for the sake of future objectives and are motivated by past events. It is not that past events do not affect future events—they do—but the determination only happens when the action is performed in the present. According to Schatzki, it is in the flow of human conduct that practical intelligibility, that is, what it makes sense to do next, determines how to proceed, and practical intelligibility is teleological, directed towards future ends.

Temporality is thus a feature of the activities of individuals. Furthermore, individuals' activities interweave in social practices as they engage in collective projects. Common ends, preferred paths, sharing places and material arrangements are brought together in nexuses of organized actions, that is, social practices that guide activity. However, according to Schatzki's Heideggerian theory of human activity, social practices do *not* determine activity. Social practices, understood as normativized nexuses of activities, can only guide action:

> Like rules and cultural as well as institutional orders, interwoven timespaces cannot predetermine activity. They explain coordinated actions because they happen *along with*, as the effect of, the performances of actions. Because, moreover, social phenomena consist in practices, and practices are composed of actions, social phenomena, too, are indeterminate. (Schatzki 2010, p. 186; emphasis in the original)

Schatzki's event ontology thus characterizes human activity as fundamentally indeterminate—determination only happens in the present as the action is performed. Many components, among which Schatzki singles out material arrangements and social practices, are active in guiding, channelling and restraining activity. But ultimately human activity is indeterminate.

Producing a Novel Genre Film: *Antboy*

The *Antboy* film project was followed ethnographically by the second author of this chapter from August to November 2013, during the film's preproduction, and in January and February 2014, during the final stages of preproduction (see Stjerne and Svejenova 2016; Stjerne 2016 for a detailed account of the ethnography and methodological reflections). *Antboy* is a movie that was initiated by the CEO of Nimbus Film, Birgitte Hald, who sought to develop a new genre and change existing practices within the Danish film industry. The vision of *Antboy* involved going beyond the predominant style of social realism within the Danish film industry in order to enrich it with elements from other genres, especially in terms of the practices performed in the United States, where filmmakers have a wide range of tools with which to tell a good story. Developing a new Danish hero genre required modifying and transcending prevalent practices within the Danish film industry. Creating this new genre meant that several challenges needed to be overcome.

Birgitte and an assistant searched through various archives and manuscripts to find a story suitable for this project. They were looking for a hero character with a human touch that would allow them to bring in social realism. First, they stumbled upon a book called *Captain Underpants*, a story about a clumsy superhero, but unfortunately the film rights had already been sold to DreamWorks Animation. Searching further, they came across a suitable book trilogy, *Antboy*, and Nimbus acquired the film rights.

The first real challenge came when searching for a suitable director for the film project. At first, Birgitte reached out to some of the experienced directors of children's movies who were semi-attached to Nimbus Film. However, none of these directors were available within a reasonable time frame and, in the end, a less experienced director was hired. Unfortunately, the manuscript was interpreted within the existing social realism genre, and did not include the American hero storylines. As a result, the team was discarded and the manuscript abandoned. The hiring process started anew, this time with a stronger focus on hiring people interested in the US hero genre. For a while, no potential candidates came to the producer's mind, and the project ended up in a drawer at Nimbus Film along with other 'orphan projects'.

One day, however, a director who was enthusiastic about the hero genre and was working on a different film project at Nimbus came across the *Antboy* project and convinced Birgitte that he was the right director for it, despite his lack of experience with feature films. Birgitte decided to give him a chance because she thought that his perspective, which was more heavily inspired by US style, would enable the vision to be brought forth. Birgitte knew that she would not get national state support without guaranteeing a deeper experience base of competencies for the project, so she added herself to the list of producers working on the movie. Following several disagreements with the national funding office and having failed to receive support, Birgitte decided to support the movie herself because she believed in a future return on her investment. *Antboy* was an investment in moving into a new market that would enable the creation of future movies and funding in this genre. Eventually, the movie received financial support from the Danish Film Institute (Det Danske Filminstitut, DFI) and the production of the movie was ready to begin.

During preproduction, the new vision was concretized by the *Antboy* team through references to several prior movies, mood boards and mood books (that is, collages of images, texts, samples of objects and colours that provide an imaginary setting for a storyline), and a manuscript that was to specify the action to be carried out during production. During production, they discovered that the manuscript was insufficient to guide onset activity. The director realized too late that some scenes could not be carried out in practice. On the set, some scenes had to be shot ad hoc, without pre-planning, requiring the team to come up with solutions to problems, or to replace and invent scenes on the spot. An example of this was a scene where Antboy was supposed to climb the walls to the top floor window of his house. The cinematographer realized that this scene would be difficult to shoot effectively because of the specific location, and he suggested having an elevator built into the house instead, connecting all three levels of the house.

In another scene, Antboy throws two bullies onto a basketball net, and the perspective of the next shot looks down from high up—creating a 'larger-than-life look'. This effect is usually carried out using cranes and expensive equipment, which the *Antboy* budget did not allow for. Solving the problem became a matter of creating new practices inspired by the techniques used in the production of American action movies. The crane equipment technique that is usually used to create this filmic expression is executed by filming both the person and the camera upside down (both hanging from the roof) making it look as if they are both standing on the ground. By rotating the camera slowly and pulling the dolly backwards, it becomes clear from the viewers' perspective that the actors are actually hanging from the roof, which creates a moment of surprise. The cinematographer came up with an idea to develop this camera technique into a new hand-held version while pulling the dolly back.

In principle, it was the same as [with] the crane, but it (hand-held camera) just does not get a (smooth) sliding movement and the elegance, but instead it gets the playful indie, low-budget feel that characterized the first movie (*Antboy 1*) and also makes it more charming (than the other two sequel movies *Antboy 2* and *3*). (*Antboy* Cinematographer, 2015 interview).

The only way to get that perspective using traditional practices was with a crane, but in *Antboy* they decided to try this out with a drone. It worked just fine and created a new look.

It was impossible at that point in time to plan everything and to foresee all the challenges that lay ahead. The screenwriter was in a different location, alone and though he had a predilection for hero movies, he had limited experience in writing manuscripts for this kind of movie. One of the difficulties he faced was that writing and budgeting go hand in hand; every small stunt added to the manuscript severely impacted the budget. The screenwriter was fully aware of this, but found that it was impossible to budget while inventing the story.

Despite the difficulties, the movie was completed, became a novelty for the local industry and was reviewed positively by the critics. The critics emphasized its positive qualities, such as fun, charm, humanity and sense of adventure, stating that the movie had struck an 'elegant balance between action, comic, and Danish family movie tradition' and acknowledged its main character as 'possibly the greatest "little" superhero from Denmark to date'. The film attracted audiences comparable to traditional Danish commercial children's movies. It also received some festival attention, and was distributed internationally; in the United States, it was dubbed in English.

What's New in *Antboy*?

How are we to understand novelty, and when and where do we find it in the process of producing the *Antboy* movie? Considering the aphorism that 'everything must change to stay the same', how can we identify the *significant* changes that brought 'novelty' to the Danish film industry? In the flow of time, what determines events in ways that mean that they qualify as novel?

Theorizing on this case allows us to bring forth two temporal approaches to social order that accentuate the roles of novelty, change and temporality first from a pragmatist perspective and second from a social practice perspective. The first approach, found in Mead's pragmatism, brings out the role of the past–present–future connection in making the new, where both past and future are more fluid forms that enter into the present actions.

To understand the *Antboy* case from a pragmatist perspective requires that we conceptualize the case as a situation (Dewey 1938). This situation is populated with actors who are engaged in transactions with one another and their environment, and it is in the situation that experience is made possible. For American pragmatists, the 'situation' is *not* a single object or event or set of objects and events. We never experience or form judgements about objects and events in isolation, but only in connection with a contextual whole. It is this contextual whole that is theorized in relation to its temporal structure by Mead. It is in the present that past and future events are given meaning in relation to the contextual whole, the situation.

Thus, it is not possible to understand events in isolation. As an example, to understand how the scene with the bullies and the basketball net was solved, we must understand the contextual whole of the situation. This includes understanding how past and future events are reconstructed as actors come to know in the present situation. Certainly, the scene was important in order to tap into the action genre that was envisioned as ideal for the production, but the economic costs of using a crane were just too high. The creative solution to the problem was to replace the crane set-up with a hand-held camera. This solution stays true to the ambition of creating 'larger-than-life' effects, but now with a twist. Solving the problem becomes a process of reconstruction in the present. Determined to achieve, in the future, a 'larger-than-life' effect to tap into the American action hero tradition, the past is reconstructed in the present: the manifesto now implies that mixing American hero movies with Danish social realism *is* to bring forward 'the playful, indie, low-budget feel'. The solution is guided by envisioning the future and accomplishing the task in ways that will bring forth the 'larger-than-life' effects sought after, and it connects to the past via the cinematographers' experiences of shooting action scenes. Whereas the 'elegant sliding effect' of the camera movement afforded by the crane could not be achieved, a similar, but different camera effect could instead create a new and more playful effect. In the activity of the present, aspirations about future states of affairs (a new Danish hero genre) are connected to past experiences (both practices belonging to the action genre as well as social realism), while also changing these past experiences (reinterpreting prior movies in the light of the projections about the future *Antboy*). In this case, it was realized that 'larger-than-life' effects need not involve an expensive technical set-up with a crane; a similar, but different effect could be achieved in other ways.

The second approach, found in Schatzki's social practice theory, also installs the event as the basic ontological unit. Like Mead, the Heideggerian conception also differentiates the event into the dimensions of past, present and future—held together by *Dasein*'s existence in time. In this perspective, novelty is *inherent* in action. When the cinematographer created a new way to shoot the 'larger-than-life' scene with a hand-held camera and positioned it in a dolly instead of a crane, this activity must be explained as 'coming toward that for the sake of which one acts, and coming or departing from that to or in the light of which one reacts' (Schatzki 2010, p. 170). The 'coming toward that for the sake of which' is the cinematographer's teleological directedness towards filming the 'larger-than-life' shot which contributes to and enacts the aspiration to take the movie towards the imagery of the American hero film genre. 'Departing from that or in the light of which the action reacts' is the restricted budget, the unavailability of a crane for the shot, and a team that draws on past practices within social realism. In Schatzki's Heideggerian framework, the actions of the cinematographer are metaphysically indeterminate, as is all action. It is only determined in the present as the act happens. In this metaphysical position, novelty and change are inherent in activity.

Many authors have pointed at the parallel themes and approaches in phenomenology and American pragmatism (e.g. Okrent 1991; Baert 1992; Svec and Capek 2017), and it is not difficult to find convergences between practice theory and American pragmatism (Buch and Elkjær 2015; Buch and Schatzki forthcoming). In the present context, discussing temporality, we have already noted that both Mead and Schatzki theorize time in relation to human experience as past, present and future events. Using the conceptual resources provided by Mead and Schatzki, let us discuss change and novelty in the *Antboy* case.

Mead's and Schatzki/Heidegger's theorization of temporality installs novelty and change as a fundamental element in human activity. Novelty is not an exceptional incidence *in* time, but rather a constitutive element *of* temporality. For Schatzki/Heidegger, the indeterminacy of human activity means that action is open-ended, both on an individual and collective level. Similarly, Mead insists that the future is 'incurable contingent' (Mead 1972, p. 313 ff.), open, and constantly reconstructed in the present. However, the contingency of human activity does not leave it as a chaotic field of arbitrary actions. Mead's social psychology of the 'I' and the 'Me' (Mead 1934/1972) and Schatzki's theorization of social life as meshes and bundles of social practices (Schatzki 2002) are attempts to better understand how social order is constituted, preserved and changed in the flow of time. Both Mead and Schatzki attempt to theorize human activity in order to understand the basic mechanisms of human action. But in both cases, these mechanisms are not nomological or deterministic.

Although Mead's and Schatzki's theorizations of social life have many similarities, they also have differences. We have stressed the convergences between their views on time and the role they ascribe to novelty, but their views are slightly different on an ontological level. As previously mentioned, Mead's philosophy is strongly influenced by Darwinian thoughts on evolution. In Mead's account, sociality is an emergent phenomenon with causal powers that has acquired a certain autonomy in the course of evolution, and this emergent sociality is a product of interactions among organisms. In contrast, Schatzki's ontology is flat, claiming that 'everything there is to phenomena of some general sort is laid out on one level of reality' (Schatzki 2016). Instead of seeing 'the social' as an autonomous emergent phenomenon produced by agents' interactions, Schatzki's flat ontology stipulates that practices are the central element in the constitution of social phenomena and that they are laid out on one level of reality. In the practice theoretical perspective, sociality is not an emergent product of agents' normatively coordinated (inter)actions. Schatzki does not evoke normatively directed interactions as an explanation for emergent social activity.[1] Instead, he sees indeterminacy:

> [as] an inherent feature of human activity generally. [...] It is ultimately because activity is indeterminate that cultural and institutional orders, like knowledge, competence, preference, desire, commitment, and conviction, cannot predetermine the forms, or 'orderly features', of interaction. (Schatzki 2010, p. 186, our emphasis)

In Schatzki's social ontology, novelty is integral in action—both social and non-social—whereas for Mead, novelty emerges as an effect of interaction, cooperation and communication. The 'scope' of the practice theoretical conception of novelty is thus broader than Mead's.

These two perspectives, *which link the novel stronger* to the present actions, provide new ways of seeing and understanding creativity and innovation. This is in line with more recent debates in the literature that suggest a stronger focus on field research to bring the complexity of creativity into real life situations (Rosso 2014) or which use the notion of 'dancing in chains', with an emphasis on the ad hoc actions conducted in between externally and internally self-imposed constraints (Ortmann and Sydow 2017). By teasing out the temporal aspects of novelty, this approach opens up new perspectives to this ongoing debate about the role of constraints in creativity (e.g. Amabile 1996; Caniëls and Rietzschel 2015). As shown in the *Antboy* case, the temporal aspects of human activity are essential for unfolding how the novel evolves in practice. In the *Antboy* case, the future-directed aspiration to develop something new was what drove the activities. Furthermore, the present obstacles and delimitations enhance the novel. Although novelty is part of any human activity because of its open-endedness, actions are constantly modified and changed, and tools, such as manuscripts and mood boards, do not easily translate into the intended 'actions of the future'. The novel emerges in the present in the temporal tensions that are inevitably there. If the novel emerges from a temporal tension of past and future, it opens new considerations for debates about how to organize for creativity.

Conclusion

Antboy sought to change the existing practices within the Danish film industry. It was part of an initiative formulated by Birgitte Hald that children's movies should become more complex to better reflect the preferences of contemporary kids. This intentional call for change set in motion a chain of actions. Directors were hired, projects formulated, manuscripts drafted and productions established. Our short description of the *Antboy* initiative cannot do justice to the immense complexity of the situation and how the chains of actions evolved. However, it is obvious that the outcome of the process could not be predicted at the time Birgitte initiated the project. As the story goes, the project was almost abandoned because no qualified director could be found. It was only by coincidence that a director, working on another project at Nimbus Film, stumbled upon the plan to make a different kind of children's movie. Furthermore, throughout the production process, inventive novel solutions and compromises were found to bring forth the movie. In the temporal theorization of both Mead and Schatzki/Heidegger, 'novelty' has the character of an event that happens (as any other event). However, as an event, the 'novel' thrusts itself forward as humans temporalize being as past, present and future in engaging with the world.

By pointing to mechanisms in social activity, Mead's social psychology and Schatzki's practice theory can help us understand how this process of activities in the *Antboy* project evolved, was channelled, orchestrated and enacted in specific socio-material situations, involving specific actors with specific backgrounds and aspirations. But in the pragmatist and practice theoretical accounts, this theoretical explanation must always be not only partial, situated and fallible, but also—in an ontological sense—incomplete. Novel events are unpredictable and, in a sense, unexplainable—they just happen. It is only as they happen, in the present, that we can explain what happened, as a reconstruction of the past in the light of the future.

We have pointed to the convergences between pragmatism and practice theory in theorizing temporality and characterizing novelty in social activity. We believe that this convergence must be understood by bringing forth the preoccupation with the *practical* dimension of human life that has been influential in philosophy and humanistic theory throughout the twentieth century, and which has also taken the central stage in process-oriented approaches to organization studies (Chia 2017). Focusing on practice, practices, and emphasizing such phenomena as practical knowledge, the contextual, processual, embodied and temporal aspects of activity, and organizing actions in time and space, has produced intellectual resources for theorizing about human social life and organizing (for) the future. However, a task still remains for future research to explore and map the intricacies and details in the theoretical landscape that promote 'the primacy of the practical'. We have pointed out that even though both Mead and Schatzki emphasize novelty in their respective accounts of human activity, their ontologies are slightly different. In Schatzki's Heideggerian practice theory, novelty is an inherent constituent of indeterminate human activity, whereas in Mead's account, novelty is considered an emergent phenomenon springing from organisms' (communicative) interactions with one another and their environments. Which of these ontologies should be preferred is open to further research (Schatzki forthcoming).

Note

1. This does not mean that normativity is absent in practice theoretical accounts—only that so-called regulist accounts of normativity are problematic. Joseph Rouse (2017) argues that practice theory must adopt a temporal conception of normativity: 'What unifies a temporally extended social practice is not some feature that its individual performances have in common, but the mutual responsiveness of those performances over time.'

References

Amabile, Teresa M. 1996. *Creativity in Context*. Boulder: Westview Press.
Baert, Patrick. 1992. *Time, Self, and Social Being. Temporality Within the Sociological Context*. Aldershot: Avebury.
Becker, Howard S. 1982. *Art Worlds*. Berkeley: University of California Press.
Buch, Anders, and Bente Elkjær. 2015. Pragmatism and Practice Theory. Convergences or Collisions. Paper Presented at the Conference of Organizational Learning, Knowledge, and Capabilities (OLKC2015), Milan, April 2015.
Buch, Anders, and Theodore Schatzki. forthcoming. *Questions of Practice in Philosophy and the Social Sciences*. New York: Routledge.
Caniëls, M.C.J., and E.F. Rietzschel. 2015. Organizing Creativity: Creativity and Innovation Under Constraints. *Creativity and Innovation Management* 24: 184–196.
Chia, Robert. 2017. A Process-Philosophical Understanding of Organizational Learning as 'Wayfinding': Process, Practices, and Sensitivity to Environmental Affordances. *The Learning Organization* 24 (2): 107–118.
Dawson, Patrick, and Christopher Sykes. 2016. *Organizational Change and Temporality. Bending the Arrow of Time*. London: Routledge.
Dewey, John. 1920/2008. In *Reconstruction in Philosophy*, The Middle Works, ed. Jo Ann Boydston, vol. 12. Carbondale: Southern Illinois University Press.
———. 1938. *Logic. The Theory of Inquiry*. New York: Henry Holt and Company.
Garud, Raghu, Barbara Simpson, Ann Langley, and Haridimos Tsoukas, eds. 2016. *The Emergence of Novelty in Organizations*. Oxford: Oxford University Press.
Joas, Hans. 1996. *The Creativity of Action*. Cambridge: Polity.
———. 1997. *G. H. Mead. A Contemporary Re-examination of His Thought*. Cambridge, MA: MIT Press.
Jones, C., M. Maoret, F. Massa, and S. Svejenova. 2012. Rebels with a Cause: Formation of the De Novo Category 'Modern Architecture'. *Organization Science* 23: 1523–1545.
Lampel, J., T. Lant, and J. Shamsie. 2000. Balancing Act: Learning from Organizing Practices in Cultural Industries. *Organization Science* 11: 263–269.

Langley, Ann, and Haridimos Tsoukas, eds. 2017. *The SAGE Handbook of Process Organization Studies.* Thousand Oaks: SAGE.
Mead, George Herbert. 1932/2002. *The Philosophy of the Present.* New York: Prometheus Books.
———. 1934/1962. In *Mind, Self, and Society. From the Standpoint of a Social Behaviorist*, ed. C.W. Morris. Chicago: Chicago University Press.
———. 1938/1972. *The Philosophy of the Act,* ed. C.W. Morris et al. Chicago: Chicago University Press.
Okrent, Mark. 1991. *Heidegger's Pragmatism. Understanding, Being, and the Critique of Metaphysics.* Ithaca: Cornell University Press.
Ortmann, Günter, and Jörg Sydow. 2017. Dancing in Chains: Creative Practices in/of Organizations. *Organization Studies.* Online First, August 2017.
Rosso, Brent D. 2014. Creativity and Constraints: Exploring the Role of Constraints in the Creative Processes of Research and Development Teams. *Organization Studies* 35: 551–585.
Rouse, Joseph. 2017. Normativity. In *The Routledge Handbook of Philosophy of the Social Mind*, ed. Julian Kieverstein, 545–562. New York: Routledge.
Sawyer, R. Keith. 2005. *Social Emergence. Societies as Complex Systems.* Cambridge: Cambridge University Press.
Schatzki, Theodore. 2002. *The Site of the Social. A Philosophical Account of the Constitution of Social Life and Change.* University Park: Pennsylvania State University Press.
———. 2010. *The Timespace of Human Activity. On Performance, Society, and History as Indeterminate Teleological Events.* Lanham: Lexington Books.
———. 2016. Practice Theory as Flat Ontology. In *Practice Theory and Research. Exploring the Dynamics of Social Life*, ed. Gert Spaargaren, Don Weenink, and Machiel Larmers, 28–42. New York: Routledge.
———. forthcoming. On Plural Actions. In *Practice, Practices, and Pragmatism. Perspectives from Philosophy and the Social Sciences*, ed. Anders Buch and Theodore Schatzki. New York: Routledge.
Stjerne, Iben. 2016. Transcending Organization in Temporary Systems. Aesthetics' Organizing Work and Employment in Creative Industries. PhD Series 50.2016, Copenhagen: Copenhagen Business School.
Stjerne, Iben, and Silviya Svejenova. 2016. Connecting Temporary and Permanent Organizing. Tensions and Boundary Work in a Series of Film Projects. *Organization Studies* 37 (12): 1771–1792.

Svec, Ondrej, and Jakub Capek. 2017. *Pragmatic Perspectives in Phenomenology*. London: Routledge.
Urry, John. 2016. *What Is the Future?* Cambridge: Polity Press.
Wijnberg, N., and G. Gemser. 2000. Adding Value to Innovation: Impressionism and the Transformation of the Selection System in Visual Arts. *Organization Science* 11: 323–329.

4

Creativity in/of Organizations for Managing Things to Come: Lessons to Be Learnt from Philosophy

Günther Ortmann and Jörg Sydow

Introduction

'The future cannot begin' (Luhmann 1990; our transl.). In a sense, this is a truism because when the future begins it is no longer the future, given that 'to begin' means 'beginning in the present'. So, Luhmann's dictum says nothing but 'the future cannot become the present', which is analytically true. Inherent to the future is a 'not yet'. This seems to make 'organizing the future' paradoxical: how could one organize something that has not yet come into existence but is still to come? On the other hand, 'organizing *for* the future' comes close to a pleonasm insofar as organizing is always about future affairs—about how to get things done in the future (by providing suitable rules and resources *hic et nunc*). Why is it, then, that 'organizing (for) the future' as a challenge to be coped with has acquired an unquestionable plausibility and even urgency in our time?

G. Ortmann (✉)
Universität Witten/Herdecke, Witten/Herdecke, Germany

J. Sydow
Freie Universität Berlin, Berlin, Germany

© The Author(s) 2018
H. Krämer, M. Wenzel (eds.), *How Organizations Manage the Future*,
https://doi.org/10.1007/978-3-319-74506-0_4

The obvious answer is (see, for instance, Giddens 1990) because we live in 'hyper-modern' times characterized by significantly increased reflexivity, regarding in particular (a) acceleration (in terms of technological, organizational and market change), (b) perceived or real systemic irreversibilities and forces such as path dependencies and (c) increased leverage effects of present decisions and actions on an expectable future. All this exerts increasing pressure to take into account, anticipate and influence developments to come—one has to do it, not the least because others will do it. So, *not* to organize for a future, which casts a stronger and longer shadow on the present than ever before, seems to no longer be an option (see also Koch et al. 2016).

The paradoxicality of 'organizing the future' comes down to its uncertainty and unknowability. It is in this context, not least, that creativity in and of organizations is needed for dealing with the increased urgency of managing the future which, while being unknown, casts a longer shadow on the present. But creativity itself has the pertinent dimensions of temporality and unknowledgeability: to search for something new is to look for something that is unknown in the present but is to become known soon, something that helps us to prepare for a notoriously unknown future. Intending the new, however, is exactly what establishes another paradox, namely the Platonic search paradox mentioned in the Meno dialogue.[1] This seems to apply particularly to managing or organizing (for) creativity because organizing means intending and is about order, stability and predictability while creativity suggests, at least at first sight, the need for disorder, change and uncertainty (see also DeFillippi et al. 2007).

In the face of these difficulties, we found it worthwhile to look at more basic ways of dealing with implied problems as suggested by philosophers and some sociologists inspired by philosophy. In this chapter, we concentrate on selected issues revolving around questions that philosophers have dealt with, while making no claim of being exhaustive. The issues we focus on concern the problems of creating something new and managing things to come: contingency, temporality, knowledgeability and related problems such as the opposition of freedom and constraint. We begin by considering the concept of hyper-modernity and the accompanying questions of escalating contingency and escalating necessity. Next, we make a plea for a strict understanding of paradoxicality and consider ways of thinking about implied oppositions in terms of complementarity and recursive constitution, rather than the concept of paradox, which is somewhat devalued by over-use these days. The following section is dedicated to the role of imagination in every act of planning and decision-making as emphasized by Alfred Schutz (1967), who builds on Henri Bergson's work in this respect. We then deal with two versions of paradoxes of (intended) creativity: the Platonic search paradox and Jon Elster's states, which are essentially by-products, which is to say, states one cannot (directly) intend. We will take a look at the opposition of freedom and constraint, drawing particular attention to Friedrich Nietzsche's view of creativity. Finally, we deal with the problem of the emergence of corporate actorhood, where we consider the creativity *of* organizations—taken to be actors with an important role in (hyper-)modernity and in particular when it comes to bringing about something new—to create *and* to implement the new, which includes winning legitimation and the acceptance of users, consumers and the public.

The guiding criteria for selecting these issues were that (1) at first glance at least, creativity as well as the concept of future—and, to a greater degree, of organizing (for) creativity regarding the future—seems to imply a whole string of oppositions, contradictions and paradoxes; (2) these issues have to be dealt with in practice and, at the very least, 'managed'; (3) creativity in and of organizations is essential in face of an unknown future, and (4) there are possibly lessons to be learnt from philosophy regarding the temporality, complementarity and (Derridean) supplementarity of pertinent oppositions such as present/future, old/new and the like.

Creativity in Times of Escalating Contingency, Necessity and Impossibility

The German philosopher Theodor W. Adorno once said (in *Minima Moralia* 1976, p. 316) that we live within a 'cult of the new'. This is true for creativity too, which is in danger of becoming an incantation in the (hyper-)modern situation of escalating uncertainty, complexity and contingency. To rely on creativity is to draw a bill payable in the future—an uncertain future. It is a specific kind of what another German philosopher, Hermann Lübbe (1998), called *Kontingenzbewältigung* ('coping with contingency') by transforming coincidence into meaningful action (*Handlungssinn*; for an English explanation see Büttner 2009, p. 27). For Lübbe (1998), one way for *Kontingenzbewältigung* to materialize is through religion. The cult of the new might bear comparison with religion's function of coping with contingency: if we rely on and trust creativity we are no longer at the mercy of chance and serendipity, but able to act purposefully and meaningfully while coping with contingency. To sing the praises of creativity, then, may be an incantation of hope, reflecting the essence of religious faith. We propose supplementing Lübbe's view with the complementary concept of escalating necessities and impossibilities implied by escalating contingency. Think of the necessities/impossibilities caused by nuclear power (e.g. to get rid of the nuclear waste). Think of path dependencies, systemic forces and constraints, structural inertia or of exhausted resources such as oil, fresh water or even sand, and of the diminishing biodiversity. When God is dead, the escalating contingency provides the opportunity for something new; the escalating necessities/impossibilities provoke an urgency to seek shelter in the very idea of human creation and creativity: shelter and solace. Derrida (2007, p. 23) even suggests a desire of invention/desire to invent (albeit accompanied by a feeling of tiredness and exhaustion; ibid., p. 23). That is, from our perspective at least, how creativity became an 'exemplary format' of the entire society or a universal social norm (Reckwitz 2012) under conditions of (hyper-)modernity.

In times when more and more becomes possible in terms of technology, economy, market changes and so on; when action chains become longer and longer; when system complexities increase; when path dependencies and leverage effects become stronger and more far-reaching, anticipations of the future—for instance, the signalling of future performance, or the next smartphone or Tesla car as things to come soon—become more and more important (Ortmann 2009, pp. 44–49). The shareholder value of firms, such as Uber or Tesla, results to a large extent from placing bets on the notoriously unknown future. In such a situation, creativity in dealing with this future, with longer action chains, stronger system complexity, expectable path dependencies and so on, becomes more and more urgent.

Amabile's (1996) widely accepted definition of creativity—creation as the generation of something novel and at least potentially valuable (cf. Shalley et al. 2004)—obviously evokes a lot of questions, many of which have not been dealt with in any fundamental way. New for whom? Valuable for whom? What does 'generating' or 'bringing about' mean in this context? Does making creative use of toothpicks or paper clips imply the same creativity as Frederick Winslow Taylor's invention of scientific management or, at that, as the invention of limited liability for corporate actors? Isn't it the case that destruction, as well as production, can be creative, including even non-desirable destruction? And wouldn't such an 'evil' kind of creativity be a worthwhile research subject for management and organization studies? As evil as the purposes for which it was used, the invention of a combustion furnace with a double (or even triple) crucible in which to cremate corpses was the outcome of a generative process, and it was valuable for the Nazis in Auschwitz. To prefabricate buildings made with concrete slabs; to make use of the toxic waste product of pesticide production, namely dioxin, as a weapon in war; fracking (hydraulic fracturing): all these creations shed light on the deeply ambivalent character of creativity and therefore on the necessity to distinguish desirable from undesirable creations and kinds of creativity. Again, however, the question arises: desirable for whom? The value of a creation is always a matter of culture, history, interests and of reference systems; a matter of relativity. When referring to certain systems for which particular creations are valuable, we need to supplement Amabile's definition: the value we talk about has somehow to be generalizable in order to deserve to be called a product of creativity (see Gordon 1961, p. 3). Otherwise, there would be nothing other than a peculiar singularity, unique and ephemeral. This requirement for generalizability has inevitably a normative or moral dimension.

In the case of creativity *in* organizations, the contingency to be coped with may be internal or external. Insofar as organization itself is a means to absorb contingency and uncertainty (Thompson 1967; Luhmann

1995), it may come into conflict with creativity as another way of coping with contingency because the latter depends on and creates certain forms of contingency and uncertainty (Schüßler et al. 2014). So, organizing creativity—or organizing (for) the future—*may* turn out to be a contradiction *in adiecto*, a contradiction not just in terms, but a matter-of-fact contradiction in itself. We will, however, stick to the complementarity of organization and creation with an eye for the Derridean supplementarity involved.

Creativity *of* organizations (as an organizational capacity) is all the more pressing because organizations as corporate actors are confronted with internal and external contingencies and impossibilities, increasingly so in the course of omnipresent contingency and impossibility escalation. Consider, for example, the technological contingencies and constraints, of the possibilities and impossibilities implied by globalization, or of new forms of interorganizational cooperation within strategic alliances and networks or regional clusters (cf. Sydow et al. 2016). Is there, however, such a thing as the creativity of an organization as distinct from the creativity of its members? This question calls for a concept of emergence of a kind of capability that is more than the sum or aggregation of individual powers and cannot be reduced to such powers (see below). Philosophy, though for the most part ignorant of the concept and importance of organizations, let alone of their capacity as corporate actors—no lesson to be learned from philosophy in that respect—shows great interest in the question of emergence.

Paradoxicality, Complementarity and Recursiveness

Paradoxes in general, and the particular paradox involved in bringing about something new, are problems philosophers have dealt with since ancient times. This leads us to the question: what can we learn from philosophy regarding creativity in general and creativity *in* and *of* organizations for organizing (for) the future? While philosophical thinking doubtless underlies most theorizing, including psychological theories, which are consulted most often when it comes to explaining how creativity comes about, we aim to search for more direct inspiration from philosophy for an understanding of creative processes, whether they are conceived from a strong or moderate process view (cf. Fortwengel et al. 2017).

The first lesson is that not every tension, dilemma, opposition and even contradiction is a paradox. We should firmly restrict the concept and speak of a paradox only *if a condition of possibility implies a condition of impossibility*.[2] For this reason, we propose to substitute, in the majority of cases, the ideas of complementarity and recursive constitution for the somewhat worn out figure of a paradox. Dealing with creativity and its problems in terms of complementarities can turn out to be fruitful for both theorists and practitioners. Complementary oppositions presuppose each other as necessary conditions of possibility. A similar form is recursive constitution as defined by Giddens (1984): action constitutes structure and vice versa.

In order to sharpen the concepts of complementarity and recursive constitution, and to take away their somewhat comforting tinge of completeness, we will, however, add Derrida's idea of supplementarity. A supplement in this sense conveys the double meaning of supplementing *and* substituting/replacing. Derrida sometimes (e.g. 1976, pp. 141–142) calls it 'that dangerous supplement' because it is filling a gap or void on the one hand, but replacing or undermining the supplemented item on the other. This may include a difference in terms of temporality, too, namely a deferment. In an admittedly very general sense, for Derrida future is that what is to come but is subject to *différance*. Think of generating something new on the one hand and implementing and using it on the other. The latter can be considered as a supplement in the sense of Derrida; it may complement or even improve the implementation and usage in the ordinary sense, but it may also defer, dilute, modify, endanger or even replace the initial new idea or product, as in the case of a new and creative corporate strategy diluted or even perverted by and through the process of implementation. These are the constellations Derrida has in mind when he says: 'The *supplement* is to fill a void'—here, to complete or finish the initial new idea—but 'the supplement supplements. It adds only to replace. It intervenes or insinuates *in-the-place-of*; if it fills, it is as if one fills a void [...]. Compensatory [*suppléant*] and vicarious, the supplement is an adjunct, a subaltern instance which *takes-(the)-place* [*tient-lieu*]. As a substitute, it is not simply added to the positivity of a presence, […] its place is assigned in the structure by the mark of an emptiness [here, the certain emptiness/openness/unfinishedness/imperfection of the initial idea]. Somewhere, something can be filled up of *itself*, can accomplish *itself*, only by allowing itself to be filled through sign and proxy' (Derrida 1976, p. 145). In a similar vein, one may think of rules and following rules, of routine and improvisation, of revolutionary and normal science, of originals, models, copies and so on.

Modo futuri exacti: Deciding, Acting and Imagination

Before we come to more specific issues of the temporal aspects of creativity, we would like to draw attention to a more basic one: Alfred Schutz' emphasis of the temporality of every kind of purposeful action, which has to be preceded by what Schutz calls an 'Entwurf' (a project). 'Entwerfen' (projecting) requires an, in some sense, creative imagination; in German, Schutz even calls it a 'Phantasieerlebnis' (a fantasy)—namely, an idea/fiction/imagination *modo futuri exacti* (in the future perfect tense; Schutz 1967, pp. 63–64) of how the world will look when the *Entwurf* (the project) has been realized. This imagination relates to the 'action phantasized about as over and done with' (ibid., p. 65). Schutz is concerned solely with individual actions. Note, however, that this is all the more true when it comes to organizational projects, decisions, actions and, therefore, imaginations. Organizing, as we noted in the introduction, is always about the future, and therefore requires us to imagine the state of the world when the anticipated organizational rules and resources have been provided, or when a restructuring has taken place, or when a strategy has been formulated and implemented.

Because the future is unknown, individual and corporate actors will have to develop an idea—'a mere sketch with many empty places', as Schutz (1967, p. 64) says—of the future they refer to in the present, an 'imagined future' as Jens Beckert (2016) calls it. An imagined and, as we

(Ortmann 2009, p. 225) have emphasized, 'enacted future' because what is needed beyond imagination is the performative establishment of this very imagined future as valid for 'us'—valid for our present thinking and acting which, in organizations, depends on the unifying fiction of some future and an implied sets of expectabilities (ibid.).

Organizations depend on imagined and enacted futures, and the enactment must be performed at the organizational, and not just at the individual level. The creativity needed for it to happen has to be creativity not only *in*, but also *of* organizations.

The Platonic Search Paradox: Certainty and Uncertainty

The bad news regarding invention, innovation and creativity is that the search for something new is subject to the Meno paradox—the Platonic search paradox. Because what is sought for is unknown, one does not and cannot know where to look for it and how to manage the search. In one German edition of Platon's work (1998), the editor, Otto Apelt, called this a product of sophistic 'Afterlogik' ('mean logic'). This is an unparalleled misjudgement. For the benefit of students of business and, in particular, supporters of institutional economics, we refer to two problems, which are both prime examples of the Meno paradox. First, it is impossible to optimize on search costs because you do not and cannot know the marginal benefit of an additional unit of search in advance. Second, the trading of information is difficult, as we know from Kenneth Arrow (1971), because the buyer does not know how useful new information will be before it has been received, but once it has been given, the buyer may no longer be willing to pay for it.

So, the Meno paradox not only turns out to be a true paradox but is also a nasty shock for those involved with organizing for creativity or with innovation management more generally. This, in our view, discredits the vast amount of mostly dispensable literature on innovation and on the secrets behind the success of innovation, reorganization, organization development and change (cf. Tidd et al. 2013). To put it bluntly, every attempt to manage innovation is threatened by futility. This looks like a rather strong argument against any attempts to organize for creativity, the importance of which, strangely enough, is reduced by most innovation scholars to the 'fuzzy front end' of the innovation process (e.g. Reid and De Brentani 2004).

The other side of this coin is that invention and innovation are not only journeys into an unknown future but also, to a great extent, a matter of good luck. Everyone and every organization know this, but there is still a strong inclination within the social sciences to play down the role of chance. An exception here is Robert Merton (1968), who emphasized a serendipity pattern within scientific research. Serendipity is 'the faculty of making happy and unexpected discoveries by accident' (*Oxford English Dictionary*). Serendipity means 'to look for a needle in a haystack and get out with the farmer's daughter' (Comroe 1977). Even within economics, business studies and the literature on innovation management, this serendipity pattern is slowly becoming accepted as an inherent feature of innovation (cf. Pina e Cunha et al. 2015; Garud et al. 2018). To find something not looked for is, in a sense, all-pervasive within the creation of the new. Serendipity is the ability, as the German saying goes, 'in sein Glück zu stolpern' ('to stumble into good luck').[3] Creativity researchers have addressed this problem by pointing to the role of quantity: experimenting a lot, trying out new methods, frequently exposing oneself to potentially unfamiliar settings and so on may increase the likelihood of stumbling into something new and potentially valuable (Csikszentmihalyi 1997).

An invitation to participate in a workshop on innovation and change (at the Social Science Center Berlin, WZB), however, posed a somewhat different question: not how do we *get to* the new idea but: 'How do new ideas, innovative methods or products … win approval …? When does the establishment embrace the new and when does it draw up its defence lines? … And in which form do new ideas reach users, consumers and audiences?' These questions seem to be all the more promising because they appear to avoid the Meno paradox.

In a sense, however, even these questions are contaminated by the search paradox, because if 'new ideas are ten a penny', as the invitation said, we have to first select the interesting/relevant/promising/feasible new ideas, separate the wheat from the chaff, and we are then confronted with the paradox, because we cannot know in advance which of these ideas may succeed. However, when actors look at and select ideas, they admittedly often know *something* about the search object and/or the search area. The search paradox, like every paradox, turns out to be a gradual affair (Sainsbury 1993). Incremental improvements of processes and products depend in particular on a considerable amount of knowledge and skill, and not merely on luck and serendipity. In addition, learning from failures involves searching oriented by extant knowledge, namely knowledge of what does not work and, at least to some extent, why it does not work (see Dörfler and Baumann 2014, on the A380 programme). To quote Martin Heidegger, in a sense, the world is revealed to us by failures, accidents, defects and faults happening to us: ' when something ready-to-hand is missing, … this makes a break. … Our circumspection comes up against emptiness, and now sees for the first time *what* the missing article was ready-to-hand *with*, and what it was ready-to-hand *for*' (Heidegger 1962, p. 103). This partial knowledge is a condition of the possibility of organizing for the future and for creativity.

That something is missing comes as a surprise or an irritation. So, the question arises as to what leads to an observer's irritability. Creativity insofar can be said to be irritability—the ability or sensitivity to recognize something as irregular and astonishing, to take the familiar as something strange and, therefore, in need of explanation. The 'lifeworld' in the sense of Husserl (1964) needs to be transcended. And this is an even more difficult task in organizational lifeworlds, because organizations depend to a great degree on fixed habits and world views. On the other hand, they may be able to incorporate strange views, unconventional thinkers, creativity techniques and the like and therefore to overcome prejudice and fixed interpretations by means of the division of labour.

Certainty—for example, that a fair evaluation of ideas or tolerance of off-the-wall suggestions will occur—seems important in stimulating or at least sustaining the creative process in and across an organization. The importance of perceived safety for individual creativity has been demonstrated at the team level (Kark and Carmeli 2009). On the other hand, creative processes are inherently uncertain, not only as regard to the output but also the process itself; and they do not in themselves provide the 'safety' net which makes some people feel comfortable. In line with Frank Knight (1921), we thereby conceive uncertainty, in sharp opposition to risk, as being not calculable and, in the extreme, including even the unexpected. Organizing for creativity, however, is less about balancing between 'too little' and 'too much' (Chen 2012) than considering the possible trade-offs between different types of (un-)certainty. One example is the transformation of environmental uncertainty organizations are exposed to when they form an innovation network into network-internal uncertainty (e.g. partner-related uncertainty) (Beckman et al. 2004; Sydow et al. 2013). In this regard, the alleged transformation of a 'society of organizations' (Perrow 1991) into a 'society of networks' (Raab and Kenis 2009) that also plays out in creativity research (Perry-Smith and Mannucci 2017), should it occur, would be accompanied by a change in type rather than by great uncertainty.

Jon Elster: States That Are Essentially By-products

'Threatened by futility' does not mean that an endeavour is futile. It simply implies an acknowledgement of the search paradox and the indispensable role of coincidence in striving for the new. 'Striving' means 'intending' and is, therefore, contaminated by the difficulties of intending, as suggested by Elster (1984): there are states one cannot intend, states one will fail to meet when and because an actor, a person or an organization directly intends them. The matter of intention is key here, but the accent is on 'directly'. While *direct* intending is impossible, indirect ways of intending may very well be feasible. This is true for intending the new, too. Organizing for creativity in order to cope with future challenges, looked at this way, is a question of 'indirectness'.

Why is it that, as suggested by most creativity researchers, no matter whether they provide an actor-centred, a context-centred or an interactional explanation of creativity (cf. Zhou and Hoever 2014), we cannot (directly) intend the new? The answer is simple enough: because we do not know of it, 'because one can only intend what one can expect as something already determinate' (Waldenfels 1990, p. 97, our transl.).

And what does it mean to say that what is impossible to achieve directly may be possible if strived for in an indirect or oblique way? To answer this question, we return to the Meno paradox and note Plato's 'solution'. It reads: 'All cognition is recognition', in the sense of remembering past lives (Polanyi 2009, p. 22) or a Platonic 'idea' or 'ideal form'. Of course, nowadays most people would reject this kind of Platonism.

Michael Polanyi's (2009, pp. 22–23) solution was: in looking for the new we refer to a kind of 'foreknowledge of yet undiscovered things' and to an 'intimation of something hidden' by and through *tacit knowledge*—with iteration taking place in searching, within iterative attempts to determine the undetermined. Against this background, it comes as no surprise that the ideas of 'undirected search' and 'creative recombination' have received some attention in understanding how the creative comes about (e.g. Stark 2009), or when creative endeavours in one domain inspire new ways of thinking in others (e.g. Padgett and Powell 2012).

It is because of the nonetheless important role of chance on the one hand and tacit knowledge on the other that it is most frequently suggested that creating new ideas comes down to 'allowing space for' creativity—to providing people within or across organizations with favourable and promising conditions for trial and error, with leeway to developing new ideas, to improvising, to going dead ends or uncertain or insecure directions and the like. 'Humus' is a widespread metaphor for this concept, known more formally as an appropriate organizational culture. But formal organization structures (sets of rules and resources; Giddens 1984) may also provide favourable or unfavourable conditions for creativity. To provide organizations with conditions of this kind—with a suitable organizational (or even interorganizational) culture and structure—is one indirect way of encouraging creativity and innovation.

Dancing in Chains: Contingency, Freedom and Constraints

Contingency is usually considered to be an achievement of modernity (e.g. Luhmann 1992, 1995). Some authors, however, regarded it as a curse. Kierkegaard (1954), for instance, was frightened by the profusion of possibilities, of all the dangers possibly still to come. Niklas Luhmann (1992, 94) called contingency 'the Midas gold of modern age' because the freedom it gives implies a compulsion to incessantly make decisions. In the face of escalating contingency this necessity becomes even more compelling (cf. Ortmann 2009). It is in this context that creativity is—or seems to be—more urgently called for than ever.

Freedom is often considered a necessary precondition for creativity (Amabile 1996; Shalley et al. 2004). Let us therefore have a look at its puzzling relationship to compulsion or constraint. On another occasion (Ortmann and Sydow 2018), we chose Friedrich Nietzsche and once again Jon Elster as authorities on that matter.

The phrase 'dancing in chains' is taken from Nietzsche's (1986) 'Human, All Too Human'.

> *Dancing in chains*. With every Greek artist, poet and writer one has to ask: what is the *new constraint* he has imposed upon himself and through which he charms his contemporaries (so that he finds imitators)? For that which we call 'invention' (in metrics, for example) is always such a self-imposed fetter. 'Dancing in chains', making things difficult for oneself and then spreading over it the illusion of ease and facility—that is the artifice they want to demonstrate to us. Already in Homer we can perceive an abundance of inherited formulae epic narrative rules *within* which he had to dance: and he himself created additional new conventions for those who came after him. This was the school in which the Greek poets were raised: firstly, to allow a multiplicity of constraints to be imposed upon one; then to devise an additional new constraint, impose it upon oneself and conquer it with charm and grace: so that both the constraint and its conquest are noticed and admired. (Nietzsche 1986, p. 343)

Innovation and change depend on what the German philosopher Bernhard Waldenfels (1985, p. 109) calls *Widerlager* ('abutment'; something to rest upon). There is no such thing as a pure primary production, no *creatio ex nihilo*. The new is dependent on 'tradition as abutment'. Waldenfels (1985, p. 96) argues: 'The paradox of innovation is that it presupposes what it is about to renew. We can only bring about change and innovation bound in the chains of the past. These chains may be material ones embodied in products, artifacts, tools and the like, or immaterial ones: rules, conventions, routines and relations, ways of thinking and acting, Nietzsche's inherited formulae and laws of epic narration. This is true even for invention and imagination.' 'Creativity', as Richard Feynman once said, 'is imagination in a straightjacket' (cited by Guntern 2010, p. 54). The positive effects of constraining structures, and scarce resources in particular, are also highlighted by management scholars interested in 'organizational ingenuity' (Lampel et al. 2014). Their argument is as follows: on the one hand, resource constraints underline the importance of creativity for coming up with organizational solutions. On the other hand, in line with the idea of 'imagination in a straightjacket', resource constraints enable the creative processes and practices needed to develop in the face of these very constraints.

Nietzsche talks of 'the new constraint which he imposes upon himself': this relates to *self-binding*, which the Norwegian sociologist and philosopher Jon Elster (1984) dealt with under the heading 'Ulysses and the Sirens'. Note that self-binding is a response to an expected future, namely to future temptations (the sirens' song!), and that it is much more readily at the disposal of organizations rather than of individuals, because organizational rules are self-imposed. Self-binding is one way to organize for the future, and a very important one if one thinks of the self-binding powers of organizational rules and, for that matter, of constitutions at the state level. We may, therefore, consider the organization, the corporate actor, as the modern Ulysses, and organizational self-binding as at least one source of cleverness and creativity. *Kaizen*, for instance, can be considered as a kind of self-binding, used to create ever-improved production procedures. Time limits and deadlines are another example of organizational self-binding which may possibly stimulate creativity. Of course, in many ways the creation of something new depends on unintended constraints, leading to *unintended* self-binding. Ulysses in the face of the Sirens, however, stands for *intended* self-binding. Elster's second book on the subject is titled 'Ulysses Unbound' (2000), and includes a chapter on 'Creativity and Constraints in the Arts' dealing with poetry, novels, dancing, composition and jazz.[4]

Invention for Nietzsche means not only dancing in chains but also finding new constraints, new conventions one will have to dance around in the future. In management and organization studies, we are used to distinguishing between product and process innovation, and process innovation means: new rules and ways of acting. In Nietzsche's terms this would translate as future constraints, future chains, which might turn out to be regrettable or even dangerous. Note, however, that rules are, to echo Samuel Weber (2001), 'enabling limits'. That is, rules are not only restricting but also enabling. To go further, they are enabling *through* restriction. This accords with Nietzsche and with Giddens and with Elster's 'Ulysses Unbound'.

The Emergence of Corporate Actors and the Creativity of Organizations

We cannot deal with the difficult question of emergence in depth in this chapter (see, however, Garud et al. 2015). Philosophers, again focusing first and foremost on the individual, are accustomed to dealing with the individual with particular reference to the body/mind problem. Does 'the mind' emerge from the body in an anti-reductionist sense? That is to say, is it impossible to *de*duce every feature of the mind from the body or, in other words, to *re*duce the mind features to corporeal ones? In our context, do organizations have features and, in particular, abilities or powers that cannot be reduced to features of their individual members? Is organizational creativity an emergent capacity in this sense? Could it even be an important ingredient of a 'dynamic capability' (Teece et al. 1997)? We are inclined to answer these questions positively because, to put it bluntly, and in short, the creativity of a chemical company, of car manufacturers like Volkswagen and BMW, of a political party or of a soccer team is indeed more than the sum of the individual creativity of its members. And some creativity researchers studying 'collaborative emergence' would agree (e.g. Sawyer 2003; Hargadon and Bechky 2006), but because of the continuing dominance of psychological approaches in this field they are still in the minority. Moreover, creativity is not only an important ingredient of organizational capacity per se, but also, more specifically, an indispensable ingredient of dynamic capability.

We can think about either synchronical or diachronical emergence. The diachronical perspective is, among others things, about evolution. Life emerges from inanimate matter. Birds emerged from fishes. The corporate actor—its powers, rights and duties—may be considered to be an evolutionary or historical product of modernity. In fact, the historical emergence of corporate actorhood occurred mainly in the nineteenth century.[5] We are inclined to say that to establish the corporate actor—and even personhood—as an institutional fact was an unprecedented way to organize for the future when seen from the point of view of the corporation. In a sense, it rang in hyper-modernity. In this—diachronical—perspective, *The Emergence of Organizations and Markets* (Padgett and Powell 2012) is up for discussion.[6] On the other hand, at any given point in time, organizations and individuals, teams and team members, creativities of organizations and of their members and so forth exist *simultaneously*. Diachronical emergence is about the emergence of the new as compared to the past, while synchronical emergence is about hierarchies or levels of reality at one point in time—of 'supervenient' (features of) objects at a higher level of emergence. In conclusion, in (hyper-)modern times, the creativity needed for organizing (for) the future is mainly a matter of emergent organizational capacities.

Acknowledgements An earlier version was presented at WK ORG 2015 at the University of Zurich, Switzerland.

Notes

1. '[A] man cannot search … for what he does not know, because he does not know what to look for.' (Plato, *Meno*, 80e, Grube's translation).
2. For more details and a somewhat different definition, see Sainsbury (1993).
3. This is why an article about strategic management—about preparing for an unknown future—was called 'Stumbling Giants' (Ortmann and Salzman 2002). The authors wanted to say: even strategic management, also in big corporations, cannot but *stolpern in ihr Glück*.

4. For more on the use of jazz as a metaphor within organization studies, see for example Weick (1998) and Hatch (1999).
5. For more on corporate personhood in the United States, see Nace (2003).
6. See Sawyer (2003) for a general discussion of diachronical emergence and creativity.

References

Adorno, Theodore W. 1976. *Minima Moralia*. Frankfurt: Suhrkamp.
Amabile, Theresa M. 1996. *Creativity in Context*. Boulder: Westview Press.
Arrow, Kenneth J. 1971. *Essays in the Theory of Risk-Bearing*. Chicago: Markham.
Beckert, Jens. 2016. *Imagined Futures. Fictional Expectations and Capitalist Dynamics*. Cambridge, MA: Harvard University Press.
Beckman, Christine M., Pamela R. Haunschild, and Damon J. Phillips. 2004. Friends or Strangers? Firm-Specific Uncertainty, Market Uncertainty, and Network Partner Selection. *Organization Science* 15 (3): 259–275.
Büttner, Gerhard. 2009. Children's Concepts of Contingency as a Subject of Philosophizing. In *Hovering Over the Face of the Deep. Philosophy, Theology and Children*, ed. G.Y. Iverson, G. Mitchell, and G. Pollard, 25–36. Münster: Waxmann.
Chen, Katherine K. 2012. Organizing Creativity: Enabling Creative Output, Process, and Organizing Practices. *Sociology Compass* 6 (8): 624–643.
Comroe, Julius H. 1977. *Retrospectroscope: Insights into Medical Discovery*. Menlo Park: Von Gehr Press.
Csikszentmihalyi, Mihaly. 1997. *Flow and the Psychology of Discovery and Invention*. New York: Harper.
DeFillippi, Robert, Gernot Grabher, and Candace Jones. 2007. Introduction to Paradoxes of Creativity: Managerial and Organizational Challenges in the Cultural Industries. *Journal of Organizational Behavior* 28: 511–521.
Derrida, Jacques. 1976. *Of Grammatology*. Baltimore: Hopkins University Press.
———. 2007. *Psyche. Inventions of the Other*. Vol. 1. Stanford: Stanford University Press.
Dörfler, Isabel, and Oliver Baumann. 2014. Learning from a Drastic Failure: The Case of the Airbus A380 Program. *Industry and Innovation* 21 (3): 197–214.
Elster, Jon. 1984. *Ulysses and the Sirens*. Cambridge: Cambridge University Press.

———. 2000. *Ulysses Unbound, Studies in Rationality, Precommitment, and Constraints.* Cambridge: Cambridge University Press.
Fortwengel, Johann, Elke Schüßler, and Jörg Sydow. 2017. Studying Organizational Creativity as Process: Fluidity or Duality? *Creativity and Innovation Management* 26 (1): 5–16.
Garud, Raghu, Barbara Simpson, Ann Langley, and Haridimos Tsoukas. 2015. Introduction: How Does Novelty Emerge. In *The Emergence of Novelty in Organizations*, ed. R. Garud, B. Simpson, A. Langley, and H. Tsoukas, 1–24. Oxford: Oxford University Press.
Garud, Raghu, Gehman, Joel, Giuliani, Antonio P. 2018. Serendipity Arrangements for Exapting Science-Based Innovations. *Academy of Management Perspectives* 32 (1): 125–140.
Giddens, Anthony. 1984. *The Constitution of Society. Outline of the Theory of Structuration.* Cambridge: Polity.
———. 1990. *The Consequences of Modernity.* Cambridge: Polity Press.
Gordon, William J.J. 1961. *Synectics. The Development of Creative Capacity.* New York: Harper.
Guntern, Gottlieb. 2010. *The Spirit of Creativity. Basic Mechanism of Creative Achievements.* Lanham: University Press of America.
Hargadon, Andrew B., and Beth A. Bechky. 2006. When Collections of Creatives Become Creative Collectives: A Field Study of Problem Solving at Work. *Organization Science* 17 (4): 484–500.
Hatch, M.J. 1999. Exploring the Empty Spaces of Organizing: How Improvisational Jazz Helps Redescribe Organizational Structure. *Organization Studies* 20 (1): 75–100.
Heidegger, Martin. 1962. *Being and Time.* New York: Harper.
Husserl, Edmund. 1964. *Erfahrung und Urteil.* 3rd ed. Hamburg: Classen.
Kark, Ronit, and Abraham Carmeli. 2009. Alive and Creating: The Mediating Role of Vitality and Aliveness in the Relationship Between Psychological Safety and Creative Work Involvement. *Journal of Organizational Behavior* 30 (6): 785–804.
Kierkegaard, Sören. 1954. *Die Krankheit zum Tode, in: Gesammelte Werke, 24. und 25. Abteilung.* Düsseldorf: Hirsch.
Knight, Frank. 1921. *Risk, Uncertainty and Profit.* Chicago: University of Chicago Press.
Koch, Jochen, Hannes Krämer, Andreas Reckwitz, and Matthias Wenzel. 2016. Zum Umgang mit Zukunft in Organisationen – eine praxistheoretische Perspektive. *Managementforschung* 26: 161–184.

Lampel, Joseph, Benson Honig, and Israel Drori. 2014. Organizational Ingenuity: Concept, Processes and Strategies. *Organization Studies* 35 (4): 465–482.

Lübbe, Hermann. 1998. Kontingenzerfahrung und Kontingenzbewältigung. In *Kontingenz*, ed. G.V. Graevenitz and O. Marquard, 35–47. München: Fink.

Luhmann, Niklas. 1990. Die Zukunft kann nicht beginnen. Temporalstrukturen der modernen Gesellschaft. In *Vor der Jahrtausendwende: Berichte zur Lage der Zukunft*, ed. P. Sloterdijk, 119–150. Frankfurt: Suhrkamp.

———. 1992. *Beobachtungen der Moderne*. Opladen: Westdeutscher Verlag.

———. 1995. *Social Systems*. Stanford: Stanford University Press.

Merton, Robert K. 1968. *Social Theory and Social Structure*. Enlarged ed. New York: Free Press.

Nace, Ted. 2003. *Gangs of America. The Rise of Corporate Power and the Disabling of Democracy*. San Francisco: Berrett-Koehler.

Nietzsche, Friedrich. 1986. *Human, All Too Human*. Cambridge: Cambridge University Press.

Ortmann, Günther. 2009. *Management in der Hypermoderne: Kontingenz und Entscheidung*. Wiesbaden: VS.

Ortmann, Günther, and Harold Salzman. 2002. Stumbling Giants: The Emptiness, Fullness and Recursiveness of Strategic Management. *Soziale Systeme* 8 (2): 205–230.

Ortmann, Günther, and Jörg Sydow. 2018. Dancing in Chains: Creative Practices in/of Organizations. *Organization Studies* 39 (in print).

Padgett, John F., and Walter W. Powell, eds. 2012. *The Emergence of Organizations and Markets*. Princeton: University of Princeton Press.

Perrow, Charles. 1991. A Society of Organizations. *Theory and Society* 20 (6): 725–762.

Perry-Smith, Jill E., and Pierre Vittorio Mannucci. 2017. From Creativity to Innovation: The Social Network Drivers of the Four Phases of the Idea Journey. *Academy of Management Review* 42 (1): 53–79.

Pina e Cunha, Miguel, Arménio Rego, Stewart Clegg, and Greeg Lindsay. 2015. The Dialectics of Serendipity. *European Management Journal* 33: 9–18.

Platon. 1998. *Sämtliche Dialoge*. Bd. II: Menon – Kratylos – Phaidon – Phaidros (Meiner-Ed.), ed. O. Apelt. Hamburg: Meiner.

Polanyi, Michel. 2009. *The Tacit Dimension*. Chicago: University of Chicago Press.

Raab, Jörg, and Patrick Kenis. 2009. Heading Toward a Society of Networks: Empirical Developments and Theoretical Challenges. *Journal of Management Inquiry* 18 (3): 198–210.

Reckwitz, Andreas. 2012. *Die Erfindung der Kreativität*. Frankfurt: Suhrkamp.

Reid, Susan E., and Ulrike de Brentani. 2004. The Fuzzy Front End of New Product Development for Discontinuous Innovations: A Theoretical Model. *Journal of Product Innovation Management* 21 (3): 170–184.

Sainsbury, Richard M. 1993. *Paradoxien*. Stuttgart: Reclam.

Sawyer, R. Keith. 2003. Emergence in Creativity and Development. In *Creativity and Development*, ed. R.K. Sawyer, V. John-Steiner, S. Moran, R.J. Sternberg, D.H. Feldman, J. Nakamura, and M. Csikszentmihalyi, 11–30. Oxford: Oxford University Press.

Schüßler, Elke, Charles-Clemens Rüling, and Bettina B.F. Wittneben. 2014. On Melting Summits: The Limitations of Field-Configuring Events as Catalysts of Change in Transnational Climate Policy. *Academy of Management Journal* 57: 140–171.

Schutz, Alfred 1967. *The Phenomenology of the Social World*. Evanston: Northwestern University Press.

Shalley, Christina E., Jing Zhou, and Greg R. Oldham. 2004. The Effects of Personal and Contextual Characteristics on Creativity: Where Should We Go from Here? *Journal of Management* 30 (6): 933–958.

Stark, David. 2009. *The Sense of Dissonance: Accounts of Worth in Economic Life*. New York: Princeton University Press.

Sydow, Jörg, Gordon Müller-Seitz, and Keith G. Provan. 2013. Managing Uncertainty in Alliances and Networks – From Governance to Practice. In *Managing Knowledge in Strategic Alliances*, ed. T.K. Das, 1–43. Charlotte: IAP.

Sydow, Jörg, Elke Schüßler, and Gordon Müller-Seitz. 2016. *Managing Interorganizational Relations – Debates and Cases*. London: Palgrave Macmillan.

Teece, David J., Gary Pisano, and Amy Shuen. 1997. Dynamic Capabilities and Strategic Management. *Strategic Management Journal* 18 (7): 509–533.

Thompson, James D. 1967. *Organizations in Action*. New York: McGraw-Hill.

Tidd, Joe, John Bessnat, and Keith Pavitt. 2013. *Managing Innovation: Integrating Technological, Market and Organizational Change*. 5th ed. Chichester: Wiley.

Waldenfels, Bernhard. 1985. *In den Netzen der Lebenswelt*. Frankfurt: Suhrkamp.

———. 1990. *Der Stachel des Fremden*. Frankfurt: Suhrkamp.

Weber, Samuel. 2001. *Institution and Interpretation.* Expanded ed. Stanford: Stanford University Press.

Weick, Karl E. 1998. Introductory Essay – Improvisation as a Mindset for Organizational Analysis. *Organization Science* 9 (5): 543–555.

Zhou, Jing, and Inga J. Hoever. 2014. Research on Workplace Creativity: A Review and Redirection. *Annual Review of Organizational Psychology and Organizational Behavior* 1: 333–359.

5

Organizational Futurity: Being and Knowing in the Engagement with What Is Yet to Come

Seelan Naidoo

Introduction

Prominent theories of the organizational engagement with what is yet to come either are grounded in bare organizational knowing or approach this engagement as derivative among the relations of organizational temporality. In this chapter, an alternative onto-epistemological account is explored that is grounded in the notion of organizational futurity.

I begin the chapter by pursuing a line of questioning which attends to the epistemological aporetics involved in holding that organization entails some active relation—a crucial engagement—with what is yet to come. What is the status and character of organizational knowing in actualizing this organizational engagement? Knowing and knowledge lie at the hearts of two prominent theoretical perspectives on this engagement: orthodox strategy theory and sensemaking theory. I identify and problematize the paradigmatic assumption (Alvesson and Sandberg 2011) implicit in orthodox strategy theory (Calori 1998) that the organizational engagement

---

S. Naidoo (✉)
Department of Philosophy, University of St. Gallen (HSG),
St. Gallen, Switzerland

© The Author(s) 2018
H. Krämer, M. Wenzel (eds.), *How Organizations Manage the Future*,
https://doi.org/10.1007/978-3-319-74506-0_5

with what is yet to come is effected and sustained on the basis of *prospective organizational knowing*. In a similar manner, the commitment to the *retrospectivity of organizational knowing* in the theory of sensemaking and future-perfect thinking (Weick 1995) is problematized. This does not lead to an argument for a synthesis of these modes of organizational knowing as a way out. Prospective strategy theory and retrospective sensemaking are severally and jointly problematic. At bottom, both are modes of bare knowing that are increasingly debilitated in an age of higher-order contingency. Organizational knowing can no longer be taken for granted as the sole, or even the most fundamental, basis for effecting and sustaining the crucial organizational engagement with what is yet to come. In this way, more space is opened up in organization studies and strategy theory for thinking this engagement in onto-epistemological terms: on the basis of organizational *being* without excising organizational *knowing*.

In the following, more speculative section, the notion of *organizational futurity* is explored as a response to the critique unfolded in the previous section. Following the early work of Martin Heidegger, the organizational engagement with what is yet to come is given priority among the relations involved in organizational temporality. This avails an alternative approach to organizational temporality than that espoused in process organization studies and sensemaking theory, where the organizational engagement with 'the future' is taken to be derivative. The notion of organizational futurity is a conceptualization aimed at understanding that and how organization is always already oriented toward what is yet to come prior to organizational knowing. The emphasis is shifted backward, from trying to study organization as responsive to 'the future' or 'a future' on the basis of bare knowing and knowledge, to the more basic problematization of organization as a practical coping (Chia and Holt 2006) with the prior ontological fact of organizational futurity.

Points of Departure

Approaching organization as always underway implies that it is a phenomenon that is temporally stretched out across the past and present and into the future. For Hernes (2014), organizational temporality from a process perspective involves the organizational experience of the temporally 'spread' 'present-past-future relationship'. Organization is not a stable, entitative phenomenon which changes intermittently. Rather, organization is characterized as 'indivisible', and 'continual movement' 'in the flow of time'. For Rescher (1996), 'processes develop over time'—they are 'transtemporal': 'it is of the very essence of an ongoing process that it combines existence in the present with tentacles reaching into the past and the future'. Let us call this a horizontal notion of organizational temporality wherein 'past and future extend beyond the real' (Bakken et al. 2013). In heeding Augustine (1961), however, our hastily derived horizontal notion becomes problematic on both ontological and epistemological grounds: 'By whatever mysterious means it may be that the future is foreseen, it is only possible to see something which exists; and whatever exists is not future but present.'

If neither 'the past' nor 'the future' exist, how can existent organization be temporally stretched or spread into regions of non-existence? How can we see what does not exist yet, or what no longer exists? And how can we know what we cannot see? Augustine offers a way out of these difficulties. He gives us a vertical notion of organizational temporality as simultaneously stretched across 'a present of past things' in memory, 'a present of present things' in direct perception, and 'a present of future things' in expectation (Augustine 1961).

These horizontal and vertical notions, despite their apparent differences, provide more fundamental insights into organizational temporality which they share. Interrelated points of departure for the inquiry pursued in this chapter are drawn from this intersection. The first point, taken as basic, is that organization is understood as a phenomenon that is always underway—as temporally stretched out—and is thus inconceivable in atemporal terms. As Bergson (2007) would say, organization as durational cannot be captured in a snapshot without sacrificing it *as* organization. The second point, taken as a prescription, is that organization as temporally stretched entails some active relation—a crucial organizational engagement—with what is yet to come. A solar system is underway but is not in any way *engaged* with what is yet to come—organization is taken here to be always underway and engaged with what is yet to come. The third point, this time taken as a proscription, is that this engagement is not to be approached as an analytically separable 'part' of organizational temporality. The engagement with what is yet to come cannot be cogently partitioned from the engagement with what is and the engagement with what has been. There is no determinate moment—a 'time-zero'—at which even nascent organization has no history; and, there is no moment at which 'organization' has no future since that would be the very moment at which it ceases *as* organization. Hernes (2014) avoids this pitfall by approaching organizational temporality as the indivisible 'present-past-future relationship' which, nevertheless, has a specific emphasis and temporal directionality. Thus, the focus in this chapter on the organizational engagement with 'what is yet to come'[1] is an emphasis that leads to a specific argument about the directionality of organizational temporality and the priority of this engagement—it is not a dissection of organizational temporality.

The Aporetics of Organizational Knowing in the Age of Higher-Order Contingency

Problematizing Prospective Organizational Knowing

Organizational strategy is commonly understood as forward-looking: as 'based on a longer view into the future' (Ackoff 1990); as 'shaping the course of an organization' (Hickson et al. 1995). It is said to be about the 'long-term direction of the organization' (Johnson et al. 2008); and, in everyday management speak, it is 'about knowing where you are, deciding where you want to be, and working out how to get there'. A prospective orientation underlies otherwise multifarious notions of strategy. The term 'prospectivity', derived from a conjunction of the Latin root words *pro-* and *specere* and translated literally as fore-looking, refers here to the way in which organizational strategy is epistemologically oriented toward what is yet to come. It is an organizational looking ahead to discern what is yet to come. In this sense, the more general and dispersed organizational engagement with what is yet to come is concentrated in the prospectivity of strategy. Even if strategic planning unfolds chronologically by first reviewing past patterns, or by considering the configurations of the current situation, this is only done in order to work out and actualize the organizational engagement with what is yet to come. Even if strategic planning is undertaken to merely justify past managerial actions, perhaps in highly questionable ways, this is only for the high-stakes effects that even mythical justifications might have 'down the road'. Strategy is generally taken as both inherently prospective and eminently so in the context of organization. The organizational engagement with what is yet to come is the locus of strategy. To better understand this engagement, it makes sense to begin by considering its expressions in and as strategy theory and strategic practice.

It is in the dominant orthodoxy in strategy theory that the prospectivity of strategy is most explicitly espoused. Calori (1998) identifies the three 'prescriptive schools' and 'orthodox models of strategic management', which he subjects to an 'epistemological critique'. He does so by questioning these 'rational models of strategy formation on their own "terrain": reasoning'. A strong epistemological commitment to prospective organizational knowing and the prognostic organizational knowledge availed thereby is definitive of these models and especially of the strategic planning model. Prognostic organizational knowledge[2] refers here to organizational knowledge garnered by 'rational prognosis' (Koselleck 2002, 2004): predictions, projections, and descriptions as specified claims about what is yet to come. Such claims are made in reference to, for example, future organizational actions, means, states, events, trends, and outcomes. Strategic planning typically involves detailed situation analyses and forecasts of the organizational environment, which are translated into even more detailed forecasts in the form of plans and budgets for achieving some desired future state. Formal strategic plans are detailed specifications of the organizational future constructed primarily out of myriad prognostic claims. Prospective organizational knowing and the prognostic organizational knowledge availed thereby are of central importance in orthodox strategic planning. It is rational, deliberate, and assertively proactive in relation to the future (Mintzberg 1973). The underlying assumption of orthodox strategic planning theory and formal strategy practice is that the organizational engagement with what is yet to come is effected and sustained—and ultimately circumscribed—by the extent to which 'the future' is amenable to prospective organizational knowing and prognostic knowledge. Here, reasoning about 'the future' is exhausted in prospective knowing.

However, 'the future' has since ancient times been thought as contingent and thus as epistemologically problematic. What is to come does not yet exist. Propositions about future events are indeterminate with respect to their truth or falsity. Taken together, these problems describe Aristotelian *in-principle* future contingency (Williams 2008). The major implication of in-principle contingency is that there is no transtemporal epistemological principle that holds equally to what has been and what is, *and* to what is yet to come. What is yet to come is not knowable in the same way as what is present to observation or experience. As Koselleck (2004) says: 'The legibility of the future, despite possible prognoses, confronts an absolute limit, for it cannot be experienced.'

If the future was not contingent in principle, there would be no need for strategic planning. It is in order to try to cope organizationally with in-principle future contingency that people strategize at all. Thus, organizational knowledge claims of what 'the future' will be like, typically the products of strenuous strategizing, are understood as conjectural and tenuous to begin with. And to the extent that such claims are made and taken seriously as the basis for future action, may turn out in unforeseen ways. It is not surprising then that formal organizational strategy practice is found to be thoroughly imbued with a sense of contingency and is indelibly marked by ambiguity (Lindblom 1959; March and Olsen 1976; Weick 1995; Orlikowski 2015; Czarniawska 2003). The people who strategize know that they cannot know *ex ante* how their strategies will turn out. Since the future cannot be ignored in strategizing, even tenuous forms of knowledge of what is yet to come are taken as rationally better than 'flying blind' or gambling on the basis of pure chance. Strategic planning is not a seeking to overcome in-principle future contingency; it is a means of coping with it as an ineradicable condition of organization.

However, the in-principle contingency of what is yet to come has been greatly compounded by *historically induced contingency.* Contingency itself is increasingly on the move and on the rise. Generally accelerating change, higher degrees of social multiplicity and complexity all give rise to increased Knightian uncertainty (Knight 1964). For Koselleck (2004), modernity is characterized by the increasing 'divergence between experience and expectation'. For Luhmann, uncertainty is pervasive, the future is fundamentally unpredictable, even unknowable (Best 2012). Organization itself, as Orlikowski (2015) says, 'is [also] contingency all the way down'.

And so, organizational knowing of 'the future', approached in strategic planning as contingent in principle, must now be approached as contingent to a higher order. We no longer live and organize under mere in-principle contingency. We must now live and organize in an age of *higher-order* future contingency which is both quantitatively and qualitatively more intense. If what is yet to come is to be approached as increasingly contingent (Orlikowski 2015; Beckert 2013, 2014), 'non-calculable' (Callon 1998), 'incalculable' (Arendt 1958), and ever less amenable to 'rational prognosis' (Koselleck 2002, 2004), then prospective knowing and prognostic claims in relation to 'the future' or even 'a future' become doubly problematic. It is the very prospectivity of strategy and strategizing that is becoming ever more epistemologically problematic.

Although strategic planning remains the mainstream mode of strategy, it has been roundly critiqued since the 1960s (Lindblom 1959; March and Olsen 1976; Knights and Morgan 1991; Weick 1995) with the result that numerous alternative organizational perspectives and theories have been offered. Scenario-planning (Van der Heijden 2011), foresight (Tsoukas and Shepherd 2004) and effectuation (Sarasvathy 2001) are leading contemporary examples. These may be read as critical reactions, primarily to the strong claim to prognostic organizational knowledge that underlies orthodox strategic planning theory. Scenario-planning, foresight, and effectuation all eschew prognostic organizational knowledge to varying degrees. However, although contemporary developments in strategy theory are away from the strong commitment to prognostic knowledge, this has not led to the relinquishment of prospective organizational knowing. This brings to light a substantive yet implicit problematics that is shaping the development of contemporary strategy theory: in the retreat from prognostic knowledge, how might prospective knowing be sustained as the basis for strategy? The study of these retreats from prognostic organizational knowledge and the shifts in how strategic prospectivity has been re-conceptualized requires more detailed study than is practicable here. The point to hold on to is that strategy theory is caught on the horns of a dilemma in the age of higher-order contingency: it must gradually give up on prognosis without relinquishing the possibility of other modes of prospective organizational knowing. This dilemma is due to the commitment to the epistemological that underlies strategy theory in general—the commitment to organizational knowing as the sole basis for effecting the organizational engagement with what is yet to come.

Paradoxically, strategy, including formal strategic planning, is becoming more pervasive in practice, and strategy theory is a burgeoning field of research (Laamanen 2017). Strategy is not only becoming more widespread among organizations of every kind, it is also becoming more widespread within organizations. 'Nowadays, nearly everything seems to be strategic' (Schreyögg 1993). In an age in which prospective knowing and prognostic knowledge are increasingly questioned, and in which 'one can discern a "retreat from rationality"' (Reed 1991) in organization theory, it is surprising that strategy is becoming ever more pervasive. Perhaps it is precisely because prospective knowing is becoming more problematic that strategy is not only burgeoning but also becoming more pluralistic as an ameliorating response. In any case, the problems remain. If the inherent, intensive prospectivity of strategy resides wholly in the possibilities of prospective knowing, is orthodox strategy at stake in an age of higher-order contingency? If not by prospective knowing and prognostic knowledge, how else is strategy being sustained as a pervasive practical coping?

Problematizing Retrospective Organizational Knowing

It is this problematization that underpins the retrospectivity of 'organisational sensemaking' theory and 'future-perfect thinking' (Weick 1995) which is counterposed to the prospectivity of strategy theory. Weick's pejorative view of strategic planning as based on 'magical probes into the future' expresses the suspicion that prospective organizational knowing is deeply problematic as the epistemological basis for actualizing the organizational engagement with what is yet to come. For Weick, actors involved in organizing can only look back on past action to make meanings now of what has transpired, since 'the future is actually indeterminate, unpredictable'. Although Weick accepts the Bergsonian 'pure duration' of experience from an ontological point of view, retrospective sensemaking is an 'attentional' epistemology wherein 'it is only possible to direct attention to what exists, that is, what has already passed'. In this, Weick follows Mead and Schutz in their strong philosophical commitment to a retrospective epistemology.

For Mead (Hernes 2014), the extent to which we can think 'the world to come' differently from 'the world that is' is *circumscribed* by and depends upon the extent to which we can rewrite 'the world that has been' differently under the present circumstances. We proceed in 'what is' from 'has been' to 'to come'. It is only by retrospectivity that we can be prospective—we reconstruct the present and future by reworking the past. Thus, the meanings of the past are interpretatively malleable and future prospects depend upon the extent of this malleability of past meanings under the circumstances in the emerging present. On this view, 'the future' is never epistemologically available to our efforts at reconstruction. The only knowing that is available is what we know of the past, including what we know of the emerging present as it comes to pass. The temporal relation is ordered in the present from past to future as a *one-way road*. In sensemaking theory, as in much of process organization studies, 'the future' cannot affect the past or the present—'the future' and the engagement therewith is derivative. Hernes (2014), also following Mead, emphasizes an ordered temporal orientation of organization in the emerging present from past to future. Primacy is accorded to the emerging present tethered to a more or less malleable but inescapable field of meanings of the past—the relation to 'the future' is derivative among the relations of organizational temporality.

What this leads up to is whether sensemaking and future-perfect thinking provide theoretical answers to the questioning posed in this chapter. Does retrospective organizational knowing fill the epistemological gap left by the erosion of prospective knowing? Furthermore, is sensemaking an epistemological *substitute* for strategy, or is it a *complement* to strategy? Weick (1995) is understandably ambivalent on the latter question. On the one hand, prospective knowing in general is rejected as impossible, which would amount to a rejection of strategy as premised on the very possibility of prospective knowing. On the other hand, strategists are advised to incorporate retrospective sensemaking in their strategizing:

> The dominance of retrospect in sensemaking is a major reason why students of sensemaking find forecasting, contingency planning, strategic planning, and other magical probes into the future wasteful and misleading if they are decoupled from reflective action and history. (Weick 1995)

Weick (1995) is right in pointing out that strategic planning also involves retrospective knowing as part of its 'stock in trade'; and doubtless it happens that 'strategists take credit for their foresight when they are actually trading on their hindsight'. Thus, Weick may be interpreted as holding that, while prospective knowing is problematic at best and impossible at worst, the engagement with *what is yet to come* may instead be effected and sustained on the basis of retrospective modes of knowing such as sensemaking and future-perfect thinking.

Proceeding from this interpretation and returning to the former question, there is a substantive reason to suggest that retrospective sensemaking and future-perfect thinking might not be able to make up the epistemological gap. Like all retrospective modes of organizational knowing, sensemaking and future-perfect thinking also increasingly suffer debilitation under higher-order contingency. Schutz (1970) acknowledges that future-perfect thinking, also referred to as 'anticipated hindsight', 'depends on our knowledge at hand before the event, and therefore leaves open what will be irrevocably fulfilled'. Retrospective and prospective organizational knowing are in the same boat on the seas of higher-order contingency. As Stacey (2010) points out: 'The organizational reality of uncertainty means more than an inability to reliably predict the future; it also means that it is not at all clear what is currently going on and even what happened some time ago is open to many interpretations.'

Although Weick (1995) acknowledges the in-principle indeterminacy and unpredictability of the future, he does not pay sufficient attention to *historically induced* contingency. The relevance and efficaciousness of the meanings that are made on the basis of hindsight must also be approached as increasingly questionable when change in general is accelerating. As Purser and Pertranker (2005) say: 'The extrapolations from past experience are bound to be inaccurate given our contemporary business environment where change is rapid and planning horizons are shrinking (Hamel and Prahalad 1994; Stacey 1996). The future will be different from the past in ways that cannot be predicted or accurately forecasted (Cunha 2002).'

In an age of higher-order contingency, a preoccupation with 'perpetual change' (MacKay and Chia 2013), speed, and even high velocity (Tsoukas and Shepherd 2004) becomes belated and must increasingly give way to the compounding powers of acceleration further compounded by its discontinuity. Higher-order contingency involves a qualitatively higher order of changefulness than that indicated by 'continuous change'. Due to discontinuous accelerating change (which includes deceleration) even the sensemaking of the immediate past becomes less and less useful to the sensemakers in their concernful 'practical coping' (Chia and Holt 2006) with what is yet to come, which cannot be wished away even if it is unknowable.

Organizational Futurity

The Insufficiency of Bare Knowing

At one vertex, orthodox strategy theory proceeds from a commitment to prospective organizational knowing, which avails prognostic organizational knowledge, as the basis for effecting and sustaining the organizational engagement with what is yet to come. At another vertex, organizational sensemaking theory offers retrospective organizational knowing as the basis for the meaning-making that effects and sustains this engagement. Both retrospective sensemaking and prospective strategy are problematic and diminishing epistemological means for effecting and sustaining the crucial organizational engagement with what is yet to come in an age of higher-order contingency. While in-principle contingency is the limited condition of prospective knowing, higher-order contingency cuts both ways. That is the qualitative difference: we now suffer the devaluation of hindsight, memory and tradition as epistemological bases for approaching what is yet to come, just as we suffer the erosion of foresight, anticipation and utopias as the epistemological bases for approaching what is yet to come.

What underlies the signifiers pro-*spect*-ive, retro-*spect*-ive, fore-*sight*, and hind-*sight* is the primacy of *see*-ing—the primacy of the *sighted*-ness of the epistemological. Even the theories of future-perfect thinking (Schutz 1970; Weick 1995) and scenario-planning (Van der Heijden 2011) which lie between the vertices of orthodox strategic planning and organizational sensemaking are subtended by a strong epistemological commitment. As Schutz (1970) says of 'thinking in the future perfect tense': '[f]oresight, an anticipated hindsight, depends on the stock of our knowledge at hand before the event'. Although these more recent developments in strategy theory place less reliance on prognostication, they do not relinquish prospective knowing. Scenario-planning and future-perfect thinking require the 'projection' (Schutz 1970) of whole future states specified in their completion, which always involves a combination of prospective and retrospective knowing. That the descriptions of such completed future states are more numerous, accorded higher degrees of fictionality, and allow for greater imaginative range does not mean that the primacy of the epistemological is thereby relinquished.

Nevertheless, although they are problematic and even diminishing possibilities, we must accept that organizational knowing and knowledge—both prospective and retrospective—are necessary for actualizing the crucial organizational engagement with what is yet to come. Koselleck (2002) is mindful of the unavoidability of knowing in effecting and sustaining this engagement:

> In order to even act, one must take into account and plan for the empirical inexperience of the future. Whether it makes sense or not, one must foresee the future.

For Koselleck, this leads to a questioning of foresight and 'prognostic rationality': 'What do humans foresee, what can they foresee? The coming reality, or only possibilities?' Even for Weick (1995), 'the present' and 'the future' cannot be ignored.

'Future-perfect thinking' is posited as the means by which: '… sensemaking can be extended beyond the present. As a result present decisions can be made meaningful in a larger context than they usually are and more of the past and future can be brought to bear to inform them.'

The problematization of strategic planning is not a dismissal of prospective organizational knowing and prognostic organizational knowledge. Rather, the argument is that the primacy and exclusivity of the underlying epistemological commitment to prospective knowing is untenable. The problematization of organizational sensemaking is also not a dismissal of retrospective organizational knowing. Rather, the argument is that the primacy and exclusivity of the epistemological commitment to retrospective knowing is equally untenable in an age of higher-order contingency. Although they are necessary, retrospective and prospective organizational knowing, severally and jointly, *are not sufficient* for sustaining the crucial organizational engagement with what is yet to come. Something more basic is implicated.

From the Futurity of *Dasein* to Organizational Futurity

The exploration we have undertaken so far has been productive largely of problems and aporias. Prospective strategy and retrospective sensemaking perform a theoretical reduction to the epistemological—to bare organizational knowing. In an age of higher-order contingency, this exclusive commitment is becoming more aporetic and is running aground. Can we think the crucial organizational engagement with what is yet to come beneath the theorization of bare organizational knowing?

A more comprehensive understanding of this problematics does not lie in bare knowing as separable and separated from the distinctive being of organization—it does not lie in knowing excised from being. The kairotic time (Czarniawska 2003) has come for more imaginative speculation. Let us consider the crucial organizational engagement with what is yet to come as having ontological antecedents that have been theoretically covered over.

Going back to Augustine (1961), the engagement with what is yet to come is said to involve 'the present of future things', epistemologically available as 'anticipation'. This seems right, since for Augustine 'the present of future things' does indeed have the epistemological implications that he sought so fervently. However, the formulation 'the present of future things' may be transposed into more ontological terms as *the presence of future-ness*. Koselleck's (2004) description of 'expectation' provides some support for this transposition in that it accords more with *the presence of future-ness* than with Augustine's notion of 'anticipation' as the 'present of future things':

> ... expectation also takes place in the today; it is the future made present; it directs itself to the not-yet, to the nonexperienced, to that which is to be revealed. Hope and fear, wishes and desires, cares and rational analysis, receptive display and curiosity; all enter into expectation and constitute it.

Koselleck's 'expectation' is not self-evident in bare knowing. Expectation is constituted in a mode of being that is *futural*—it is an emanation that involves knowing entwined among other facets of temporal being: effectiveness, concernfulness, purposiveness. For Koselleck, expectation is the crucial engagement with what is yet to come that is grounded in the futurity of being. The terms 'futurity' (*Zukunftigkeit*) and 'futural' (*Zukunftig*), which are central in Heidegger's (1962, 2007a, b) early works, refer to the mode of human being-in-the-world that is fundamentally oriented toward what is to come: 'being out toward what is not yet, but can be' (Polt 2010). The futurity of '*Existenz* [is] the self-projecting by the self of its possibilities' (Gadamer and Palmer 2007). Heidegger's (2007b) description of being-in-the-world resonates with themes of relevance in the study of organization and is suggestive of an opening for thinking organizational temporality in terms of the notion of futurity.

Dasein as being-in-the-world means: being in the world in such a way that this be-ing means: having to do with the world, sojourning within it in the routines of working, of managing and taking care of things, but also of examining, interrogating, and determining them by way of examination and comparison. Being-in-the-world is characterised as concern.

The 'phenomenology of purposiveness', wherein the emphasis is on 'radical futurity' and 'a fundamental connection to self-concern' (Stendera 2015), that is offered in *Being and Time* lends further support to such a transposition from Heidegger's description of the temporality of *Dasein* to thinking organizational futurity. Furthermore, the conception of futurity 'in terms of radical indeterminacy' (Stendera 2015) resonates with the historically induced condition of higher-order contingency.

In this vein, organization may be re-described as underway toward what is yet to come: as inherently and primally futural; as characterized by the 'presence of future-ness' *(Zukunftigkeit)*, or better, by 'futurity'. For Heidegger (1962), '[t]he primary meaning of existentiality is the future'. Existent organization also 'exists as that which is always running ahead of itself; always pressing ahead into possibility' (Bakken et al. 2013). Thus, the organizational engagement with what is yet to come is given priority among the relations involved in organizational temporality. This avails an alternative onto-epistemological approach to that espoused in process organization studies, where the organizational engagement with what is yet to come is approached as derivative among the relations of organizational temporality.

We arrive at the notion of *organizational futurity* as a contemplative response to the questioning we have been pursuing. This notion is aimed at understanding that and how organization already involves a futural orientation prior to any organizational knowing of what is yet to come, and indeed, what this might mean for such knowing. The emphasis is shifted backward from thinking how organization is a coping with in-principle contingency by bare knowing, to a more basic problematization of how organization is a practical coping with the prior fact of futurity at the core of organizational being. Organization already involves a standing toward what is to come—it is an inherently futural phenomenon. If prospective knowing is a straining, looking ahead to discern what is to come, and retrospective knowing is a looking behind to discern what has been in order to better understand what is to come, then organizational futurity is the prior orientation of engagement with what is yet to come.

The speculation then is that organizational futurity is constitutive of the organizational engagement with what is yet to come. The compound hypothesis is that the being of organization as futural is the fount and a sustenance of the organizational engagement with what is yet to come, which is prior to, effects and shapes all modes of organizational knowing but is also affected by these in return, albeit as a secondary movement. What is yet to become of organization is not exhausted in the possibilities of organizational knowing. Organizational futurity is the basis of the crucial orientation of organization toward what is yet to come that is presupposed in strategic planning and in retrospective sensemaking. We would read a strong commitment to prognostic knowledge as a *modality*, among other modalities, of organizational futurity; just as we would read retrospective sensemaking as a modality of organizational futurity. The processes of organizational knowing are animated by organizational futurity wherein the significance of organizational knowledge and meaning is stipulated and sifted. In this way, we gain entry to understanding how organizational futurity *precedes* organizational knowing but might also *exceed* it. As the possibilities of organizational knowing and knowledge wax and wane, so the engagement with what is yet to come continues to be effected and is also sustained in the intelligibility and ongoing working out of organizational futurity.

Inconclusion

This chapter explores the possibility of a more expansive, onto-epistemological account of the crucial organizational engagement with what is yet to come than is offered by extant theories, which tend to be grounded in bare organizational knowing, or which approach the engagement with 'the future' as derivative. In the notion of organizational futurity, a more fundamental phenomenon is brought into thought. Organizational futurity points to a way of renewing current conceptualizations of the temporality of organization and the organizational engagement with what is yet to come. It has meta-theoretical significance in that it opens up a new way by which the central concepts of organization, organizational temporality, and strategy may be approached by giving priority to the engagement with what is yet to come. The questioning posed and pursued in this inquiry call to be answered in strategy practice as much as it calls to be answered in strategy theory. Perhaps the notion of organizational futurity provides another point of confluence between organization theory and practice.

More generally, this inquiry shares in the growing significance of understanding how organizations engage with what is yet to come, not only in terms of organizational performance but also in terms of the broader effects of organizational performance that have so quickly reached the planetary scale of significance. Organizational performance is becoming more fraught and uncertain, and the socio-environmental effects and risks produced by organizational failure have escalated dangerously. Perversely, even organizational 'success' all too often also produces reprehensible effects. But we only come to know this in hindsight when it is too late for anything but defensive apology and critical disgust. Much critique of organization theory and organizational practice is belated and merely feeds into reproducing the 'crisis of the future', where opportunities for cogent, a posteriori critique abound while ways out are less prevalent (Montuori 1998). New critical approaches and instruments are needed to confront the immense, pervasive, active, and powerful engagement between organization and what is yet to come. Both in theory and in practice, we need to come to terms with organizational futurity. If what is yet to come is beyond bare knowing, how will we *care* for it?

A Mere Opening Toward the *Intelligibility* of Organizational Futurity

The thinking of organizational futurity thus far is merely promissory. To be productive, this would need to be developed from imaginings and concepts to theories of the real. This calls for moving among the possibilities from speculative thinking to the *intelligibility* of organizational futurity.

In the making of promises it seems right to at least point out difficulties that might beset fulfilling them (Arendt 1958). I am aware of three interrelated groups of difficulties that would need to be navigated in the research that is wanting. The first group of difficulties has to do with how far Heidegger's futurity of *Dasein* will take us toward a more detailed understanding of organizational futurity. While it provides an essential opening, Heidegger's notion of futurity is not to be uncritically imported into the notion of organizational futurity. For example, although the phenomenon of organization may be held to incorporate an *organizational concern* for 'existence-relevance' (Rüegg-Stürm and Grand 2015), it seems excessive to hold that it also incorporates *Dasein*'s 'being-unto-death' as a certainty. Thus we can only go so far on the basis of Heidegger's descriptions of *Dasein,* approached as *the* task of 'first philosophy' (Heidegger 1962, 2000), the ontology of 'being as such' (Davis 2010). The thinking of organizational futurity undertaken here is not on the same plane. It is what Heidegger would perhaps disparagingly call a 'regional ontology' (Davis 2010), and any transpositions must therefore be approached with caution.

The second group of difficulties has to do with how the *intelligibility* of organizational futurity might be approached beyond contemplation. Heidegger's notion of disclosure (*Erschlossenheit*) is not truth or knowledge, but intelligibility more generally as the background of meaning (Dahlstrom 2010). Intelligibility is prior to knowing and knowledge—it is a sublation of knowing and knowledge. Only that which is intelligible can then become knowable, but that which is intelligible is not necessarily knowable. In trying to work out the intelligibility of organizational futurity, we are 'thrown into the labor of mediation, condemned to (or better, liberated for) making sense of things both practically and theoretically' (Sheehan 2014). In thinking organizational futurity, we do not do so for its own sake but must push on to consider what it means in and for organizational engagements with what is yet to come. Thus, we need to get beyond Heidegger's notion of a speculative imagination which is critiqued for its incapacity for a 'critical consciousness of the difference between the imaginary and the real' (Ricoeur in Piercey 2011). If organizational futurity cannot be approached directly in knowing or by knowledge, how is it intelligible? How might it be disclosed?

The third group of difficulties has to do with the clarification of the signifiers 'organization' and 'organizational' which are much-used throughout this inquiry. Organization has been described above as 'always underway—as temporally stretched out', and as 'always underway towards what is yet to come—as futural'. Such descriptions suffice as precursors, but they remain rather free-floating signifiers that do not help in distinguishing 'organization' in the sense of, say, a *social* process from say, biological organization, or from *Dasein* for that matter. What does it mean to refer to *organizational* knowing and knowledge? What is organizational about such knowing that is distinguishable from individual knowing, knowledge or cognition? These are not new questions. Nevertheless, they need to be attended to in the context of a more detailed study of organizational futurity which is … well … yet to come, if at all.

Acknowledgements I acknowledge the generous and valuable commentary on earlier drafts of this chapter by an anonymous reviewer, the editors of this collection, my colleagues Michael Festl and Emmanual Aloha, and Prof. Premesh Lalu (UWC-CHR). I acknowledge the South African National Research Foundation (NRF) for funding my PhD studies.

Notes

1. The expanded nomenclature, 'what is yet to come', is distinguished from the more common usage, 'the future'. This is to avoid questionable presumptions that may be connoted by the signifier 'the future': (1) that it is a singularity; (2) that it actually exists as such; and, (3) that it is a temporal partition.
2. Strictly speaking, the term 'prognostic knowledge' contains a redundancy since *pro-gnostic* already means knowledge of what is yet to come. But it is a useful redundancy in the context of this inquiry.

References

Ackoff, Russell L. 1990. Redesigning the Future: Strategy. *Systems Practice* 3 (6): 521–524.
Alvesson, Mats, and Jörgen Sandberg. 2011. Generating Research Questions Through Problematization. *Academy of Management Review* 36 (2): 247–271.
Arendt, Hannah. 1958. *The Human Condition*. 2nd ed. Chicago: The University of Chicago Press.
Augustine. 1961. *Confessions*. London: Penguin Books.
Bakken, Tor, Robin Holt, and Mike Zundel. 2013. Time and Play in Management Practice: An Investigation Through the Philosophies of McTaggart and Heidegger. *Scandinavian Journal of Management* 29: 13–22.
Beckert, Jens. 2013. Imagined Futures: Fictionality in Economic Action. *Theory Society* 42: 219–240.
———. 2014. *Capitalist Dynamics: Fictional Expectations and the Openness of the Future*, MPIfG Discussion Paper. Vol. 14/7. Köln: Max-Planck-Institut für Gesellschaftsforschung.
Bergson, Henri. 2007. *The Creative Mind: An Introduction to Metaphysics*. Trans. Mabelle L. Anderson. Newy York: Dover Publications.
Best, Jacqueline. 2012. Bureaucratic Ambiguity. *Economy and Society* 41 (1): 84–106.
Callon, Michel. 1998. An Essay on Framing and Overflowing: Economic Externalities Revisited by Sociology. *The Sociological Review* 46: 244–269.
Calori, Roland. 1998. Essai: Philosophizing on Strategic Management Models. *Organization Studies* 19 (2): 281–306.
Chia, Robert, and Robin Holt. 2006. Strategy as Practical Coping: A Heideggerian Perspective. *Organization Studies* 27 (5): 635–655.
Czarniawska, Barbara. 2003. Forbidden Knowledge: Organization Theory in Times of Transition. *Management Learning* 34 (3): 353–365.
Dahlstrom, Daniel O. 2010. Truth as *alētheia* and the Clearing of Beyng. In *Martin Heidegger: Key Concepts*, ed. Bret W. Davis. Durham: Acumen.
Davis, Brett W. 2010. In *Introduction to Martin Heidegger: Key Concepts*, ed. Bret W. Davis, 1–15. Durham: Acumen.
Gadamer, Hans-Georg, and Palmer, Richard. 2007. *The Gadamer Reader: A Bouquet of Later Writings*. Evanston: Northwestern University Press.
Hamel, Gary, and Prahalad, CK. 1994. *Competing for the Future*. Harvard Business School Press.
Heidegger, Martin. 1962. *Being and Time*. Trans John Macquarrie and Edward Robinson. New York: Harper Perennial.

―――. 2000. *Introduction to Metaphysics*: New Translation by Gregory Fried and Richard Polt. Yale.

―――. 2007a. The Concept of Time in the Science of History. In *Becoming Heidegger: On the Trail of His Early Occasional Writings 1910–1927*, ed. Theodore Kisiel and Thomas Sheehan, 60–72. Evanston: Northwestern University Press.

―――. 2007b. The Concept of Time. In *Becoming Heidegger: On the Trail of His Early Occasional Writings 1910–1927*, ed. Theodore Kisiel and Thomas Sheehan, 196–213. Evanston: Northwestern University Press.

Hernes, Tor. 2014. *A Process Theory of Organization*. Oxford: Oxford University Press.

Hickson, David John, and Pugh, Derek Salman (eds.). 1995. *Management Worldwide: The Impact of Societal Culture on Organizations Around the Globe*. Penguin.

Johnson, Gerry, Kevan Scholes, and Richard Whittington. 2008. *Exploring Corporate Strategy: Text & Cases*. New York: Pearson Education.

Knight, Frank. 1964. *Risk, Uncertainty, and Profit*. New York: Sentry Press.

Knights, David, and Glen Morgan. 1991. Corporate Strategy, Organizations, and Subjectivity: A Critique. *Organization Studies* 12 (2): 251–273.

Koselleck, Reinhart. 2002. *The Practice of Conceptual History: Timing History, Spacing Concepts*. Stanford: Stanford University Press.

―――. 2004. *Futures Past: On the Semantics of Historical Time*. New York: Columbia University Press.

Laamanen, Tomi. 2017. Editorial: Reflecting on the Past 50 Years of Long Range Planning and a Research Agenda for the Next 50. *Long Range Planning* 50: 1–7.

Lindblom, Charles E. 1959. The Science of "Muddling Through". *Public Administration Review* 19 (2): 79–88.

MacKay, R.B., and R. Chia. 2013. Choice, Chance, and Unintended Consequences in Strategic Change: A Process Understanding of the Rise and Fall of NorthCo Automotive. *Academy of Management Journal* 56 (1): 208–230.

March, James G., and J.P. Olsen. 1976. Organizational Choice Under Ambiguity. In *Ambiguity and Choice in Organizations*. Oslo: Universitetsforlaget.

Mintzberg, Henry. 1973. Strategy-Making in Three Modes. *California Management Review* 16 (2): 44–53.

Montuori, Alfonso. 1998. Complexity, Epistemology, and the Challenge of the Future. *Academy of Management Proceedings* (K1–K8): 31–41.

Orlikowski, Wanda. 2015. Technology and Organization: Contingency All the Way Down. In *Technology and Organization: Essays in Honour of Joan Woodward*. Greenwood: Emerald Group Publishing.

Piercey, Robert. 2011. Kant and the Problem of Hermeneutics: Heidegger and Ricoeur on the Transcendental Schematism. *Idealistic Studies* 41 (3): 187–202.

Polt, Richard. 2010. Being and Time. In *Martin Heidegger: Key Concepts*, ed. Bret W. Davis, 69–81. Acumen.

Purser, Ronald E., and Jack Petranker. 2005. Unfreezing the Future: Exploring the Dynamic of Time in Organizational Change. *The Journal of Applied Behavioural Science* 41 (2): 182–203.

Reed, Mike. 1991. Review Article: Scripting Scenarios for a New Organization Theory and Practice. *Work, Employment & Society* 5 (1): 119–132.

Rescher, Nicholas. 1996. *Process Metaphysics: An Introduction to Process Philosophy*. Suny Press.

Rüegg-Stürm, Johannes, and Simon Grand. 2015. *The St. Gallen Management Model*. Haupt.

Sarasvathy, Saras D. 2001. Causation and Effectuation: Toward a Theoretical Shift from Economic Inevitability to Entrepreneurial Contingency. *Academy of Management Review* 26 (2): 243–263.

Schreyögg, Georg. 1993. Book Review: Richard Whittington – What Is Strategy and Does It Matter?

Schutz, Alfred. 1970. In *On Phenomenology and Social Relations: Selected Writings*, ed. R. Helmut. Wagner: The University of Chicago Press.

Sheehan, Thomas. 2014. What, After All, Was Heidegger About? *Continental Philosophy Review*. DOI 10.1007/s11007-014-9302-4. Springer.

Stacey, Ralph D. 1996. *Complexity and Creativity in Organizations*. Berrett-Koehler Publishers.

Stacey, Ralph D. 2010. *Complexity and Organizational Reality: Uncertainty and the Need to Rethink Management After the Collapse of Investment Capitalism*. London: Routledge.

Stendera, Marilyn. 2015. Being-in-the-world, Temporality and Autopoiesis. *Parrhesia*, 24: 261–284.

Tsoukas, Haridimos, and Jill Shepherd. 2004. Introduction: Organizations and the Future, from Forecasting to Foresight. In *Managing the Future: Strategic Foresight in the Knowledge Economy*, ed. Haridimos Tsoukas and Jill Shepherd. Malden: Blackwell.

Van der Heijden, Kees. 2011. *Scenarios: The Art of Strategic Conversation*. 2nd ed. New York: Wiley.

Weick, Karl E. 1995. *Sensemaking in Organizations*. Sage.

Williams, Robert. 2008. Aristotelian Indeterminacy and the Open Future. (https://philpapers.org/rec/WILAIA-4)

Part II

Theoretical and Methodological Perspectives

6

Open(ing up) for the Future: Practising Open Strategy and Open Innovation to Cope with Uncertainty

Maximilian Heimstädt and Georg Reischauer

Introduction

The diagnosis that 'the future is open' has recently (re-)emerged at the forefront of the social sciences. More specifically, we witness a growing interest concerning the question of how economic actors in general (Beckert 2016) and organizations in particular (Koch et al. 2016) deal with a future that is increasingly conceived as unknowable and unpredictable. A promising avenue for addressing this question is the study of 'temporal practices' (Kaplan and Orlikowski 2012; Reckwitz 2002) or, more specifically, 'future-oriented practices'. Examining these practices allows us to attain a better understanding of how organizations cope with the growing certainty that the future is genuinely uncertain (Koch et al. 2016; Reckwitz

---

M. Heimstädt (✉)
Reinhard Mohn Institute of Management, Witten/Herdecke University, Germany

G. Reischauer
Department of Strategy and Innovation, WU Vienna University of Economics and Business, Austria

2016). Although the uncertainty of the future has been a long-standing interest in management and organization scholarship (e.g. Cyert and March 1963), this new perspective enables researchers to move beyond organizational practices such as strategic planning and technological forecasting that aim at predicting the future towards practices that allow organizations to work with uncertainty in a much broader sense.

In this chapter, we argue that organizational practices of openness are paradigmatic examples of future-oriented practices. These practices help organizations cope with the uncertainty of the future without promising to resolve it altogether. We illustrate how these practices do so by focusing on the two most prominent bundles of organizational practices in management research that are based on the principle of openness: *open innovation* and *open strategy*. Organizations that open up their innovation process probe the future. Rather than trying to make accurate predictions about future customer preferences, they try to co-create these preferences (e.g. by the external sourcing of ideas from the crowd) or create multiple pathways for addressing preferences in the future (e.g. by corporate incubating). Organizations that open up their strategy process import the future; rather than secretly planning for a generally unforeseeable future, they engage stakeholders in a dialogue about their expectations regarding the future (in the case of transparent strategizing) or try to increase stakeholders' commitment by allowing them to partake in certain decisions (in the case of inclusive strategizing).

Our chapter proceeds as follows. In a first step, we show how openness presents an organizing principle that scholars have linked to the uncertainty of the future in v arious ways. After that, we develop our understanding of organizational practices of openness as paradigmatic examples of future-oriented practices. We then demonstrate this understanding with examples from the two bundles of the most prominent open practices: open innovation and open strategy. Finally, we close with a discussion on the limits of openness as a practice to address uncertainty.

Openness as an Organizing Principle

Looking to the past, we find at least three distinct understandings of openness as an organizing principle. First, openness can be understood as a general law that not just constrains but also enables organizations.

In the late 1940s and 1950s, a group of scholars from diverse academic backgrounds worked on a scientific programme that tried to establish the 'system' as a common denominator of different academic fields (Hammond 2002). In his work on 'general system theory', the Austrian-born Ludwig von Bertalanffy (1969), one of the group members, argued that the idea of closed systems might apply to static or mechanical systems, yet is inappropriate when describing living systems. For von Bertalanffy, living systems needed to be described as open systems, whereby he understood openness as a system's constant interaction with its environment.[1] This interaction, he argued, is necessary for the system's continuity. Organization scholars quickly picked up on the recommendation to describe their research object through the language of systems (Scott 2003). In this tradition, openness is described as a necessary condition for organizations. The principle of openness ensures an organization's future; however, the organization is very restricted in deliberately shaping this future.

A second understanding pictures openness as a humanistic ideal, an organizing principle that is ethically superior to the principle of closedness. This perspective can be traced back to the work of Karl Popper. In *The Open Society and Its Enemies*, Popper (1945) described closed societies as those that are founded on collectivism and a belief in the certainty of knowledge. According to Popper, however, an open and desirable society is one that allows its guiding assumptions to be tested and eventually modified, and hence is one that allows its leaders to be 'falsified' through democratic elections. Armbrüster and Gebert (2002) adapted Popper's socio-philosophical ideas as a frame of reference for studying management and organizational trends and proposed using this frame of reference to examine whether certain practices follow open or closed patterns of thinking. One of their key findings was that management practices that follow the principle of closedness are those that favour collectivism as opposed to individualism, and the certainty of knowledge as opposed to continuous learning. In this understanding of openness, actors can deliberately apply the principle to themselves. By choosing openness as an organizing principle, organizations increase the contingency of the future and avoid taking a direction that does not allow for readjustment of means and ends later on.

A third understanding portrays openness as an efficient mode of production. Popper's contemporary, the Austrian economist Friedrich von Hayek, personifies this principle. In his opus magnum *The Road to Serfdom*, Hayek (1944), like Popper, rejected the idea of an authority with an uncriticizable claim to truth. Like Popper, Hayek was sceptical of political systems that rely (solely) on central planning, and supported the 'conviction that where effective competition can be created, it is a better way of guiding individual efforts than any other' (Hayek 1944, p. 37). Hence, both argued that the way in which the future is performed in the present should not be closed but open. However—and this may present the most striking difference to the thinking of Popper—Hayek understood openness not as the scrutiny of the government by the people, but as a general decentralization of decisions that shape the future (e.g. allocation of resources through market mechanisms, not state planning). Openness in this tradition can thus be understood as a principle that prescribes the decentralization of ideas on what the future might look like, meritocratic decision-making and a preference for emergence over planning. At the same time, this Hayekian understanding of openness as an organizing principle implies a paradox: on the one hand, it increases the contingency of the future by decentralizing the mechanisms that shape future; on the other hand, it decreases contingency, as it sees decentralization as the most superior organization of work. This resembles what Ortmann (2009, p. 19) describes as the 'Golden Touch of modernity', a principle that, from a distance, looks like one that allows for utmost contingency yet which, once embraced, turns a contingent future into a necessary one.

Towards Organizational Practices of Openness

The three understandings of organizational openness described above share the assumption that openness as an organizing principle is closely linked to the uncertainty of the future. In the following section, we present practices as a promising lens through which to explore this connection in greater depth. Following Giddens (1984), practices can be understood as social actions that recursively produce and reproduce the structures that constrain and enable actions (cf. Feldman and Orlikowski 2011). As a tool to study time not as an objective 'container' but as the malleable structures described by Giddens, Andreas Reckwitz has proposed the concept of 'temporal practices, that are practices that go beyond the organization of temporalities inherent in every practice, but that are *focused* and *specialized* on organizing time' (2016, pp. 42–43, own translation, emphasis in original).

We can think of temporal practices as being oriented towards one or more temporal modes: the past, the present and/or the future. Focal to our interest are practices that are focused and specialized on organizing the future, for example, through imagination, calculation or planning. Future-oriented practices may include the calculation of risk in decision-making, scientific prediction or the development of alternative scenarios for the future. These future-oriented practices allow a colonization of time reaching out from the present into the future, whereby the future seems directly contingent on decisions made in the present (Reckwitz 2016).

Organizational practices of openness are paradigmatic examples of future-oriented practices that allow organizations to work with the uncertainty of the future in novel ways. The rise of such novel ways of dealing with the future is grounded in the recent diagnosis by Reckwitz (2016) of the 'crisis of modern-day rationalization of the future'. Since the 1980s, he argues, organizations have perceived the future less as an empty space to be filled out, but rather as a space that is filled with uncertainty. When uncertainty prevails, it becomes intriguing to find out how organizations form expectations, as a 'shadow of the future' (Axelrod 1984) that motivates decisions in the present (Beckert 2016). Against this background, we demonstrate in the following section how the two most prominent bundles of organizational practices—open innovation and open strategy—allow organizations to work with uncertainty in novel ways.

Open Innovation: Probing the Future

Innovation management is a bundle of organizational practices strongly oriented towards the future. When organizations innovate, they attempt to develop new products and/or services that match future preferences.

In traditional innovation management, organizations try to predict these preferences and feed these anticipations into their innovation processes. However, market forecasts continue to fail (Beckert 2016, p. 221 et seq.), and product failure becomes more expensive in times of growing competition (Wiggins and Ruefli 2005). Thus, it becomes much harder to make these forecasts and to form expectations about future preferences. A key response to this challenge has been the open innovation approach. Introduced by the seminal work of Chesbrough (2003), it initiated a major shift in perspective with regards to practising innovation. Instead of seeking 'to discover new breakthroughs; develop them into products; build the products in its factories; and distribute, finance, and service those products—all within the four walls of the company', an organization that turns to open innovation uses 'purposive inflows and outflows of knowledge to accelerate internal innovation, and expand the markets for external use of innovation' (Chesbrough 2003, p. 4). In the following section, we describe two practices of open innovation and their link to the future: crowdsourcing and corporate incubating. As we illustrate, both forms of open innovation work with uncertainty by probing the future, by creating small tests of the future in the present.

Crowdsourcing

Crowdsourcing is a form of open innovation through which knowledge that ultimately should lead to innovation is gathered from external sources. Crowdsourcing refers to 'the act of outsourcing a task to a "crowd" rather than to a designated "agent" (an organization, informal or formal team, or individual), such as a contractor, in the form of an open call' (Afuah and Tucci 2012, p. 355). An example of crowdsourcing is Procter & Gamble's Connect + Develop programme, to which individuals and organizations can submit ideas and proposals (Zimmermann et al. 2014). In general terms, tapping into the wisdom of a crowd is a promising innovation practice for solving a problem that requires understanding of a knowledge domain that, from the perspective of the focal organization, is distant. More specifically, crowdsourcing has been found to be a valuable form of innovation if the problem is easy to delineate and to communicate to the crowd; the knowledge required to address the problem falls outside the organization's established knowledge domain; the capability to promptly evaluate and integrate the solution does exist; access to a large crowd is at hand; and all involved actors have easy access to the needed information technologies (Afuah and Tucci 2012).

How far does this practice relate to the future? On a general level, it probes the future but attempts to avoid the risk of present innovations falling short of future customer preferences. Rather than estimating the future preference, they involve potential customers in a collaborative innovation process to co-create these preferences (Djelassi and Decoopman 2013). The novel way in which these practices probe the future is that uncertainty is moved closer to the present and is considered during the stage of developing ideas, the so-called fuzzy front end of innovation (van den Ende et al. 2015). In other words, the imagining of possible futures and how they might shape preferences is omnipresent in the early stages of the innovation process. In addition, the crowd presents a diverse source of knowledge and hence a variety of possible futures. By tapping into the ideas of the crowd, an organization gains access to a range of very different ideas about how the future may look like. A key mechanism that allows organizations to utilize the variety of different futures is what Powell (2017, p. 7) describes as the 'feedback dynamics' of the crowd. The crowd constantly checks whether ideas hold up to ideals or criteria set by the innovating organization. This iteration allows the emergence of a variety of futures that has already successfully passed a first selection stage.

Corporate Incubating

Corporate incubating is described as a property-based and corporate-backed administrative apparatus that aims at promoting the commercialization of knowledge (Enkel et al. 2009; Phan et al. 2005, p. 166; West and Bogers 2014). This highlights that, in contrast to the form of open innovation described above, spatial arrangements of social goods and the co-presence of persons are the key ingredients of incubators. The basic idea of corporate incubators is that new ventures—the incubatees—can launch innovations better and quicker than the corporation as a whole. More specifically, the incubator assists by diagnosing business needs, selecting and monitoring the processes of the new venture, providing access to financial capital and individuals, and fostering quick learning (Hackett and Dilts 2004). This basic idea of corporate incubating includes several variants with regard to the dimension of time. For example, corporate accelerators like the Siemens Technology Accelerator perform a rather competitive and cyclical selection of new ventures and have a short incubation period (Kohler 2016). In contrast, technology business incubators, as increasingly found in universities to commercialize research outputs, have a more complex and less time-pressured intake policy (Mian et al. 2016).

The open innovation practice of corporate incubating probes the future by creating several possible pathways to the future. These pathways are explored through new ventures in a supervised and time-limited context. Corporate incubating produces a stream of nascent innovations that, depending on market conditions, may be nurtured or rejected. The way in which possible future pathways are created is a routinized trial-and-error process. While traditional innovation processes also involve trial-and-error, they are deeply embedded into existing strategies and organizational structures. By outsourcing the iterative commercialization of ideas into relative autonomous new organizations—which are somewhat 'protected' by the incubator, but still able to fail—a less restricted probing of the future can take place. In sum, corporate incubating allows an organization to build a portfolio of possible futures to be probed. In contrast to traditional innovation management that aims at building a portfolio of possible products, a more exploratory approach to innovation can take place. Thus, a portfolio of possible futures does not reduce uncertainty by simply spreading the risk across several innovations, but by having the opportunity to continue or discontinue nurturing possible pathways into the future as time unfolds.

Open Strategy: Importing the Future

Strategy is seen as the organizational function that is most strongly oriented towards the future. Traditionally, strategizing is understood as the determination of the long-term goals of an organization (Chandler 1962). Some strategy professionals engage with all sorts of techno-rational instruments that are expected to most accurately predict the future to set these goals. The general perception of an open and unpredictable future, however, reached the domain of strategy some decades ago (Hill and Westbrook 1997), an event best captured by the change in terminology from 'forecasting' to 'foresight' (Tsoukas and Shepherd 2004). By opening up the strategy process, organizations work with the uncertainty of the future in novel ways. In the following section, we focus on two forms of open strategy: transparent strategizing and inclusive strategizing (Hautz et al. 2017; Whittington et al. 2011). As we show, both open strategy practices work with uncertainty by 'importing the future', by dragging certain aspects of the future into the present.

Transparent Strategizing

Historically, academics and professionals have understood strategy as a highly secret endeavour. Accordingly, a sustained competitive advantage can only be achieved and sustained when information about strategy is withheld from competitors (Makadok and Barney 2001), or at least sufficiently obscured to avoid imitation (Vicente-Lorente 2001). Accounts of transparent strategizing have challenged this conviction. Transparency hereby refers to the 'visibility of information about an organization's strategy, potentially during the formulation process but particularly with regard to the strategy finally produced' (Whittington et al. 2011, p. 536). In practice, this transparency is oftentimes mediated by means of digital information and communication technology, such as internal and external strategy blogging. Organizations have experimented with blogs as a tool within the larger toolbox of outbound corporate communication, for example, when, in 2004, Sun Microsystems' Chief Operating Officer used the corporate employee blog to harshly criticize Hewlett Packard's product strategy and in return received a cease-and-desist order from HP (Cox et al. 2008). Like many other corporations to follow, Sun responded to this incident with blogging policies that create certain restrictions within the openness of strategy blogging.

Gegenhuber and Dobusch (2017) recently found more radical and thorough practices of strategy blogging that vividly exemplify how transparent strategizing can help organizations to import the future. In a comparative study, they showed how two start-ups use strategy blogging to engage with actual and (potential) users, the media and to attract investors. Using a practice lens, the authors analysed strategy blog posts and found that the two software start-ups inform the public about their plans ('broadcasting'), receive feedback ('dialoguing'), and even include stakeholders in democratic decision processes ('including'). Zooming into the data provided by the authors, the particularities of open strategy as a bundle of future-oriented practices unfolds. In a blog post from 2009, one of the organizations addresses its audience directly:

> Now over to you. You can and should participate in the priority of our task list for new improvements! One decision criterion: what systems do you use most often or which would you likely use in the near future. I will develop a [product name] plugin for the 2–3 highest ranked ideas, ideally in the order that you suggested. (Gegenhuber and Dobusch 2017, p. 8)

What happens in this episode of strategy blogging is that the complex and resource-intensive process of traditional market research that includes large-n surveys and handpicked focus groups is replaced with a process that is functionally equivalent. Instead of making strategy based on traditional means of forecasting, the software start-up defines a question, collects user input, categorizes the input into 'tasks' and eventually sorts these tasks into a list. By doing so, the start-up replaces the fiction that individuals in a statistical sample utter preferences 'as if' they were a broader population with the fiction that the preferences of the actual users in the present remain stable into their future. Thereby the start-up eliminates the risk of a flawed statistical representation, but at the same time keeps up the façade of 'calculative rationality' (Levinthal and March 1993, p. 96). The unpredictability of the future is thereby not resolved, yet in a certain way imported into the present.

Inclusive Strategizing

The boundary between transparency and inclusion in strategizing is not entirely clear-cut. Transparency can be understood primarily as intentional acts of information disclosure, whereby inclusion refers primarily to feedback mechanisms that are meaningful in a sense that the feedback can, at least potentially, shape the evolution of an organization's strategy. It is this potential inclusion that is linked to the uncertainty of the future. Traditionally, academics and professionals understood strategizing as an elitist task that needs to be performed by a closed group of experts. This circle of 'elite staff' (Williamson 1970, p. 125), trained in analytical tools, would be able to deliver the most rational decision advice (gathered through in-depth data analysis) to the top management. In this traditional perspective of strategy, the top management is able to perform strategic rationality by limiting inclusion to a small group of employees who devote their entire capacity to the strategy process. Open strategy has challenged this orthodoxy by widening strategy-making to a broader group of employees, each of whom would only devote a fraction of their entire capacity to the process. Besides strategy consultants, who have been included in strategy-making for decades, open strategy refers to the inclusion of, for example, civil society, consumers, suppliers or complementors.

Inclusive strategizing can help organizations to deal with the uncertainty of the future by increasing stakeholders' commitment to the organization. In the postmodern condition, in which actors are confronted with an 'exponential growth of *concurring* events' (Reckwitz 2016, p. 49), employees are tempted to switch their employer more quickly than in the past. Organizations, on the other hand, require a certain degree of stability to function. It has been found that inclusive practices allow individual participants to reflect on their 'role, identity, and future in the organization' (Mantere and Vaara 2008, p. 351), which in turn can lead to an increase in motivation and overall commitment to the organization

(Antikainen et al. 2018; Dobusch and Müller-Seitz 2012). By including a wider array of stakeholders from inside and outside the organization in the strategy process, organizations can increase the duration of these stakeholders' commitment to the organization when traditional instruments of remuneration seem unlikely to do so (Sheridan 1992).

Studies on inclusive practices in the strategy process are still relatively rare and oftentimes focus on 'alternative' organizations (e.g. Dobusch 2012; Luedicke et al. 2017). However, the relation between more inclusive strategizing and organizations' efforts to work with an increasingly uncertain future becomes particularly clear in corporations as the *locus classicus* of elitist and closed strategizing. A vivid example of this is the 'ValuesJam' organized by IBM 2003, a three-day discussion via the corporate intranet about the company's values (Palmisano 2004). Fifty-thousand employees were estimated to have joined the jam, whereby 10,000 comments were posted. By the end of the process, analysts pored over the postings, mined the million-word text for key themes using a specially tailored 'jamalyzer' tool, and came up with a revised set of corporate values, which the CEO announced to employees in an intranet broadcast shortly afterwards (Palmisano 2004, p. 5 et seq.). In an interview, CEO Sam Palmisano describes how he perceived the jam had changed IBM employees' perception of their future, from something that might be just a continuation of IBM's crisis-shaken past in the 1990s towards something shapeable:

> You lay out the opportunity to become a great company again—the greatest in the world, which is what IBM used to be. And you hope people feel the same need, the urgency you do, to get there. Well, I think IBMers today do feel that urgency. Maybe the jam's greatest contribution was to make that fact unambiguously clear to all of us, very visibly, in public. (2004, p. 11)

Through more inclusive strategizing, organizations can not only import the uncertainty of stakeholder commitment from the future into the present, but can also actively try to reduce the risk of 'exit' (employees leaving the firm) by providing channels for employees to 'voice' their concerns (Hirschman 1970).

Discussion and Conclusion

In this chapter, we illustrated how far the two prominent bundles of organizational practices that are based on the organizing principle of openness—open innovation and open strategy—present future-oriented practices (Table 6.1).

Both examples of open innovation—crowdsourcing and corporate incubating—have in common their attempt to probe the future. Crowdsourcing attempts to capture the risk that present innovations might miss customer preferences in the future. The means to capture these preferences is the involvement of potential customers, which does not predict but rather co-creates future customer preferences. Corporate incubating probes the future by creating possible pathways an organization might take in the future. To achieve this, corporate incubators incorporate routinized trial-and-error processes that allow them to build a portfolio of innovative ideas. However, neither crowdsourcing nor corporate incubating allows organizations to absorb and overcome the uncertainty of the future. In each case, the decisions on which ideas to further develop and commercialize are not delegated to the crowd or the innovation intermediary. Both of these open innovation practices face limitations when it comes to addressing uncertainty. With crowdsourcing, organizations frequently face a large number of possible solutions that can be overwhelming and result in the paradoxical outcome that,

Table 6.1 Future-oriented practices based on openness

Bundle of practices and link to the future	Exemplary practices	Implications for how organizations work with uncertainty
Open innovation: Probing the future	Crowdsourcing	Capturing the risk that present innovations miss customer preferences in the future
	Corporate incubating	Generating multiple pathways from the present into the future
Open strategy: Importing the future	Transparent strategizing	Moving uncertainty about acceptance of future strategy decisions into the present
	Inclusive strategizing	Creating commitment in the present to avoid lack of commitment in the future

despite their initial efforts to acquire solutions from distant and thus less familiar knowledge domains, ultimately more familiar solutions are chosen (Piezunka and Dahlander 2015). Also, in the case of innovation intermediaries, the key task of integrating the external knowledge into the innovation-seeking organization is not resolved but demands particular attention (Wallin and von Krogh 2010).

Both examples of open strategy—transparent and inclusive strategizing—attempt to import the future. Through transparent strategizing, organizations move the uncertainty about the acceptance of future strategy decisions into the present. This effect seems particularly strong when stakeholders do not only access strategy information but also provide feedback on it. Through this process of 'dialoguing' (Gegenhuber and Dobusch 2017), both organization and stakeholder become entangled in the performative illusion that a stakeholder's attitude to a strategic idea in the present will be the same as in the future. Through inclusive strategizing, organizations create commitment in the present to avoid lack of commitment in the future. When including stakeholders in strategy decisions, organizations can import the uncertainty about an employee's commitment in the future into the present and reduce it by providing room for reflection on role and identity (Mantere and Vaara 2008). There are also clear limitations to open strategy practices in addressing future uncertainty. Analogous to the idea that leadership requires not only leaders but also a certain degree of cooperation from those who are led, organizations can only work with the future behaviour of other actors when these actors are willing to accept openness and engage with the organization in the present. For example, if potential customers refuse to share their opinions on the strategy ideas produced by an organization, the organization has no opportunity to influence the customer's future satisfaction with strategic decisions.

We have restricted our discussion of open innovation practices and open strategy practices to their positive effects as far as the future is concerned. However, there are also several potential downsides. On the one hand, the outputs of these future-oriented practices might be highly structured from the very beginning and thus are more closed than open. For example, Wenzel and Koch (2017) argue that corporate incubating practice may be close to the strategic core of a firm and will therefore be unable to probe the future as we argued above. Conversely, organizations that fully expose their innovation and strategy process to externals may become dependent on these externals. Organizations in the sharing economy that depend on their online community to create value exemplify this argument (Reischauer and Mair 2018).

Recently, the media scholar Nathaniel Tkacz mused that 'the open is increasingly used to "look forward"' (2012, p. 387). As we demonstrated, organizational practices of openness are also increasingly used to imagine and thereby work with the uncertainty of the future. In times of rising uncertainty and unpredictable shocks, realizing such imaginary power in the form of open innovation and open strategy practices seems to be a valuable organizational feature. It remains to be seen which other organizational functions might be opened up in the future and at which point organizations might reach the boundaries of openness.

Note

1. An idea that most prominently informed Niklas Luhmann's (1995) later theory of social systems, and especially his concept of 'autopoiesis' (for the significance of Luhmann's work for the study of organizations, cf. Seidl and Becker 2006).

References

Afuah, Allan, and Christopher L. Tucci. 2012. Crowdsourcing as a Solution to Distant Search. *Academy of Management Review* 37: 355–375.
Antikainen, E., P. Sajasalo, and T. Auvinen. 2018. Participative Strategy Work. In *Navigating Through Changing Times: Knowledge Work in Complex Environments*, ed. Anne Eskola. London: Routledge.
Armbrüster, Thomas, and Diether Gebert. 2002. Uncharted Territories of Organizational Research: The Case of Karl Popper's Open Society and Its Enemies. *Organization Studies* 23: 169–188.
Axelrod, Robert. 1984. *The Evolution of Cooperation*. New York: Basic Books.

Beckert, Jens. 2016. *Imagined Futures: Fictional Expectations and Capitalist Dynamics*. Cambridge, MA: Harvard University Press.
Chandler, Alfred. 1962. *Strategy and Structure: Chapters in the History of the Industrial Enterprise*. Boston: MIT Press.
Chesbrough, Henry. 2003. *Open Innovation: The New Imperative for Creating and Profiting from Technology*. Boston: Harvard Business Review Press.
Cox, Joshua L., Eric R. Martinez, and Kevin B. Quinlan. 2008. Blogs and the Corporation: Managing the Risk, Reaping the Benefits. *Journal of Business Strategy* 29: 4–12.
Cyert, Richard, and James G. March. 1963. *A Behavioral Theory of the Firm*. Malden: Wiley.
Djelassi, Souad, and Isabelle Decoopman. 2013. Customers' Participation in Product Development through Crowdsourcing: Issues and Implications. *Industrial Marketing Management* 42: 683–692.
Dobusch, L., and Müller-Seitz, G. 2012. *Strategy as a Practice of Thousands: The Case of Wikimedia*. Academy of Management Best Paper Proceedings, doi: https://doi.org/10.5465/AMBPP.2012.43
Enkel, Ellen, Oliver Gassmann, and Henry Chesbrough. 2009. Open R&D and Open Innovation: Exploring the Phenomenon. *R&D Management* 39: 311–316.
Feldman, Martha, and Wanda J. Orlikowski. 2011. Theorizing Practice and Practicing Theory. *Organization Science* 22: 1240–1253.
Gegenhuber, Thomas, and Leonhard Dobusch. 2017. Making an Impression Through Openness: How Open Strategy-Making Practices Change in the Evolution of New Ventures. *Long Range Planning* 50: 337–354.
Giddens, Anthony. 1984. *The Constitution of Society: Outline of the Theory of Structuration*. Berkeley: University of California Press.
Hackett, Sean M., and David M. Dilts. 2004. A Systematic Review of Business Incubation Research. *The Journal of Technology Transfer* 29: 55–82.
Hammond, Debora. 2002. Exploring the Genealogy of Systems Thinking. *Systems Research and Behavioral Science* 19: 429–439.
Hautz, Julia, David Seidl, and Richard Whittington. 2017. Open Strategy: Dimensions, Dilemmas, Dynamics. *Long Range Planning* 50: 298–309.
Hayek, Friedrich A. 1944. *The Road to Serfdom*. London: Routledge.
Hill, Terry, and Roy Westbrook. 1997. SWOT Analysis: It's Time for a Product Recall. *Long Range Planning* 30: 46–52.
Hirschman, Albert O. 1970. *Exit, Voice, and Loyalty: Responses to Decline in Firms, Organizations, and States*. Cambridge, MA: Harvard University Press.

Kaplan, Sarah, and Wanda J. Orlikowski. 2012. Temporal Work in Strategy Making. *Organization Science* 24: 965–995.
Koch, Jochen, Hannes Krämer, Andreas Reckwitz, and Matthias Wenzel. 2016. Zum Umgang mit Zukunft in Organisationen: Eine praxistheoretische Perspektive. *Managementforschung* 26: 161–184.
Kohler, Thomas. 2016. Corporate Accelerators: Building Bridges Between Corporations and Startups. *Business Horizons* 59: 347–357.
Levinthal, Daniel A., and James G. March. 1993. The Myopia of Learning. *Strategic Management Journal* 14: 95–112.
Luedicke, Marius K., Katharina C. Husemann, Santi Furnari, and Florian Ladstaetter. 2017. Radically Open Strategizing: How the Premium Cola Collective Takes Open Strategy to the Extreme. *Long Range Planning* 50: 371–384.
Luhmann, Niklas. 1995. *Social Systems*. Palo Alto: Stanford University Press.
Makadok, Richard, and Jay B. Barney. 2001. Strategic Factor Market Intelligence: An Application of Information Economics to Strategy Formulation and Competitor Intelligence. *Management Science* 47: 1621–1638.
Mantere, Saku, and Eero Vaara. 2008. On the Problem of Participation in Strategy: A Critical Discursive Perspective. *Organization Science* 19: 341–358.
Mian, Sarfraz, Wadid Lamine, and Alain Fayolle. 2016. Technology Business Incubation: An overview of the state of knowledge. *Technovation* 50: 1–12.
Ortmann, Günther. 2009. *Management in der Hypermoderne: Kontingenz und Entscheidung*. Wiesbaden: VS Verlag für Sozialwissenschaften.
Palmisano, Sam. 2004. Leading Change When Business Is Good. Interview by Paul Hemp and Thomas A. Stewart. *Harvard Business Review* 82: 60–70.
Phan, Phillip H., Donald S. Siegel, and Mike Wright. 2005. Science Parks and Incubators: Observations, Synthesis and Future Research. *Journal of Business Venturing* 20: 165–182.
Piezunka, Henning, and Linus Dahlander. 2015. Distant Search, Narrow Attention: How Crowding Alters Organizations' Filtering of Suggestions in Crowdsourcing. *Academy of Management Journal* 58: 856–880.
Popper, Karl. 1945. *The Open Society and Its Enemies*. London: Routledge.
Powell, Walter W. 2017. A Sociologist Looks at Crowds: Innovation or Invention? *Strategic Organization* 15: 289–297.
Reckwitz, Andreas. 2002. Toward a Theory of Social Practices: A Development in Culturalist Theorizing. *European Journal of Social Theory* 5: 243–263.
———. 2016. Zukunftspraktiken: Die Zeitlichkeit des Sozialen und die Krise der Modernen Rationalisierung der Zukunft. In *Die Ungewissheit Des*

Zukünftigen, ed. Frank Becker, Benjamin Scheller, and Ute Schneider, 31–54. Frankfurt/New York: Campus.
Reischauer, Georg, and Johanna Mair. 2018. Platform Organizing in the New Digital Economy: Revisiting Online Communities and Strategic Responses. *Research in the Sociology of Organizations*.
Scott, W. Richard. 2003. *Organizations: Rational, Natural, and Open Systems*. 5th ed. Upper Saddle River: Prentice Hall.
Seidl, David, and Kai H. Becker, eds. 2006. *Niklas Luhmann and Organization Studies*. Copenhagen: Copenhagen Business School Press.
Sheridan, John E. 1992. Organizational Culture and Employee Retention. *Academy of Management Journal* 35: 1036–1056.
Tkacz, Nathaniel. 2012. From Open Source to Open Government: A Critique of Open Politics. *Ephemera* 12: 386–405.
Tsoukas, Haridimos, and Jill Shepherd. 2004. Organizations and the Future, from Forecasting to Foresight (Introduction). In *Managing the Future. Foresight in the Knowledge Economy*, ed. Haridimos Tsoukas and Jill Shepherd, 1–17. Malden: Blackwell.
van den Ende, Jan, Lars Frederiksen, and Andrea Prencipe. 2015. The Front End of Innovation: Organizing Search for Ideas. *Journal of Product Innovation Management* 32: 482–487.
Vicente-Lorente, José David. 2001. Specificity and Opacity as Resource-Based Determinants of Capital Structure: Evidence for Spanish Manufacturing Firms. *Strategic Management Journal* 22: 157–177.
von Bertalanffy, Ludwig. 1969. *General System Theory: Foundations, Development, Applications*. New York: George Braziller.
Wallin, Martin W., and Georg von Krogh. 2010. Organizing for Open Innovation: Focus on the Integration of Knowledge. *Organizational Dynamics* 39: 145–154.
Wenzel, Matthias, and Jochen Koch. 2017. Acceleration as Process: A Strategy Process Perspective on Startup Acceleration. In *Accelerators*, ed. I. Drori and M. Wright. Cheltenham: Edward Elgar.
West, Joel, and Marcel Bogers. 2014. Leveraging External Sources of Innovation: A Review of Research on Open Innovation. *Journal of Product Innovation Management* 31: 814–831.
Whittington, Richard, Ludovic Cailluet, and Basak Yakis-Douglas. 2011. Opening Strategy: Evolution of a Precarious Profession. *British Journal of Management* 22: 531–544.

Wiggins, Robert R., and Timothy W. Ruefli. 2005. Schumpeter's Ghost: Is Hypercompetition Making the Best of Times Shorter? *Strategic Management Journal* 26: 887–911.

Williamson, Oliver E. 1970. *Corporate Control and Business Behavior*. Englewood Cliffs: Prentice Hall.

Zimmermann, Alexander, Peter Gomez, Gilbert Pobst, and Sebastian Raisch. 2014. Creating Societal Benefits and Corporate Profits. *MIT Sloan Management Review* 55: 18–21.

7

Antenarratives in Ongoing Strategic Change: Using the Story Index to Capture Daunting and Optimistic Futures

Tommi P. Auvinen, Pasi Sajasalo, Teppo Sintonen, Tuomo Takala, and Marko Järvenpää

Introduction

Because strategy is inevitably future oriented (e.g. Golsorkhi et al. 2011; Sajasalo et al. 2016), the character and nature of the future are the most problematic and reflected-upon issues of strategic change in organizations. While understanding the past and present situation establishes the basis for action in organizations, a more detailed grasp is needed of how future-oriented understanding(s) and responses to the projected future(s) emerge in organizations (see Beckert 2016; Chiles et al. 2007). This requires a more thorough appreciation of how emerging meanings in organizational reality related to the future and strategic organizational change are constructed in organizational discourse (Gioia and Chittipeddi 1991; Boje 2008; Sajasalo et al. 2016).

In this chapter, we aim to further the understanding of the role of stories in future-oriented (prospective) organizational sensemaking. Stories

T. P. Auvinen (✉) • P. Sajasalo • T. Sintonen • T. Takala • M. Järvenpää
Jyväskylä University, Jyväskylän, Finland

© The Author(s) 2018
H. Krämer, M. Wenzel (eds.), *How Organizations Manage the Future*,
https://doi.org/10.1007/978-3-319-74506-0_7

133

are a fundamental part of organizational discourse and a central means of conveying and constructing meanings in organizational communication (Grant and Marshak 2011). Narrative approaches have established themselves as an integral part of organizational change and strategy-as-practice literature (see, e.g., Brown and Thompson 2013; Sonenshein 2010). For instance, in 2009, the journal *Organization* devoted a special issue to the topic (see *Organization* vol. 16, no. 3). In their introduction to the special issue, Brown, Gabriel and Gherardi (2009, p. 323) highlighted the importance of stories for managing change: 'Change spawns stories and stories can trigger change. Stories can also block change and can define what constitutes change.' Consistent with this idea, Sonenshein (2010) and Vaara and Reff Pedersen (2013) addressed the role of sensemaking, narratives and discursive understanding in future-oriented strategic change. Boje (2011b) and Boje, Haley and Saylors (2016) highlighted the role of antenarration in the context of organizational change. Our chapter aligns particularly with the work of Vaara and Tienari (2011), who applied antenarratives to reveal emerging legitimation and resistance in organizational storytelling during a strategic change in a financial organization.

Narratives are generally understood as well-formed and crystallized accounts of events having a beginning–middle–end (BME) structure and a rather permanent state of being. Stories, however, differ from narratives in that they lack a stable structure and emerge in informal everyday situations in organizations (Boje 2001, pp. 1–6). In situations of strategic change, organizational discourse contains several stories conveying information, opinions, beliefs and even facts regarding the change and future of the organization, making it challenging for organizational members to make sense of the unfolding events.

Stories have an important role in making sense of dynamic and complex organizational change (see Boje 2008; Vaara and Tienari 2011). According to Weick (2001), sensemaking is an ongoing process through which people create an understanding of the everyday organizational realities they face. It is a matter of identifying, sketching, interrelating and interpreting multiple ongoing organizational discourses, particularly stories (Berti 2017). The time aspect is intrinsic to sensemaking in that sensemaking takes place here and now, but its time referent may be the past or the future.

Because strategic change is formed by a host of events and actions with a future orientation, there is always a need to understand events to come. Boje (2008) elaborated on the ideas of antenarrative and prospective sensemaking. Both are useful for our purpose in this chapter. The prefix 'ante' refers to something that comes before or first. Thus, an antenarrative is something emerging and existing before a narrative. Boje (2008, p. 13) defined antenarratives as 'prospective (forward-looking) bets (antes)'. In terms of sensemaking, narratives with a stable BME structure connect with Weick's (2001) concept of retrospective sensemaking. Antenarratives, on the other hand, represent prospective sensemaking (Boje 2001, 2008). One more conceptual clarification is still required: in line with Boje (2001, 2011a), when developing our method, we treat stories as antenarratives—characterized by fragmented, incomplete, incoherent, unplotted and nonlinear speculations.

To understand how people evaluate the 'truth value' of the stories and narratives they encounter, we will utilize the narrative rationality framework (Fisher 1989). All narrative accounts (narratives, antenarratives and stories) have a rationality of their own. Fisher (1989) proposed a narrative paradigm with its own conception of rationality enriching the logico-scientific rational world paradigm. Narrative rationality consists of two elements: coherence and fidelity. Coherence refers to the experience of how well the narrative or story is composed, while fidelity relates to its plausibility.

We will establish how strategic change can be made visible and a subject of analysis for addressing change-related meanings manifested in ongoing antenarration and narrative rationality. For this purpose, we propose a new method, the *Story Index* (SIX), offering a means of understanding prospective sensemaking and rationales related to organizational change, which are difficult to capture with traditional means of inquiry. We contribute to the understanding of how strategic change-related discourse becomes meaningful in organizations (cf. Vaara and Tienari 2011; Brown and Thompson 2013) and what rationalities are involved. This facilitates more informed responses to the future by organizations in their effort to manage things to come.

Story Index: Theoretical Framing

Due to the overemphasis on the rational aspects of organizational life, storytelling, stories and narratives have typically been considered irrational and, as such, belonging solely to the unofficial and unmanageable side of organizations (Gabriel 1995, 2000). However, an appreciation has begun to emerge of the importance of subjective ideas, beliefs, emotions and ethical assessments as the building blocks of organizational rationality—constructed and communicated through storytelling (Gabriel and Griffiths 2004). As noted, for instance, by Laine and Vaara (2011) and Grant and Marshak (2011), future-oriented strategic change becomes existent and thus discernible only in organizational discourse. Furthermore, meanings associated with issues allow responses to them, making sensemaking a crucial phenomenon for all organizational activity.

The SIX method aspires to make future-oriented strategic change discernible and available for observation by grasping the flux of meanings in organizational storytelling (Boje 2008, 2011a). An index refers to a sign that is connected to a phenomenon. Just as smoke is associated with fire (see Fiske 1990), future-oriented strategic change-related storytelling may contain 'smoke' that indicates 'fires' in the discursive organizational reality. In our analysis of organizational stories utilizing SIX, we aim to identify the fires and their meanings signaled by the smoke of the discursive and narrative elements related to ongoing future-oriented organizational change processes. The metaphor of smoke denotes the early signs that guide us to the actual strategic change process discursively constructed to have starting and end points (Grant and Marshak 2011). In this respect, SIX helps us to recognize the dynamics involved in strategic change and to sense how the organizational members perceive the future. In terms of managing organizational change, it is important to understand whether the future holds optimistic or daunting notes for organizational members.

Antenarratives, Prospective Sensemaking and Narrative Rationality

Stories and storytelling—antenarratives in particular (Boje 2001)—shape the emerging meanings of organizational reality related to the future and are therefore important influencers of the resultant responses and activity. Antenarratives may assume several forms, such as linear, cyclic, vortex or rhizomatic (Boje 2011a, pp. 7, 13), assuming differing orientations toward the future. Linear antenarratives refer to future-perfect sensemaking that is concerned with situations where complete situational knowledge of outcomes is lacking. Linear antenarratives relate to the future as a continuum of the past and present—often appearing in preparations for the future by setting goals—and are therefore common in strategic planning.

Cyclic antenarratives orient to the future in a nonlinear fashion and build on the idea that a cycle recognized in the past will repeat itself predictably at some later point. While this idea is reflected in the life cycle models that appear in the management literature, and there is some practical indication of the cyclic nature of the stock market (Boje 2011b), the foundation for such assumptions is as shaky as those that espouse linear, extrapolative thinking.

Vortex antenarratives assume a form from which there appears to be no escape. When an antenarrative takes the form of a vortex, much of the story is invisible to the author and the audience alike, appearing to be dictated by circumstances over which no one has control. In a vortex antenarrative, the future emerges haphazardly once the vortex takes over, and the connection between the past and the future is random, as the field of possibilities is countless and totally unknown.

The key facet of rhizomatic antenarratives is movement: they tend to extend in all directions (either above ground or underground) in the organizational reality. A rhizomatic antenarrative extends underground in a latent manner, and when uncertainty (e.g. organizational or market change) enters the organizational flux of stories, it shoots up sprouts around the organization and grows rampantly (Boje 2011a, b). Rhizomatic antenarratives contain mostly past connotations that resonate with the present situation, forming a web of meanings that strengthen each other and eventually influence the emerging conception of the future.

Prospective sensemaking is especially integral to future-oriented strategic change, but it is similarly important for all ongoing change endeavors in organizations. This makes the antenarrative perspective a relevant vantage point for better appreciating the nature of strategic change and managing it by allowing for considerations of the dynamics and future-oriented nature of the process. Strategic change is inevitably a form of ante-something; it is a bet (ante) on the future through which an organization aspires to seize events in order to gain control of them. Therefore, antenarratives communicated in the course of strategic change can function as transformative agents related to the future, as shown, for instance, by Vaara and Tienari (2011).

Narrative rationality (Fisher 1989, pp. 62–64) suggests that human beings have an inherent awareness of narrative probability formed by two components: coherence and fidelity. First, people examine and test the coherence of the stories they encounter. It is a matter of configuration. How do the parts of a story hold together? Do they form an understandable whole? Second, people ruminate about how the stories relate to their lived experiences. They seek to determine whether the stories portray the world in a manner that they find believable—a test of fidelity. By testing both the coherence and fidelity of experiences, human beings determine what counts as reality (Fisher 1989).

The perceived truth about a given matter is a result of juxtaposition. There is no story that is not embedded in other stories (Fisher 1994; see also Auvinen et al. 2010). Assessing what is true involves a judgment of fidelity, which is determined by the facts that appear in a story ('facts are facts'). Fidelity is also determined by the values that appear in a story—the match between the idea of subjective ethics and the soundness of the values that emerge in the interpretation. Therefore, as values inform reason, it is indispensable to weigh the values in a discourse to determine their worthiness as a basis of belief and action (Fisher 1994).

In the following, we apply the idea of narrative rationality as a framework to examine the reasoning (i.e. the rationales and motives) that emerges in the antenarration of our case organization's members related to future-oriented strategic change.

Research Site, Data and Methodology

Our illustrative case organization is the largest financial institution in Finland, the OP-Pohjola Group Central Cooperative (OP-Pohjola), with about 12,000 employees and EUR 125 billion in total assets (OP Financial Group 2016). We focus on its largest bank, Helsingin OP Bank Plc (HOP), employing some 700 people.

We gained full access to the organization in 2012 to study its strategizing (cf. Whittington 1996). In early 2014, during an interview round focused on strategy implementation, we found ourselves in the midst of a massive strategic change. The most recent round of interviews occurred during what had been announced as a major merger process that would unfold from spring 2014 onward, providing us with an exceptional opportunity to witness the strategic change process in real time. Figure 7.1 outlines recent major events concerning HOP and the involvement of the research team with the organization.

Our research strategy is qualitative and interpretative (see Eriksson and Kovalainen 2008). Altogether, 30 interviews were conducted while the strategic change was ongoing (February 2014–October 2015), covering all organizational levels: that is, OP-Pohjola's top management and the HOP top management team (Tier 1), as well as the middle management and the operative personnel at HOP (Tier 2). Snowball sampling (Patton 2002; Laumann and Pappi 1976) was utilized to find the informants. The representatives of HOP senior management were asked to identify

Fig. 7.1 Research setting

individuals representing both tiers for further interviews. All informants—16 representing Tier 1 and 14 for Tier 2—agreed to the interviews. The interviews lasted between 30 and 90 minutes each, resulting in 24 hours of recordings with 400 pages of single-spaced transcription.

The themes of the semi-structured interviews included the background of the interviewees, the communication of the ongoing strategic change, and the interviewees' subjective understanding of it at the time. The interviewees were invited to discuss their conceptions of the change process and anticipated actions, which made our data especially suitable for the antenarrative approach (cf. Boje 2001; Eriksson and Kovalainen 2008).

Producing our findings involved applying the SIX method by first resorting to antenarrative theme analysis (Boje 2001; see also Auvinen 2012) to identify emerging meanings in our data in the context of a future-oriented, ongoing strategic change. We sought to sketch the unfolding experiences of the interviewees, which resulted in capturing two antenarratives closely resembling the forms suggested by Boje (2011b). Next, to evaluate how the antenarratives hung together (coherence) and whether they appeared plausible (fidelity), we applied Fisher's (1994) narrative rationality framework. Finally, we synthetized the previous steps to produce a condensed picture of the strategic change by piecing together the antenarratives. This last step aimed at clarifying how the rationales worked as shapers of the future-oriented meanings relevant to the ongoing strategic change in order to capture its dynamics. In other words, SIX allowed us to observe the smoke in the emerging antenarratives and to identify the fire it represented in the discursive organizational reality: whether the antenarrative appeared positively or negatively charged. Figure 7.2 summarizes our process of applying SIX.

Results: Using SIX

Since early 2012, HOP has been aiming at growth with an ambitious goal of 'becoming the leading bank in the metropolitan region' (see Sajasalo et al. 2016). A major step in the projected growth path was a planned merger of two banks: HOP (wholly owned by OP-Pohjola) and Pohjola Bank (publicly listed), which would benefit the owners of

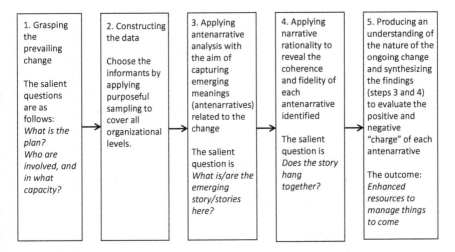

Fig. 7.2 The Story Index method

OP-Pohjola in the long run (e.g. Helsingin Sanomat 2014). The arrangement aimed to improve the competitive position of OP-Pohjola by enabling new funding and reducing overlap by creating a single organization in the Helsinki metropolitan region (OP-Pohjola 2014).

To illustrate the usability of SIX in capturing prospective sensemaking and the resultant projections of the otherwise unknown future in the form of optimistic and daunting antenarratives, we outline the elements of each and the narrative rationalities involved.

Optimistic Future: The Leading Bank Antenarrative

After the merger plan became public, the chief executive officer of HOP restated the strategic goal: 'The aim of the new bank is to reach first place in the metropolitan region in all business lines. As a group, we have a huge potential for growth here. For now, we are the contender' (OP-Pohjola 2014).

A central theme in the antenarrative, which we term the 'leading bank antenarrative', is growth. The imperative for growth appears as a canonized discourse within Tier 1 management, emphasizing HOP/OP-Pohjola's active role in industry transformation. A senior manager (Tier 1) of

OP-Pohjola frames the need for growth as a must to secure the future: 'No growth today means no result tomorrow—and the day after tomorrow, we are no longer. … Banking, you know, is a balance sheet business.'

A growth path for HOP was set in its official strategy with a time frame of 2025 (see Sajasalo et al. 2016), highlighting the assumption of steady growth, which was only to be accelerated by the planned merger. The leading bank antenarrative therefore resembles what Boje (2011a) called the 'linear antenarrative', where the past, present and future form a continuum that is expected to be realized as planned.

Linear antenarratives, while problematic in terms of simply extrapolating from the past into the future, remain widely used in strategic planning (e.g. Hayes 2014). Linear antenarratives resort to retrospective sensemaking, with the expectation that the past will repeat itself. Therefore, change is interpreted as a logical and rational step that inevitably leads to the future goal. While the leading bank antenarrative outlines an end for the process in 2025, a senior manager (Tier 1) of OP-Pohjola provides a rationale for setting such a concrete milestone and tones down the generally held perception of it within the organization as binding: 'A given year [2025] was set to mark the time by which we want to achieve the goal. It really doesn't matter if the goal is met that exact year. It symbolizes that we believe the goal is achievable within some reasonable time frame.'

The rationality embedded in the leading bank antenarrative mostly emerged through fidelity, particularly in the form of sound reasoning (Fisher 1994). The setting of a publicly listed part and a cooperative part co-existing within the same group is framed as not serving the best interests of the main owner, OP-Pohjola, the group as a whole, or the owner-customers of the cooperative group. The recurring need to consider minority shareholders' interests in the listed Pohjola Bank was portrayed as a hindrance to the unity and best interests of the whole group.

From the majority owner's perspective, the constant balancing between the differing interests of the owner groups was counterproductive to the growth effort. Therefore, eliminating the influence of the minority owners represented sound reasoning from the group's perspective, as explained by a senior manager (Tier 1) of OP-Pohjola:

> Managing a hybrid organization was becoming harder. Making it work at all required a very permissive style of management toward the listed part of

the group ... it can't be that the majority owner [over 1.5 million owner-customers] needs to constantly be asking 30,000 minority owners' [of Pohjola Bank] permission: 'Is it okay if we do this?'

Likewise, coherence (Fisher 1989, 1994) emerged in the leading bank antenarrative. The narrative revolved around the imperative for growth, which is in line with stories in other relevant discourses, such as the universal economic growth discourse (e.g. Rodrik 2003) and the imperative business growth discourse (see Binswanger 2009; Gordon and Rosenthal 2003), emphasizing the importance of various external forces seen to force business organizations to seek growth. The organization appears in control of its destiny in the leading bank antenarrative: while challenged by the external environment, it is able to achieve the needed growth through methods of its own choosing, and by doing so, achieve its future aspirations. Therefore, the future view constructed in the leading bank antenarrative clearly represents optimism.

To synthesize, we find that the leading bank antenarrative gained fidelity and coherence for those involved in the growth imperative discourse. Growth appears as an inescapable necessity for the banking business and the overriding rationale for securing the future. Consequently, from the perspective of ongoing strategic change and prospective sensemaking, the leading bank antenarrative is the smoke that indicates the fire of the growth imperative.

Daunting Future: The Digitalization Antenarrative

One major external force appearing to drive change in the banking business, ostensibly exceeding all others, is digitalization. The main feature of this antenarrative is intensifying competition brought about by a new breed of international and domestic competitors at the fringes of the industry building on digital service provision. The organization is portrayed as in urgent need of preparation for the unconventional competition enabled by digitalization. Ultimately, digitalization appears to challenge the entire existence of industry incumbents. An excerpt from the top management of OP-Pohjola (Tier 1) typifies the firmly held belief that digitalization will fully and irreversibly revolutionize banking: 'The disruption caused by digitalization means the whole financial sector will be totally reinvented in the next few years … the business model needs to be totally constructed anew.'

While digitalization appears as a force of nature from the perspective of top management, this assessment raises some criticism lower down in the organization as being a distortion of reality. This means that top management either has been persuaded by the digitalization hype without due critical thinking or has become alienated from the everyday reality of the organization. For Tier 2 representatives, digitalization appears less revolutionary, giving rise to dissatisfaction with the top management's digitalization excitement:

> Digitalization seems to drive strategy nowadays … sure, it will change things … there are still those of us who believe face-to-face interaction is needed; not everything will be digitalized. Looking at things from the HQ may give the illusion that everyone operates digitally. Lots of average Joes and Jills, however, still need real people to advise them—and an occasional pat on the back when dealing with the major financial questions of their lives.

The digitalization discourse portrays features of what Boje (2011a, b) referred to as a vortex antenarrative. The digitalization antenarrative assumes the form of a pressing external force that is perceived to have unspecified—yet unavoidably coercive—implications for the organization. The issues in the digitalization antenarrative present solely negative implications for the organization. The likelihood of the organization maintaining its current mode of operation appears nonexistent: fundamental changes are depicted as being inescapable in the immediate future.

The financial sector incumbents see the effects of digitalization as posing severe threats beyond anyone's control. The external force is so pressing that even the prospect of opportunities created by the emerging competitive landscape does not feature in the antenarrative. The digitalization antenarrative paints a picture of a matter of life and death. To survive the projected turmoil, the incumbents must reinvent both their business models and the organizations themselves to justify their existence in the future.

In terms of narrative rationality, the digitalization antenarrative appears to have gained coherence (Fisher 1994) for those involved with the strategic change, especially at the top of the organization. The digitalization antenarrative represents an inevitable and insurmountable problem for them, as digitalization and its effects simply cannot be avoided. The strategic change is therefore constructed as being a compulsion in the face of an inescapable fact. While the overall excitement about digitalization met some resistance at the lower reaches of the organizational hierarchy, it clearly had no impact on the received wisdom regarding the effects of digitalization on the financial sector. Therefore, the future view constructed in the digitalization antenarrative presents a daunting future and paints a picture of an immediate need for thorough strategic change to avoid peril.

To synthesize, the rationality of the digitalization antenarrative emerges through coherence. Several elements in the digitalization antenarrative itself, and in the discourses related to the external environment, adhere to create coherence for the antenarrative, which thus lends fidelity to the prospective sensemaking upon which it is based. The digitalization antenarrative is closely connected and aligns with recent global developments in business, such as the effects of digital convergence on the hard-hit media industry (e.g. *The Economist* 2012). These recent trajectories elevate the importance of the external forces that are seen to coerce business organizations into seeking ways in which to transform themselves at the risk of otherwise being eliminated by new, nimble competitors. The digitalization antenarrative is the smoke that indicates the fire of a threat to the existence of the organization. The smoke is so thick that it appears to disarm critical thinking at the top of the organization.

Discussion and Conclusion

In our application of SIX, we identified two emerging future-oriented storylines: the leading bank antenarrative (linear) and the digitalization antenarrative (vortex), with contrasting orientations toward the future of the organization and the industry. The leading bank antenarrative appears both legitimate and empowering in terms of prospective sensemaking.

The digitalization antenarrative appears legitimate as well but, in terms of prospective sensemaking, it is discouraging. However, both are examples of antenarratives in which external influences feature prominently. As discussed above, they differ from one another in that the leading bank antenarrative revolving around substantial growth in the future (2025) depicts the external environment as enabling and malleable through the organization's own initiatives, whereas the digitalization antenarrative portrays the external environment as hostile and unavoidably coercive, even life-threatening.

While both growth and digitalization appear to be widely accepted, almost self-evident imperatives within the business community, they manifest rather differently for the members of the case organization. Both the growth and digitalization imperatives imply changes that must occur within the organization. The growth-oriented, leading bank antenarrative assigns strong agency to the organization: the organization is in control of its destiny and the outlook is therefore positive. The digitalization antenarrative portrays the organization as a business survivalist, pressured by an almost omnipotent digital revolution. In the emerging digitalized competitive landscape, the question is fundamentally about survival through transformation under severe pressure. In this antenarrative, the organization has little or no power to control events. The digitalization antenarrative strips the organization of its agency and places it at the mercy of malicious external forces, making the organization's future look daunting.

However, the response of OP-Pohjola to the projected optimistic and daunting futures captured here through SIX illustrates how prospective sensemaking, the emerging meanings related to the future, and responses to the projections interrelate in an attempt to manage things to come. In the fall of 2015, OP-Pohjola commenced a process in which both the optimistic and daunting future outlooks intertwined to produce a bold new direction for the organization. The strategy was clearly a response to the earlier prospective sensemaking, especially the daunting future view of the digitalization antenarrative.

What previously presented itself as a threat in the form of digitalization now appeared as a tentative opportunity to be captured based on the strengths of the organization (wide customer base and strong balance sheet) to offset its weaknesses by investing EUR 2 billion over five years (IT systems, R&D, mobile platforms/applications, etc.). The organization was projected to change from 'a plain financial services provider to a diversified services company of the digital era with strong financial services expertise' (OP Financial Group 2017). Thus, the organization—clearly recognizing the need to respond to the threat of digitalization to keep alive the positive future dominating the growth antenarrative—effectively switched its orientation toward digitalization and redirected its focus from a defensive stance to an offensive one.

This finding adheres with the critique of the traditional, rational and linear unfreezing–change–refreezing modeling of change processes (cf. Sonenshein 2010; Brown and Humphreys 2003). Rather than following a linear process, organizations only become altered through the perpetual sensemaking of their members regarding both the present situation and unknown future states. The vision-state of our case organization of transforming into a modern diversified services company appears as a reversal of the traditional logic of the industry, and therefore challenges the clearly outlined progress of change processes questioned lately (Sonenshein 2010). However, the management is still considered a key group in overcoming resistance in organizations by breaking down existing meaning constructions. This attitude implicitly assigns the rest of the organization the narrow role of change resister and leads to overlooking of the perspective of the change recipients (Bartunek et al. 2006; Ford et al. 2008). According to our findings, promoters and resisters emerge in all organizational levels: resistance evidently wells from the constantly emerging organizational meanings rather than from individual members or organizational positions.

Our findings further show that it is important to make the prospective sensemaking and experiences of organizational members at all levels visible to facilitate a better understanding of how organizational change takes shape in the discursive reality before it materializes in concrete terms. Change emerges through the activities of individuals in their daily work, which makes the change-related sensemaking of individuals and small groups an important subject of study for change management, as Vaara, Sonenshein and Boje (2016) noted in their review of the literature addressing organizational stability and change. Our findings show how

SIX offers guidance for managing change by bringing the change recipients and the discursive elements of ongoing change to the fore, as called for by Bartunek et al. (2006) and Ford, Ford and D'Amelio (2008), among others.

Moreover, our findings highlight the need to pay closer attention to the socially constructed nature of change that SIX is able to capture; SIX therefore provides an alternative to the tendency in functionalist accounts of change to focus on observable actions alone (Brown and Humphreys 2003). This is crucial not only for a better understanding of the nature and dynamics of organizational change, which essentially is about occurrences in the tentative future, but also for a better sense of how future-oriented understanding in organizations is constructed through prospective sensemaking. As sensemaking can be said to occupy a central role in the materialization of organizational change, prospective sensemaking can be said to be equally important—if not more so—in attempts to grasp the otherwise unknown future.

While the importance of language and discourse has recently gained recognition in the management literature (see Gabriel 2000; Sonenshein 2010; Vaara and Tienari 2011; Boje et al. 2016), the applications of storytelling and antenarratives are still underdeveloped (cf. Vaara et al. 2016). Emerging from our findings, one theme that stands out is the importance of discourse and its capacity to do things in organizations. Both change and the future are fundamentally socially constructed phenomena and are promoted or blocked through the use of language (Bartunek et al. 2006; Brown and Humphreys 2003; Ford et al. 2008). It is important to recognize that organizational stories act as powerful change agents, and therefore antenarratives provide resources for managing things to come.

Acknowlegement The authors wish to thank OP Group Research Foundation for their support (Grant # 201600095).

References

Auvinen, Tommi. 2012. The Ghost Leader: An Empirical Study on Narrative Leadership. *Electronic Journal of Business Ethics and Organization Studies* 17 (1): 4–15.

Auvinen, Tommi, Esa Mangeloja, and Teppo Sintonen. 2010. Is Narrative a Content of Economics and Business Administration? *Annual Review of Management and Organizational Inquiry* 6 (1): 1–13.

Bartunek, Jean M., Denise M. Rousseau, Jenny W. Rudolph, and Judith A. De Palma. 2006. On the Receiving End: Sensemaking, Emotion, and Assessments of an Organizational Change Initiated by Others. *Journal of Applied Behavioral Science* 42 (2): 182–206.

Beckert, Jens. 2016. *Imagined Futures: Expectations and Capitalist Dynamics*. Cambridge: Harvard University Press.

Berti, Marco. 2017. *Elgar Introduction to Organizational Discourse Analysis*. Cheltenham: Edward Elgar.

Binswanger, Mathias. 2009. Is There a Growth Imperative in Capitalist Economies? *Journal of Post Keynesian Economics* 31 (4): 707–727.

Boje, David M. 2001. *Narrative Methods for Organization and Communication Research*. New York: Sage.

———. 2008. *Storytelling Organizations*. London: Sage.

———. 2011a. Introduction to Agential Antenarratives that Shape the Future of Organizations. In *Storytelling and the Future of Organizations*, ed. David M. Boje, 1–22. New York: Routledge.

———. 2011b. Postscript—An Antenarrative Theory of Socioeconomic in Intervention Research. In *Storytelling and the Future of Organizations*, ed. David M. Boje, 383–392. New York: Routledge.

Boje, David M., Usha Haley, and Rohny Saylors. 2016. Antenarratives of Organizational Change: The Microstoria of Burger King's Storytelling in Space, Time, and Strategic Context. *Human Relations* 69 (2): 391–418.

Brown, Andrew D., and Michael Humphreys. 2003. Epic and Tragic Tales: Making Sense of Change. *The Journal of Applied Behavioral Science* 39 (2): 121–144.

Brown, Andrew D., and Edmund R. Thompson. 2013. A Narrative Approach to Strategy-as-Practice. *Business History* 55 (7): 1043–1067.

Brown, Andrew D., Yiannis Gabriel, and Silvia Gherardi. 2009. Storytelling and Chance: An Unfolding Story. *Organization* 16 (3): 323–333.

Chiles, Todd H., Allen C. Bluedorn, and Vishal K. Gupta. 2007. Beyond Creative Destruction and Entrepreneurial Discovery: A Radical Austrian Approach to Entrepreneurship. *Organization Studies* 28 (4): 467–493.
Eriksson, Päivi, and Anne Kovalainen. 2008. *Qualitative Methods in Business Research*. London: Sage.
Fisher, Walter R. 1989. *Human Communication as Narration: Toward a Philosophy of Reason, Value, and Action*. Columbia: University of South Carolina Press.
———. 1994. Narrative Rationality and the Logic of Scientific Discourse. *Argumentation* 8 (1): 21–32.
Fiske, John. 1990. *Introduction to Communication Studies*. London: Routledge.
Ford, Jeffrey D., Laurie W. Ford, and Angelo D'Amelio. 2008. Resistance to Change: The Rest of the Story. *Academy of Management Review* 33 (2): 362–377.
Gabriel, Yiannis. 1995. The Unmanaged Organization: Stories, Fantasies, and Subjectivity. *Organization Studies* 16 (3): 477–501.
———. 2000. *Storytelling in Organizations: Facts, Fictions, and Fantasies*. Oxford: Oxford University Press.
Gabriel, Yiannis, and Dorothy S. Griffiths. 2004. Stories in Organizational Research. In *Essential Guide to Qualitative Methods in Organizational Research*, ed. Catherine Cassell and Gillian Symon, 114–126. London: Sage.
Gioia, Dennis A., and Kumar Chittipeddi. 1991. Sensemaking and Sensegiving in Strategic Change Initiation. *Strategic Management Journal* 12 (6): 433–448.
Golsorkhi, Damon, Linda Rouleau, David Seidl, and Eero Vaara. 2011. Introduction: What Is Strategy as Practice? In *Cambridge Handbook of Strategy as Practice*, ed. Damon Golsorkhi, Linda Rouleau, David Seidl, and Eero Vaara, 1–20. Cambridge: Cambridge University Press.
Gordon, Myron J., and Jeffrey S. Rosenthal. 2003. Capitalism's Growth Imperative. *Cambridge Journal of Economics* 27 (1): 25–48.
Grant, David, and Robert J. Marshak. 2011. Toward a Discourse-Centered Understanding of Organizational Change. *Journal of Applied Behavioral Science* 47 (2): 204–235.
Hayes, John. 2014. *The Theory and Practice of Change Management*. 4th ed. Basingstoke: Palgrave Macmillan.
Helsingin Sanomat. 2014. OP:n Karhinen: Pohjolan miljardikauppa hyödyttää pitkällä aikavälillä asiakkaita. http://www.hs.fi/talous/a1391659551057. Accessed 12 Dec 2016.
Laine, Pikka-Maaria, and Eero Vaara. 2011. Strategia Kuuluu Henkilöstölle! Dialoginen Näkökulma Strategiatyöhön. In *Toisinajattelua Strategisesta Johtamisesta*, ed. Saku Mantere, Kimmo Suominen, and Eero Vaara, 29–42. Helsinki: WSOYPro.

Laumann, Edward O., and Franz U. Pappi. 1976. *Networks of Collective Action*. New York: Academic Press.
OP Financial Group. 2016. OP Financial Group's Earnings Analysis and Balance Sheet. https://op-year2015.fi/en/report-by-the-executive-board-and-financial-statements/report-by-the-executive-board/op-financial-group-s-earnings-analysis-and-some-key-balance-sheet-indicators. Accessed 3 June 2016.
———. 2017. Strategy. https://www.op.fi/op/op-financial-group/op-financial-group/strategy?id=80101&srccid=161502194&WT.ac=161502194_sisalto_-_strategia&kielikoodi=en&srcpl=3. Accessed 30 May 2017.
OP-Pohjola. 2014. OP-Pohjolan Fuusio. https://www.op.fi/op/op-pohjola-ryhma/uutishuone/?id=80300&srcpl=1#/uutiset/8185/fuusio_vahvistaisi_op-pohjolan_asemaa_paakaupunkiseudulla!1417519754. Accessed 28 Nov 2016.
Patton, Michael Q. 2002. *Qualitative Research and Evaluation Methods*. 3rd ed. Thousand Oaks: Sage.
Rodrik, Dani. 2003. "Introduction: What Do We Learn from Country Narratives?" In In Search of Prosperity: Analytic Narratives on Economic Growth, Dani Rodrik, 1–19. Princeton: Princeton University Press.
Sajasalo, Pasi, Tommi Auvinen, Tuomo Takala, Marko Järvenpää, and Teppo Sintonen. 2016. Strategy Implementation as Fantasizing—Becoming the Leading Bank. *Accounting and Business Research* 46 (3): 303–325.
Sonenshein, Scott. 2010. We're Changing—Or Are We? Untangling the Role of Progressive, Regressive, and Stability Narratives During Strategic Change Implementation. *Academy of Management Journal* 53 (3): 477–512.
The Economist. 2012. The Third Industrial Revolution. http://www.economist.com/node/21553017. Accessed 16 Feb 2016.
Vaara, Eero, and Anne Reff Pedersen. 2013. Strategy and Chronotypes: A Bakhtinian Perspective on the Construction of Strategy Narratives. *M@n@gement* 16 (5): 593–604.
Vaara, Eero, and Janne Tienari. 2011. On the Narrative Construction of Multinational Corporations. *Organization Science* 22 (2): 370–390.
Vaara, Eero, Scott Sonenshein, and David M. Boje. 2016. Narratives as Sources of Stability and Change in Organizations. *The Academy of Management Annals* 10 (1): 495–560.
Weick, Karl. 2001. *Making Sense of the Organization*. Oxford: Blackwell.
Whittington, Richard. 1996. Strategy as Practice. *Long Range Planning* 29 (5): 731–735.

8

What Scenarios Are You Missing? Poststructuralism for Deconstructing and Reconstructing Organizational Futures

Ricarda Scheele, Norman M. Kearney,
Jude H. Kurniawan, and Vanessa J. Schweizer

Introduction

The human capacity to imagine possible future developments is a vital mechanism in any organization: it enables individuals to make sense of present and future situations, tell stories and, from those insights, derive

---

R. Scheele (✉)
Stuttgart Research Center for Interdisciplinary Risk
and Innovation Studies (ZIRIUS),
University of Stuttgart, Stuttgart, Germany

N. M. Kearney
School of Environment, Resources, and Sustainability,
University of Waterloo, Waterloo, Canada

J. H. Kurniawan
Department of Geography and Environmental Management, University of Waterloo, Waterloo, Canada

V. J. Schweizer
University of Waterloo, Waterloo, Canada

© The Author(s) 2018
H. Krämer, M. Wenzel (eds.), *How Organizations Manage the Future*,
https://Doi.org/10.1007/978-3-319-74506-0_8

153

steps for actions. Despite the omnipresence of 'the future' in individual and organizational thinking and behaviour, its ontological underpinnings are far from settled. As imaginations or expectations, 'the future' seems intangible both for the imagining individual and for third parties. Yet, even while being literally intangible, 'the future' exerts more influence on the behaviour of organizations and its members than merely being an open and empty 'time not-yet-passed'. Acknowledging the importance of sense-making processes of the future, scholars across the social sciences have emphasized how actors' behaviour and decision-making *in the present* is anchored in their perceptions of the future. Beckert (2013, p. 219) speaks about 'fictional expectations' as mental representations in the form of narratives, theories or discourses which inhabit the individual's mind as 'an imagined future state of the world and the belief in causal mechanisms leading to this future state'. The idea that human reasoning is informed by framings is also applicable at the organizational level when we think about how metaphors, such as the organization as a political system, a culture or a machine buttress its self-concept and thus its operations (Morgan 1986).

For organizations, the future may contain one or a number of possible scenarios. These scenarios are influential, because they are mentally acted out and may serve as organizations' instruments or 'devices for living in the present' (March 1995, p. 427). In doing so, particular specifications of 'the future'—as scenarios—emerge as social realities for the organization in the present, becoming, in a sense, tangible for its members (Adam 2004).

How then can organizational researchers and practitioners study this interplay between organizations' beliefs and scenarios, which are their specifications of 'the future'? Our chapter draws on futures studies—a discipline particularly invested in moving questions of ontology (what *is* the future) towards epistemological and methodological approaches (from what perspective and with what knowledge can we study the future), as shown in Fig. 8.1. Much effort in organizational and methodological research focuses on *looking into the future*, that is, to develop scenarios in order to explore the possible future contextual environment of organizations and to draw out scenarios' implications for organizations. However, less attention is often paid to how the methods organizations apply to create alternative scenarios in order to make sense of their future have

What Scenarios Are You Missing? Poststructuralism...

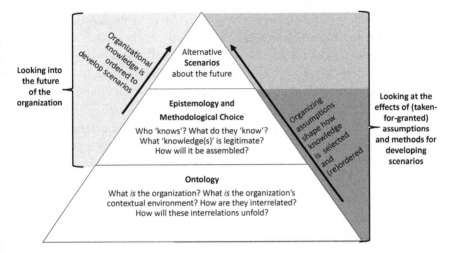

Fig. 8.1 A perspective for organizational researchers and practitioners examining how methodological choices shape the scenarios an organization accepts as plausible

consequences in and of themselves. The inability to resolve what the future really *is* and how it should be studied inevitably gives rise to power struggles in the creation of organizational futures so that 'every effort to plan the future is submerged in an overarching politics of the real' (Inayatullah 1990, p. 116). Brown et al. (2000, p. 4) have stated that the objective of interrogating this is 'to shift the discussion (…) to looking at how the future as a temporal abstraction is constructed and managed, by whom and under what conditions'. We argue that such investigations are of practical relevance: the methodologies used by an organization to make sense of the future ultimately shape the kinds of scenarios that an organization accepts as plausible and actively prepares for.

Our analysis moves away from studying 'the future' per se, meaning it shifts the analytical perspective from the objective of creating plausible and relevant scenarios towards a reflection on *the way* those alternative scenarios are created. The responsibility of researchers and practitioners, then, is not to simply ask how concrete future developments may affect an organization (i.e. equivalent to producing ever-new scenarios), but to inquire how the notion of a particular future development has made its way into an organizational scenario, what assumptions were involved in developing the scenario, how a set of alternative scenarios would look without the notion and what other possible developments have been excluded. It looks at how an organization's typically implicit ontological and epistemological assumptions and their applied methods, or 'real time activities' (Brown et al. 2000), shape the creation of its alternative scenarios. 'Real time activities' imply different means through which organizations make sense of the future. This reflects recent scholarly attention in organizational studies that views strategy not simply as a property or asset of organizations, but attends to the thought processes, activities and decisions happening within an organization (Spee and Jarzabkowski 2009). In using a practice-based perspective, Koch et al. (2016) demonstrated how everyday processes and practices are a meaningful unit of analysis for studying how an organization generates and processes time and the future.

To investigate such questions, we propose a critical research methodology, whereby 'critical' implies analysing what *other* scenarios could have been developed and understanding *why* a scenario looks this way. Thereby, we seek a better appreciation of the influences that scenario development practices have on how organizations in the present plan for the future. Poststructuralism is a promising conceptual, theory-informed methodology for this pursuit.

In the scholarly field of futures studies, critical traditions have appeared from time to time, applying, for instance, Causal Layered Analysis (Inayatullah 1998a, b) to an investigation of underlying myths and metaphors of produced scenarios, or discussing the social construction of reality as a conceptual lens (Slaughter 2002a). Yet, critical reflections on how scenarios are created have often been derided as 'impractical', in that their purpose of decomposing scenarios or establishing theoretical accounts is kept separate from actual scenario development processes. Simultaneously, Ahlqvist and Rhisiart (2015, p. 94) note that '(…) the standard futures approach does not engage critically with its own perspective (…) [and] fails to engage with the inescapable issue that defining the present is always an act of selection'. Thus, a key contribution of our chapter is that we present the method of Cross-Impact Balance Analysis, or CIB (Weimer-Jehle 2006), which is a scenario development methodology that holds great potential for simultaneously applying a critical poststructural perspective. This is useful for revealing how underlying beliefs within organizations influence alternative scenarios of the future as well as for pointing out implications of alternative ontological beliefs. CIB also is capable of feeding those reflections back into scenario development processes, hence interlinking critical inquiry with scenario development.

Poststructuralism as a Research Methodology for Scenario (Re)development

Poststructuralist ideas, as influenced by Foucault, Derrida, Deleuze, Laclau and others, have long found their way into organizational studies and strategy-related research (Kilduff and Mehra 1997; Calas and Smircich 1999) and have been shaped by Foucault's (1977) ideas on the relationship between structure, truth (or knowledge) and power. Unlike behaviouralist views on power (Dahl 1957; Bachrach and Baratz 1962), where power is something that a person or group 'holds', according to Foucault (1977), power and knowledge are inseparable and co-constitutive: what people believe to be true affects what can be done, and what is done affects what people believe to be true.[1] In organizational studies, this argument has been used to explain how discourse—as a form of organizational assumptions and practices, that is, as the 'sayings' and 'doings' in organizations—constitutes and legitimizes authority (Ezzamel and Willmott 2010).

Poststructuralism invites both practitioners and researchers to study the 'politics of the real', that is, the particular ontological and epistemological commitments embedded in methodological choices for scenario development. To highlight poststructuralism as a research methodology, this section:

- explains poststructuralist concerns with the role of knowledge and power residing in taken-for-granted forms of scenarios (e.g. narratives, quantitative projections);

- proposes *deconstruction* as the analytical approach for revealing the 'politics of the real' embedded in scenarios (development), along with *reconstruction* to suggest further scenarios that have previously been left out.

The Role of Knowledge and Power Residing in Scenarios

Investigations into the way meaning is assigned to scenarios and into the way materialized scenarios constitute social reality reveal processes as being underpinned by 'interests, power relations, definitional power and a wide range of civilizational "givens"' (Slaughter 2002b, pp. 503–504). When it comes to scenario development, this, for instance, includes decisions on what constitutes 'predetermined elements', that is, what are assumed stable trends and what are 'critical uncertainties' of the future (Wack 1985). Poststructuralism suggests that those decisions are the expression of prevalent narratives. Narratives, in the sense of 'global worldview[s] that assume(s) the validity of its own truth claim' (Rosenau 1992, p. xi), may even act as 'future imperatives': the more they receive social attention and meaning, the more they serve as imperatives to act upon, for example, in the cases of globalization and constant economic growth (Ahlqvist and Rhisiart 2015). Hodgkinson and Wright (2002) mention dynamics of 'cognitive inertia', or the potential that actors' mental models—while supporting and being supported by common narratives—stabilize to such a degree that changes in the business environment go unnoticed. Lahsen (2005) suggests that unpacking underlying assumptions of scenarios while they are being created can counter the very assumptions and practices that are taken for granted and may avoid the scenarios taking on undue authority to the detriment of the organization's viability.

Deconstruction and Reconstruction as Poststructuralist Approaches to Analysis

Poststructuralism is a worthwhile methodology for revealing the 'politics of the real' that has shaped the creation of some sets of scenarios. Additionally, and as a consequence of this perspective, poststructuralism emphasizes the value of investigating scenarios that have been overlooked. For the purposes of such 'alternative meaning-making', Inayatullah (1998b, p. 59) proposes to reorder knowledge and pursue different approaches towards 'knowledge' about the future in order to entertain scenarios that cause 'cognitive dissonance'. In pursuit of this twofold interest, poststructuralists refer to approaches of *deconstruction* and *reconstruction* while emphasizing a 'productive fusion' (Slaughter 2002b) between both approaches to realize the practical relevance of poststructuralism.

Inayatullah (1998a, pp. 818–819) proposes a 'poststructural toolbox', including different concepts that show how deconstruction and reconstruction go hand in hand conceptually. Four of the concepts[2] are especially relevant to our analysis:

- *Deconstruction:* Breaking apart a text, such as a scenario, into its components and investigating why certain components are included versus those that are excluded, for example, what 'politics of the real' are at play?
- *Distance*: Establishing a degree of distance from current categories or modes of thinking enables them to be viewed as embedded in contingent social orders, fostering the emergence of other conceptions of the future.
- *Alternative pasts and futures*: Not only the development of different futures, but also ex-post, alternative readings of the past can help for understanding the effects of 'historical' interpretations.
- *Reordering knowledge*: In the vein of deconstruction enabling reconstruction, a focus on how categories of thought 'order' knowledge, that is, in clusters around certain civilizational aspects, can help organizations and organizational scholars to displace categories and 'reorder' knowledge.

In relation to our arguments, Inayatullah's concepts imply that a poststructuralist method of inquiry is needed that operationalizes forms of deconstruction (of assumptions and practices that have led to alternative scenarios) and that, in turn, informs reconstruction (in order to explore overlooked scenarios). We propose CIB as a formalized method that strikes this balance. While qualitative discourse analysis has been applied in a poststructural mode for either deconstructing or reconstructing organizational discourses (McKinlay and Starkey 1998), CIB can go further by integrating, in a practical manner, a deconstructive approach to how alternative scenarios are created with a reconstructive approach to reveal overlooked scenarios.

A Method for Practical Poststructuralism: Cross-Impact Balance Analysis

Over the past few decades, futures studies have developed diverse empirical methods with the purpose of exploring possible future developments relevant for individuals, organizations or for society as a whole. These methods include scenario planning, roadmapping, horizon scanning or visioning. In the context of scenario planning alone, the discipline is active in applying, advancing, but also critiquing available methods (Amer et al. 2013; Wright et al. 2013b). In futures studies, rationalist, empirical approaches to the future are popular but also increasingly challenged: the recognition that conceptions of the future do not exist entirely independently of the observer, but are imagined with reference to conceptions of time, history and culture has brought about interpretivist, culturally driven approaches. Those epistemologies feed into different methodological operationalizations—including what type of data (quantitative vs. qualitative) and which analytical approaches to use (formalized modelling vs. narrative storytelling)—and naturally produce different sets of alternative scenarios for an organization.

What we wish to make clear is that no one method is able to eliminate the deep controversy that results from pluralistic societies (or organizations) and their diverse views, ideas, values, hopes and fears about the future. Grunwald (2013, p. 4) notes how, instead of reaching 'optimal' decisions, any empirical approach to studying the future reveals controversy regarding (1) the extent to which we believe today's knowledge can and should be extrapolated to the future, (2) the resulting legitimacy of the created scenarios, and (3) the extent to which those scenarios should be relied upon for 'deriving' present decisions.

The CIB method is unique in that, as a precursor to developing scenarios, it can also help to elucidate the aforementioned controversies. CIB comes from a line of scenario development methods characterized by recombination, for example, morphological analysis (Zwicky 1969) and cross-impact analysis (Helmer 1981).[3] These methods were developed to answer questions about *looking into the future*. However, CIB can also enable reanalysis, which is valuable for helping organizations to re-examine scenario components that might have been selected, or might *not* have been selected, at least in part due to organizations' assumptions about what is 'true' and imaginable as real. The CIB method is introduced in the following section, and its poststructuralist relevance is briefly illustrated through a case study, where CIB was used to reanalyse emissions scenarios commissioned by the Intergovernmental Panel on Climate Change (Schweizer and Kriegler 2012). The original scenarios were published in a *Special Report on Emissions Scenarios*, also known as SRES (Nakicenovic et al. 2000).

Context for the Poststructuralist Inquiry of Emissions Scenarios

SRES scenarios have exerted their own organizing force on climate change research, with approximately 5500 citations according to Google Scholar. This is because the SRES aimed to standardize long-term projections used as inputs for researching changes in the climate system due to emissions. In turn, researchers who focused on potential damages due to climate change would make use of climate simulations reflecting alternative possible climate scenarios (Hibbard et al. 2007): as explained below, the so-called A1, A2, B1 or B2 worlds.

The dominant approach to developing scenarios is discourse-based and called 'Intuitive Logics' (Bradfield et al. 2005). The way the SRES was developed was no exception. In the SRES case, scenario builders followed the deductive format of Intuitive Logics to develop a short list of key uncertainties and narrow their focus to two uncertainties deemed most important.[4] In turn, each uncertainty was assigned polar outcomes such as high/low or cooperation/conflict. In SRES, the key uncertainties for the twenty-first century are globalization trends (global/regional) and styles of development (economic/sustainable). These key scenario uncertainties are represented as axes with each polarity pertaining to a quadrant. This results in a 2 × 2 matrix producing four (2^2) possible scenario families, which are called A1 (scenarios characterized by globalization and economic development), A2 (regionalization and economic development), B1 (globalization and sustainable development) and B2 (regionalization and sustainable development).[5] Under Intuitive Logics, all scenarios—whether depicting high emissions or low emissions—are deemed 'equally plausible'.

By 2008, concerns were raised that the SRES had systematically produced underestimates for emissions (Pielke et al. 2008; Raupach et al. 2007). This was because observed rates of emissions exceeded the near-term projections for high emissions featured in SRES and was primarily due to the unprecedented rate of construction of coal plants in China.

The Reanalysis of Emissions Scenarios Using CIB

CIB debuted as a scenario method in 2006 (Weimer-Jehle 2006). Compared to Intuitive Logics, CIB includes a number of different practices for *looking into the future*, some of which strongly lend themselves to poststructuralist inquiry. The following explains how CIB is performed— and its potential for being a practical method for poststructuralism— through the case of the reanalysis of the SRES scenarios.

Scenario factors in CIB may be qualitative or quantitative as shown in Fig. 8.2 and they are referred to as 'descriptors'. In CIB, scenarios are combinations of outcomes, or states, for each descriptor. To identify which scenarios are internally consistent, CIB uses a series of calculations. The CIB method thus involves three steps: (1) specifying the descriptors and their possible states; (2) specifying judgements (or assumptions) of how the descriptors are interrelated through their possible states; and (3) evaluating the internal consistency of descriptor-state combinations (Schweizer and Kriegler 2012; Lloyd and Schweizer 2014).

A variety of procedures may be employed in support of steps (1) and (2), such as surveys of experts and stakeholders, and literature reviews

(Weimer-Jehle 2006; Schweizer and O'Neill 2014, ESM 1, p. 3). For the SRES reanalysis, Schweizer and Kriegler performed a literature review. During step (2), judgements of interrelations between descriptors are translated into comparable numerical units through a Likert scale. The (mental) model specifications (i.e. descriptors and their respective possible states, and judgements about descriptor interrelations) are represented within a cross-impact matrix (Fig. 8.2). Using the cross-impact matrix, a key difference in the practice of CIB compared to Intuitive Logics is that the number of 'key uncertainties' systematically explored is no longer limited to two, and the possible outcomes for each uncertainty can also be larger than two. For the reanalysis performed by Schweizer and Kriegler (2012), the cross-impact matrix represents 1728 possible scenarios (1728 = $2^2*3^3*4^2$, as specified by the number of descriptors and their respective states) compared to the four that are possible with Intuitive Logics. A primary benefit of systematically exploring a large number of scenarios is the materialization of new ways to 'order knowledge' about the future (Inayatullah 1998b). While CIB can dramatically expand the number of ways to reorder knowledge, as explained below, CIB calculations also isolate a small number of scenarios with the strongest internal consistency. Thus, among the 1728 scenarios possible, Schweizer and Kriegler found that only 11 were perfectly internally consistent.

Distinguishing differences in internal consistency across scenarios is another key difference between the method of CIB and that of Intuitive Logics, which presents all scenarios as 'equally plausible'. CIB is able to measure differences in scenario consistency through interrelations between descriptors recorded in the cross-impact matrix. These can be used to identify 'self-reinforcing' effects that make particular combinations of descriptor outcomes more coherent. Unlike discourse-based scenario methods, the CIB method requires explicit accounts of underlying assumptions and opens up organizational processes for scenario development that are typically hidden, such as particular beliefs and how they interrelate (Weimer-Jehle 2006; Lloyd and Schweizer 2014, p. 259). Values in each matrix cell summarize the influence of the descriptor shown in the row direction on the descriptor in the column direction. Thus, in Fig. 8.2, positive numbers indicate encouraging influences, negative numbers discouraging influences and zeroes no direct influence.

DESCRIPTORS *END-STATES*	Population L	M	H	GDP per Capita L	M	H	VH	FFA L	Co	H	C Intensity VLC	LC	B	HC	PE Intensity L	M	H	Econ Pol R	G	Env Pol R	G
Population																					
L: Low				0	0	0	0	**-1**	**0**	**1**	0	0	0	0	0	0	0	0	0	0	0
M: Medium				1	1	-1	-1	**0**	**1**	**-1**	0	0	0	0	0	0	0	0	0	0	0
H: High				1	1	-1	-1	**1**	**1**	**-2**	0	0	0	0	0	0	0	0	0	0	0
GDP growth per capita																					
L: Low	-2	1	1					**0**	**0**	**0**	-1	-1	0	2	0	-1	1	2	-2	0	0
M: Medium	1	1	-2					**0**	**0**	**0**	-1	0	0	1	0	1	-1	1	-1	0	0
H: High	1	1	-2					**0**	**0**	**0**	0	1	0	-1	1	1	-2	-2	2	0	0
VH: Very High	3	-1	-2					**0**	**0**	**0**	1	1	0	-2	2	1	-3	-3	3	0	0
Fossil fuel availability																					
L: Low fossils	0	0	0	0	0	0	0				3	3	-3	-3	2	1	-3	0	0	0	0
Co: Low oil/gas (High coal)	0	0	0	0	0	0	0				-2	-2	2	2	-1	-1	2	0	0	0	0
H: High fossils	0	0	0	0	0	0	0				-2	-2	1	3	-2	-1	3	0	0	0	0
Carbon Intensity																					
VLC: Very low C	0	0	0	0	0	0	0	**0**	**0**	**0**					0	0	0	0	0	-3	3
LC: Low C	0	0	0	0	0	0	0	**0**	**-1**	**1**					0	0	0	0	0	-2	2
B: Balanced	0	0	0	0	0	0	0	**0**	**1**	**-1**					0	0	0	0	0	-2	2
VH: Very High	0	0	0	0	0	0	0	**1**	**1**	**-2**					0	0	0	0	0	3	-3
Primary energy intensity																					
L: Low	0	0	0	0	0	0	0	**-1**	**-1**	**2**	1	1	1	-3				0	0	0	0
M: Medium	0	0	0	0	0	0	0	**0**	**1**	**-1**	-1	1	2	-2				0	0	0	0
H: High	0	0	0	0	0	0	0	**1**	**1**	**-2**	-1	-1	-1	3				0	0	0	0
Economic policy orientation																					
R: Regional	0	0	0	2	2	-2	-2	**0**	**0**	**0**	-2	-1	1	2	-1	-1	2			0	0
G: Global	0	0	0	-2	-2	2	2	**0**	**0**	**0**	0	0	0	0	0	0	0			0	0
Environmental policy orientation																					
R: Regional	0	0	0	0	0	0	0	**0**	**0**	**0**	-1	-1	-1	3	-2	1	1	0	0		
G: Global	0	0	0	0	0	0	0	**0**	**0**	**0**	1	1	1	-3	1	1	-2	0	0		
Given Scenario States	▼						▼			▼			▼			▼			▼		▼
Impact balance scores:	3	-1	-2	-2	-2	2	2	**-1**	**2**	**-1**	-1	1	4	-4	1	1	-2	-3	3	-2	2
Target Scenario States	▲						▲		▲				▲			▲			▲		▲

Fig. 8.2 A cross-impact matrix with impact balance calculations for the Special Report on Emissions Scenarios commissioned by the Intergovernmental Panel on Climate Change. Highlighted rows specify a 'given scenario' being inspected for internal consistency. (Source: Adapted from Schweizer and Kriegler 2012)

The assessment of internally consistent scenarios is carried out by a calculation called 'impact balances' on selected values in the cross-impact matrix. The impact balance scores (Fig. 8.2, bottom row outside cross-impact matrix) are derived by analysing a particular scenario configuration extracted from the cross-impact matrix (Fig. 8.2, highlighted rows inside cross-impact matrix). For the case shown in Fig. 8.2, the scenario configuration being assessed is Population (Low), GDP growth (Very High), Fossil Fuel Availability (High), Carbon Intensity (Balanced), Primary Energy Intensity (Medium), Economic Policy Orientation (Global) and Environmental Policy Orientation (Global). The impact balance score is the columnar sum of all highlighted matrix cells for the selected configuration. For example, for the Carbon Intensity descriptor, the impact balance score for the Very Low Carbon end-state would be −1 (derived from 0+1−2 to −1+0+1). When all the impact balance scores for each outcome for each descriptor have been calculated in a similar fashion, CIB can analyse whether the selected scenario configuration is internally consistent. For each descriptor, the internally consistent end-state is indicated by the outcome, or 'target state' with the highest impact score (labelled in the bottom row of Fig. 8.2 with an upward-facing arrow). To determine whether the initial scenario configuration is internally consistent, target states are compared to the initial scenario configuration (labelled 'given scenario states' in the bottom row of Fig. 8.2, indicated with a downward-facing arrow). When target descriptor states remain unchanged compared to a given scenario's initial states (the alignment of the upward and downward-facing arrows), this is evidence that the given scenario embodies self-reinforcing (or internally consistent) interrelationships. For the initial configuration provided in Fig. 8.2, all descriptors are internally consistent except for Fossil Fuel Availability. Under the combined influences of all of the descriptor states in the given scenario, the Coal end-state of Fossil Fuel Availability (impact balance score, Co = 2) is the highest in comparison to the Low end-state (L = −1) and High end-state (H = −1). Simply put, significant use of coal is the most consistent end-state based on the given scenario.

In their reanalysis of the SRES, Schweizer and Kriegler (2012) found 11 scenarios that were perfectly consistent. Of the four SRES scenario families, only three were represented in the set of perfectly consistent scenarios. Meanwhile, five of the remaining eight perfectly consistent scenarios reflected 'interesting futures characteristically different from those featured in the SRES', namely 'coal-powered growth' worlds with high emissions (Schweizer and Kriegler 2012, pp. 9–10). Importantly, these plausible futures were consistent with the high rate of emissions observed from 2000 to 2008, but they were not featured in the SRES. That these latent scenarios were discovered through deconstruction using CIB demonstrates the practical value of expanding different approaches of coming to knowledge on future pathways through a poststructuralist methodology.

Conclusions and Reflections

For organizations, the imperative to sustain achievements and make further progress towards organizational objectives is the main rationale for outlining possible future developments. Simultaneously, deep uncertainty about the future makes those hypothetical future developments a product of organizations' sense-making processes. In this dynamic interaction, we have drawn a distinction between two types of analysis. The first focuses on organizations' desires to *look into the future* to explore the possible future contextual environment (scenarios) and to draw out scenarios' implications for organizations' *modi operandi*. The second delves deeper into the epistemological assumptions that shape the development of scenarios; it asks why certain factors or trends are selected or *not* selected for analysis. Why are certain scenarios constructed, and others not? Does the set of scenarios considered by the organization change when previously excluded factors are included?

For the latter type of analysis, we discussed poststructural concepts (Inayatullah's 'toolbox') and demonstrated how the method of CIB can be used to exert those concepts in a way that simultaneously deconstructs assumptions underlying scenarios and reconstructs new (possibly overlooked) scenarios. Our case study on the SRES published by the Intergovernmental Panel on Climate Change (Schweizer and Kriegler 2012) illustrated how CIB was used to *deconstruct* scenarios into their constituent factors and underlying judgements regarding scenario factor interrelations. Decomposing the scenarios then allowed for *re-ordering* this knowledge, that is, reconstructing a 'hidden' family of *alternative futures*, namely 'coal-powered growth' scenarios. Compared to the prevailing method used to develop the SRES scenarios (Intuitive Logics), the careful accounting of assumptions required for CIB—and the alternative futures it uncovered—provided *distance* from methodological conventions for Intuitive Logics that had been largely unquestioned (c.f. Rounsevell and Metzger 2010; Kemp-Benedict 2012; Kosow 2016).

Two important insights can be drawn from our case. First, as the original SRES scenarios differed in important ways from the scenarios developed with CIB, the reanalysis emphasizes how the choice of methods (discursive vs. formalized models) is consequential. Each method for looking into the future had decisive effects on what scenarios would gain ontological status (see Adam 2004), that is, become recognized as 'real' and thereby affect an organization's actions in the present.

Second, our case suggests how the transparent and flexible matrix structure of CIB presents an organization with opportunities to uncover and 'make real' a more diverse set of beliefs, contributing, for instance, to greater awareness of and planning for potential uncertainties. Because CIB allows for a wider variety of futures to 'become real', the method can create distance from an organization's prevailing 'politics of the real', providing those who hold alternative perspectives with greater opportunities to shape how the organization thinks about and acts towards its future. Thereby, the formality of CIB offers no contradiction to the prevalence of qualitative discourse analysis in poststructuralist theorizing. When CIB is deployed not simply as a rigid technique but as a specific mode of inquiry, discussions that lead to the development of the CIB matrix are good opportunities to exercise poststructuralism.

A key message of our chapter is that by adopting a poststructuralist standpoint, scenario practitioners can become aware of how their assumptions curate discourses. In doing so, they can contribute to exposing dominant discourses about the future to new criticism and create space for the inclusion of marginalized ones. In doing so, CIB is able to acknowledge the diversity of organizational members—for example, managers, investors, clients, stakeholders—and their motivations and expectancies of engaging in scenario work. Their engagement is likely to be underpinned by convictions of what constitutes adequate and 'helpful' knowledge with regard to an organization's future.

Finally, by presenting a method of inquiry that bridges the gap between the worlds of scenario development and poststructural critique, we demonstrate that poststructuralism can be of practical use for organizational research. Poststructuralism's alleged tendency towards relativism and the related problem of exerting advocacy and criticism have come under attack (c.f. Weiss 2000). However, several authors have emphasized nuances within poststructuralism. Kilduff and Mehra (1997) move from 'skeptical postmodernism', which dismisses any judging criteria in relation to knowledge and truth, towards an 'affirmative postmodernism', that does allow for differentiations between competing interpretations. We see our proposal of CIB as a method for poststructuralism that follows the affirmative path, in that it demonstrates and contrasts organizational scenarios as well as the beliefs that underlie them. This broadens the utility of CIB for organizational researchers and practitioners along the epistemological spectrum (Hetherington 2001). For relativists unwilling to accept the prioritization or recommendation of any organizational scenario, CIB deconstructs taken-for-granted futures while representing and exploring the logical coherence of alternative imaginaries. For those who have a more positivist concept of knowledge, CIB can be used for generating and reordering (new) comprehensive knowledge of plausible and perhaps unimagined futures, which can be helpful for managing uncertainties. Where discourses traditionally receive less attention, CIB can promote reflection in revealing 'marginalized' assumptions, thereby surfacing difficult-to-imagine but potentially relevant scenarios. Lastly, for epistemological moderates, CIB's target of eliciting divergent cultural, moral and epistemic claims helps to clarify, focus and expand the range of debates about organizational futures.

Acknowledgements The authors wish to thank one anonymous reviewer for helpful comments on an early draft of the chapter. RS and JHK first discussed collaborating on this topic at the 2016 Annual Meeting of the Society for Risk Analysis, where JHK was supported by travel grants provided by the Society for Risk Analysis and University of Waterloo Graduate Studies Office. RS contribution to the chapter was made possible through the German Research Foundation

(DFG) and its financial support within the Cluster of Excellence Simulation Technology (EXC 310/2) at the University of Stuttgart. NMK was supported by the Dean's Doctoral Initiative within the Faculty of Environment at the University of Waterloo. JHK was supported by an Energy Policy Research Fellowship awarded by the Energy Council of Canada and a University of Waterloo SSHRC (Social Sciences and Humanities Research Council) Institutional Grant.

Notes

1. Foucault (1977) describes this relationship as giving rise to 'regimes of truth' that are reproduced by societal or organizational practices, shaping what is accepted as true and thereby influencing what is done. Inayatullah's 'politics of the real' is closely related to this concept.
2. As a fifth concept, Inayatullah proposes 'genealogy', which suggests a more 'historic' perspective on paradigms, trends and categorizations. Due to word constraints, this concept is not elaborated in our chapter.
3. Early hints of the potential for a poststructuralist methodology can be seen in Zwicky's principle of 'negation and construction', which parallels our pairing of deconstruction with reconstruction.
4. Intuitive Logics can be applied deductively and/or inductively (van der Heijden 2005). In the deductive approach, one or multiple axes are used to explore contrasting future possibilities, whereas the inductive approach develops networks of factors from which scenarios can emerge. Further enhancements of Intuitive Logics are reviewed by Wright et al. (2013a).
5. See Nakicenovic et al. (2000, Figure 1–4).

References

Adam, Barbara. 2004. Memory of Futures. *KronoScope* 42: 297–315.
Ahlqvist, Toni, and Martin Rhisiart. 2015. Emerging Pathways for Critical Futures Research: Changing Contexts and Impacts of Social Theory. *Futures* 71: 91–104.
Amer, Muhammad, Tugrul Daim, and Antonie Jetter. 2013. A Review of Scenario Planning. *Futures* 46: 23–40.

Bachrach, Peter, and Morton S. Baratz. 1962. Two Faces of Power. *The American Political Science Review* 56 (4): 947–952.
Beckert, Jens. 2013. Capitalism as a System of Expectations. *Politics & Society* 41 (3): 323–350.
Bradfield, Ron, George Wright, Georg Burt, George Cairns, and Kees van der Heijden. 2005. The Origins and Evolution of Scenario Techniques in Long Range Business Planning. *Futures* 37: 795–812.
Brown, Nik, Brian Rappert, and Andrew Webster. 2000. *Contested Futures. A Sociology of Prospective Techno-science.* Burlington: Ashgate.
Calas, M., and L. Smircich. 1999. Past Postmodernism? Reflections and Tentative Directions. *Academy of Management Review* 24 (4): 649–671.
Dahl, Robert. 1957. "The Concept of Power." Systems Research and Behavioural. *Science* 2 (3): 201–215.
Ezzamel, Mahmoud, and Hugh Willmott. 2010. Strategy and Strategizing: A Poststructuralist Perspective. In *The Globalization of Strategy Research*, Advances in Strategic Management, ed. Joel A.C. Baum and Joseph Lampel, 75–109. Bingley: Emerald Group Publishing Limited.
Foucault, Michel. 1977. Truth and Power. In *Power/Knowledge: Selected Interviews and Other Writings (1972–77)*, ed. C. Gordon. New York: Pantheon.
Grunwald, Armin. 2013. Modes of Orientation Provided by Futures Studies: Making Sense of Diversity and Divergence. *European Journal of Futures Research* 15 (30): 1–9.
Helmer, Olaf. 1981. Reassessment of Cross-Impact Analysis. *Futures* 13: 389–400.
Hetherington, Stephen. 2001. *Good Knowledge, Bad Knowledge. On Two Dogmas of Epistemology.* Oxford: Oxford University Press.
Hibbard, K.A., et al. 2007. A Strategy for Climate Change Stabilization Experiments. *Eos* 88 (20): 217–221.
Hodgkinson, Gerard, and George Wright. 2002. Confronting Strategic Inertia in a Top Management Team: Learning from Failure. *Organization Science* 23 (6): 949–977.
Inayatullah, Sohail. 1990. Deconstructing and Reconstructing the Future: Predictive, Cultural and Critical Epistemology. *Futures* 22 (2): 116–141.
———. 1998a. Causal Layered Analysis: Poststructuralism as Method. *Futures* 30 (8): 815–829.
———. 1998b. Listening to Non-western Perspectives. In *World Yearbook of Education 1998*, ed. R. Slaughter and D. Hicks. London: Kogan Page.

Kemp-Benedict, Eric. 2012. Telling Better Stories: Strengthening the Story in Story and Simulation. *Environmental Research Letters* 7 (4): 1–14.
Kilduff, Martin, and Ajay Mehra. 1997. Postmodernism and Organizational Research. *Academy of Management Review* 22 (2): 453–481.
Koch, Jochen, Hannes Krämer, Andreas Reckwitz, and Matthias Wenzel. 2016. Zum Umgang mit Zukunft in Organisationen – eine praxistheoretische Perspektive. *Managementforschung* 26 (1): 161–184.
Kosow, Hannah. 2016. The Best of Both Worlds?: An Exploratory Study on Forms and Effects of New Qualitative-Quantitative Scenario Methodologies. PhD Dissertation, University of Stuttgart.
Lahsen, Myanna. 2005. Seductive Simulations? Uncertainty Distribution Around Climate Models. *Social Studies of Science* 35 (6): 895–922.
Lloyd, Elisabeth A., and Vanessa J. Schweizer. 2014. Objectivity and a Comparison of Methodological Scenario Approaches for Climate Change Research. *Synthese* 191: 2049–2088.
March, J.G. 1995. The Future, Disposable Organizations and the Rigidities of Imagination. *Organization* 2 (3/4): 427–440.
McKinlay, Alan, and Ken Starkey. 1998. *Foucault, Management and Organization Theory: From Panopticon to Technologies of Self*. London: SAGE Publications.
Morgan, Gareth. 1986. *Images of Organization*. Beverly Hills: SAGE.
Nakicenovic, Nebojsa, et al. 2000. *Special Report on Emissions Scenarios*. New York: Cambridge University Press.
Pielke, Roger, Tom Wigley, and Christopher Green. 2008. Dangerous Assumptions. *Nature* 452 (3): 531–532.
Raupach, Michael, Gregg Marland, Philippe Ciais, Corinne Le Quere, Josep Canadell, Gernot Klepper, and Christopher Field. 2007. Global and Regional Drivers of Accelerating CO_2 Emissions. *Proceedings of the National Academy of Sciences* 104: 10288–10293.
Rosenau, Pauline. 1992. *Postmodernism and the Social Sciences: Insights, Inroads, and Intrusions*. Princeton: Princeton University Press.
Rounsevell, Mark, and Marc Metzger. 2010. Developing Qualitative Storylines for Environmental Change Assessment. *WIREs Climate Change* 1: 606–619.
Schweizer, Vanessa J., and Elmar Kriegler. 2012. Improving Environmental Change Research with Systematic Techniques for Qualitative Scenarios. *Environmental Research Letters* 7: 044011.
Schweizer, Vanessa J., and Brian C. O'Neill. 2014. Systematic Construction of Global Socioeconomic Pathways Using Internally Consistent Element Combinations. *Climatic Change* 122: 431–445.

Slaughter, Richard. 2002a. From Forecasting and Scenarios to Social Construction: Changing Methodological Paradigms in Future Studies. *Foresight* 4 (3): 26–31.

———. 2002b. Beyond the Mundane: Reconciling Breadth and Depth in Futures Enquiry. *Futures* 34: 493–507.

Spee, Andreas, and Paula Jarzabkowski. 2009. Strategy Tools as Boundary Objects. *Strategic Organization* 7 (2): 223–232.

Van der Heijden, Kees. 2005. *Scenarios: The Art of Strategic Conversation*. 2nd ed. Chichester: John Wiley & Sons.

Wack, Pierre. 1985. Scenarios: Shooting the Rapids. *Harvard Business Review*, November–December.

Weimer-Jehle, Wolfgang. 2006. Cross-Impact Balances: A System-Theoretical Approach to Cross-Impact Analysis. *Technological Forecasting and Social Change* 73 (4): 334–361.

Weiss, Richard M. 2000. Taking Science Out of Organization Science: How Would Postmodernism Reconstruct the Analysis of Organizations? *Organization Science* 11 (6): 709–731.

Wright, George, Ron Bradfield, and George Cairns. 2013a. Does the Intuitive Logics Method – And Its Recent Enhancements – Produce "Effective" Scenarios? *Technological Forecasting and Social Change* 80 (4): 631–642.

Wright, George, George Cairns, and Ron Bradfield. 2013b. Scenario Methodology: New Developments in Theory and Practice. *Technological Forecasting and Social Change* 80 (4): 561–565.

Zwicky, Fritz. 1969. *Discovery, Invention, Research Through the Morphological Approach*. New York: Macmillan.

9

Historical Methods and the Study of How Organizations Manage the Future

Yves Plourde

Introduction

Studying the future has a long history in management and organization theory, being an ongoing concern for scholars and practitioners alike. All organizations attempt to prepare for the future in one way or another, either to anticipate changes they might see in their environment in the future or to think about what the future should be like and what steps need to be made to create it (van der Heijden 2004). While adapting to changes in the environment is a necessity for a firm's survival, creating the future is a path filled with uncertainty and foolishness, with many attempts and few successes. Firms who have attempted to do so include Tesla, Amazon and Google, all aspiring to impact the way we use information and technology to improve our daily lives. In the process, they create change for others, influencing our environment. Through their choices, these organizations make 'the future out of a range of possible futures' (Fear 2014, p. 183) and contribute to changing the futures we can imagine.

Y. Plourde (✉)
HEC Montréal, Montréal, Canada

© The Author(s) 2018
H. Krämer, M. Wenzel (eds.), *How Organizations Manage the Future*,
https://Doi.org/10.1007/978-3-319-74506-0_9

While most scholars agree that focusing on those who make the future is important, there are many different ways in which to study them. A focus on the future from the present provides a rich playground for students of organizations. Studying firms like Tesla and Apple, for instance, allows us to examine their actions and internal processes in real time. Yet, a focus on the future from the present has its own set of limitations. The future is unknown, which creates uncertainty. This uncertainty stems from a lack of knowledge about system conditions and underlying dynamics, prospects for innovation and surprises and the intentional nature of human decision-making (Robinson 2003). Without knowing what comes next, we cannot distinguish between actual knowledge and beliefs, between rationality and foolishness and between laggards and game changers. What I argue in this chapter is that history is also part of the future: the question is, what future and from whose perspective? By focusing on the future from the past, we can learn how historical actors approached problems concerning the future, what they did in particular circumstances and how they adapted their vision as new knowledge was being created and shared and as they became more knowledgeable about issues and opportunities.

In this chapter, I explain why and how historical methods provide a suitable way to study the future. To illustrate how historical methods can be used to study the future from the past, I draw on my research on Greenpeace, a non-governmental organization whose mission is to address the most salient issues threatening the planet. In this project, my goal was to understand how Greenpeace members organized their activities to become more effective at what they called 'shaping the future' (Plourde 2015). The project, which covers the years 1971 to 2004, draws primarily on 200,000 pages of archives from the organization (including, among other documents, meeting minutes, proposals about issues and communications between the secretariat and affiliates), as well as histories of the organization, interviews with former Greenpeace members and media coverage. It focuses on different aspects of Greenpeace's history, including episodes of sense-making about the priorities of the organization, its engagement with specific issues and the way the organization structured its activities across time to enhance its effectiveness.

Although historical approaches to the study of organizations offer benefits when it comes to studying how organizations manage the future, they also come with challenges and limitations. First, the future from the past is now known—we have lived through the future that was the subject of past projections and we now know how events have unfolded. Yet, the things that we take for granted today were not necessarily known about in the past. It thus requires 'recovering [of] alternative choices and potential paths' (Fear 2014, p. 183) in order to interpret the future from the past in a meaningful way. Second, the available evidence of how actors envisioned the future can be sparse and incomplete. Moreover, the evidence that is used cannot be taken at face value and must be rigorously analysed (Burgelman 2011). This chapter makes the case for the use of historical methods to study how organizations manage the future, and provides an explanation as to how the challenges mentioned above can be dealt with. The case of Greenpeace serves to illustrate these challenges.

Historical Methods and the Future

Historical methods correspond to the use of traces of history to revisit past events (White 1987). Traces of history are essentially artefacts remaining from the past, but they can take many forms. The main focus of historical methods is on the intersection of continuities (patterns that extend beyond time), contingencies (phenomena that do not form a pattern) and the role of context for the study of complex systems (Burgelman 2011). In the study of continuities and contingencies in complex systems, historians recognize the intentional nature of human decision-making. In this case, we need to understand actors as historical agents and not just as actors who are primarily responsive to economic, social and political conditions (Wadhwani and Bucheli 2014). They create new conditions that sometimes have a lasting influence on the development of new institutions and their diffusion, hence the need to understand the role they played in history. Yet, understanding their role can only be achieved by looking at their actions in relation to what came before and after them. In the absence of this type of understanding, we run the risk of misinterpreting the meaning that we attach to actors, their actions and their role in the construction of institutions.

With the epistemology of historical methods in mind, the case for a historical approach to the study of how organizations manage the future becomes both practical and philosophical. The future from the present is unknown and still in the making; no one can predict with certainty what will happen (or not) in the years to come. The future from the past, on the other hand, has now unfolded. That future—the future from the past—can be studied with the benefit of hindsight, which allows us to evaluate the meaning and significance of events that can 'hinge on developments which take place after, sometimes *long* after, the original events takes place' (Fear 2014, p. 173). As such, 'access to information that contemporaries did not have about the future' allows for judging 'outcomes or the long-term consequences of (quiet) choices for their *significance*—a luxury theorists studying organizations in the present cannot have' (Fear 2014, p. 173). Hence, by knowing what happened after focal events took place, we can identify changes in their context and draw on this knowledge to investigate what caused the events and why certain actions led to certain events, while others did not. From there, the analysis of traces of history can be used for seeing the future as experienced by historical actors of significance, how they were thinking about it and what actions they undertook based on what they believed was to come.

Applications of the Study of How Organizations Manage the Future

But how can historical methods be used to study how organizations manage the future? What distinguish historical methods from other types of inquiry are its sources (Lipartito 2014). Sources used by historians can be categorized into two distinct types of evidence: primary data and secondary data. Primary data corresponds to documents produced at the time focal events took place (e.g. meeting minutes, personal correspondence, media coverage and other documents used internally and/or externally by an organization) (Gottschalk 1969). Secondary data corresponds to crafted narratives and histories revisiting the past (e.g. corporate histories, memoirs from CEOs and other types of narratives that revisit past events) (Gottschalk 1969). Using these sources, historians will focus on different phenomenon through different theoretical lenses and types of analysis (Vaara and Lamberg 2016; Rowlinson et al. 2014).

Due to the limitations associated with historical documentation, it is important to consider how this evidence can be used. The type of history on which I focus here is the use of the past to study organizations (Godfrey et al. 2016; Rowlinson et al. 2014). Building on my project on Greenpeace mentioned in the introduction, I present three applications where historical sources can be leveraged to investigate how organizations manage the future: how actors make sense of the (possible) future(s); how they enact the(ir) future; and how they organize (for) it. It is worth mentioning that the three applications are closely related to one another and can all be considered part of an overall process that includes three phases: envisioning, enacting and structuring. What I present here is the analytical distinction that is required for the study of each of these phases, as they require a focus on different units of analysis with different types of evidence and analysis.

Application #1: How Actors Make Sense of the (Possible) Future(s)

The first application refers to how actors make sense of the (possible) future(s). Questions about what the future will be, what it could be or what it should be are all questions at the core of future studies (although through a focus on the future from the present). When it comes to understanding how actors make sense of the (possible) future(s), a focus on the past can be used to uncover the becoming of past imaginations and to address questions such as how historical actors viewed the future (e.g. about a technology, an issue or a potential opportunity), how they shared their views (e.g. with other organizational members or stakeholders) and why they made the choices they made (e.g. to favour one technology over another). This can be achieved through the study of sense-making episodes (Magnússon and Szijártó 2013; Levi 2001).

In my investigation of the Greenpeace archives, discussions about the future were conducted at different levels and for different types of futures (i.e. the world, the organization and for specific issues). The main future of concern, however, remained the natural environment and what that environment would look like if the world kept on pursuing the same path. Examining this organization's archives allowed me to see how individuals were thinking about the future and how they verbalized it. What became clear through my investigations of the Greenpeace archives was that a focus on the future was not explicit until long after the organization's first actions in 1971. Discussions about the future became explicit only from 1985, and became particularly salient during the years 1986–1988, when the senior leadership attempted to define its overarching goals. Moreover, the vision they laid out during that period had a lasting impact on the organization, becoming part of the mission statement that is still in use today. Questions of interest for Greenpeace members at the time were about the most salient issues threatening the planet, what should be done to address those issues and what Greenpeace's role could be regarding those issues. These first observations led me to explore additional paths of inquiry, which went beyond the original question about how actors within Greenpeace were thinking about the future. What were the triggers for those discussions? Why were they having these conversations at that particular moment in time? How did they share their views about what the future was likely to be and how it should look? What was the long-term effect of these conversations on the subsequent decisions made by Greenpeace leaders? These questions came to light only because it was possible to analyse their sense-making process using knowledge about what came *before* the discussions, and what came *after* the discussions.

Application #2: How Actors Enact The(ir) Future (or Adapt to Others' Enactment)

The second application concerns how actors shape the future. The process of undertaking actions to shape the future can be called 'enactment' (Smircich and Stubbart 1985): by acting, individuals and organizations create structures, constraints and opportunities that did not exist or were not necessarily noticeable, before their actions. Internally, it requires the persuading of organizational members to espouse one vision of the future and to decide on a path that could make it a reality. Externally, it requires conducting actions that have the potential to alter others' view of reality, to favour one future over alternative possibilities. In doing so, an organization is likely to elicit resistance, as altering others' view of reality implies changing beliefs and taken-for-granted behaviours. In this process, a focal organization will have to adapt to others' enactment. As to how actors enact the(ir) future, a focus on the past allows us to see how actors were thinking about these possibilities, how they engaged in activities to bring these possibilities closer to fruition and how they adapted their actions as new knowledge was being created as a result of their actions. Here, a focus on events or a focal issue across time appears as an appropriate way to investigate this set of questions.

Enacting the(ir) future is the core of Greenpeace's mission. Sharing their vision for the future within the organization has never been much of a challenge (although deciding on priorities always has been). Bringing the real world closer to the world they would like to see, on the other hand, has been an ongoing concern. By backtracking the actions that led to some of their successes (e.g. international agreements adopted by international organizations or changes in the practices of industries), I observed that many of their successes (e.g. Brent Spar, genetically modified organisms [GMOs]) were the result of initiatives for which the outcome could not be anticipated in advance, and that were not even on the radar of the organization when the problems they were targeting started to gain momentum. Nevertheless, their actions contributed to changing our reality. Other successes (e.g. Antarctica, the Moratorium on Commercial Whaling), however, were the result of a well-thought through process on how to get there. Nonetheless, the identification of a path to follow was largely the result of random encounters that triggered a sense-making process that led to the establishment of an action plan to reach their goals. In addition, a focus on the past allowed me to observe what they were seeing at the time as steps which were necessary to influence the world to act in a more sustainable way, what actions they undertook based on what they thought were the necessary steps to meet their goals and how they adapted their subsequent actions in response to others' enactments as they succeeded (or failed) in reaching their goals. Observing their actions in relation to their own sense-making, and in relation to other historical actors' actions, allowed me to observe the necessity for Greenpeace to have clear goals while also being flexible in their plans. This was necessary because of the complexity of the systems they were attempting to impact and because of the apparent state of chaos surrounding the dynamics of these systems. Without knowing the outcome in advance, it would not have been possible for me to make sense of the importance of certain actions in relation to other actors' actions, and to observe how their sense-making process impacted the ultimate outcome of their actions.

Application #3: How Actors Organize (for) the Future

The third application concerns how activities can be structured so that an organization can become more effective at managing the future. The questions that relate to this third application concern not so much on how organizations envision the future as much as how they can organize for it. Being effective can have different meanings, depending on how an organization approaches the future. For an organization adapting to current trends and challenges, being effective might mean being able to respond to emerging threats. For an organization aspiring to shape the future, being effective might mean being able to identify and pursue opportunities that align with its vision for the future. In both cases, the organization cannot predict the future, but it can favour the adoption of specific structures, processes and practices that enhance the organization's ability to engage with the future. In that regard, a focus on the past allows for an in-depth investigation of the 'everyday trivialities [...] and processes to reveal long-term dynamics and structures' (Vaara and Lamberg 2016). It also permits a study of how actors engaged with questions related to an organization's structure, to revisit what they did and how and to what effect.

My data on Greenpeace allowed me to observe more than just their practices across time, but also the way they were thinking about these practices, especially during their strategic planning exercises (1986–1988, 1992–1993, 1996–1999) which focused specifically on the effectiveness of the organization. The exercise of 1992–1993 was particularly insightful because it was the result of a major organizational crisis. Failure to organize their activities to adapt to these priorities led to a decline in influence, thereby restricting the ability of the organization to have a say in the decisions that would determine the future of the planet. The consensus at the time was that although they had the vision for what they wanted for the future, they did not have the structure to enact that vision. This mismatch forced them to openly discuss how they should organize for the future. This provided me with an opportunity for an in-depth investigation of what they did, why and to what effect. Overall, what resulted from this exercise was an agreement that they could not predict where opportunities to shape the future would come from or what actions would succeed. They could, however, organize their activities to act swiftly when opportunities arose. For this, they needed to clarify their goals, develop greater flexibility and further integrate their activities. The subsequent changes contributed to their ability to seize opportunities, with the result that Greenpeace regained some of its influence. By looking at Greenpeace's future through its past, I was able to revisit their past choices, the sense-making process surrounding these choices as they happened and their effect.

Historical methods can be used for each of the three applications mentioned above, and the three applications are also entwined. Sense-making about possible futures will guide actions. Actions and adaptations to others' enactment will create new information that can lead to revised interpretations about possible futures or new ways to think about possible paths for the future. Sense-making and actions will then impact the structures and practices that can be used to enhance the ability of an organization to enact the future. While each of these applications is related to the others, they do require a distinct approach from an analytical perspective. In the next section, I present principles for analysing historical evidence in relation to the above applications.

Analysing Historical Evidence

Building on historical evidence to interpret the past presents a number of challenges. First, we can only count on sparse and often incomplete evidence to see how historical actors envisioned the future. Second, not all documents have the same value (see Rowlinson 2004; Lipartito 2014; Yates 2014 for an extensive discussion on the topic of sources) nor do they serve the same purpose when it comes to looking at how historical actors managed the future. Third, the future from the past is now known, which was not the case for the actors who experienced it. This last point is perhaps the most challenging of all three because it requires us 'to read evidence "forward", that is, from the point of view of actors who had no other way to know anything about the future' (Fear 2014, p. 183). To explain how historians cope with these challenges, Kipping, Wadhwani and Bucheli (2014) identify a set of guidelines that serve as the generally agreed principles used by historians: source criticism; triangulation; and the 'hermeneutic circle'. In this section, I present these principles in relation to the study of the future from the past.

Principle #1: Source Criticism

The first principle is source criticism, which consists of determining the validity and credibility of each text (Kipping et al. 2014). This evaluation process is necessary because historical sources are not created by the researcher—they are created by historical actors with their own agendas—and the process behind the creation of the documents that remain from the past was largely determined by the context of the time, a context that differs in many ways from the one of the researcher (Lipartito 2014). Validity, which concerns primary sources, can be assessed by looking at the provenance of a source (including the author, the time and the place a document was produced), the intended audience and purpose, and the context under which it was written (Donnelly and Norton 2011). Credibility, on the other hand, concerns secondary sources. It consists of establishing whether or not an account of past events can be trusted to inform one's interpretation. Establishing the credibility of an account is important. Events narrated years later (through corporate histories, memoirs or interviews) can have little to do with what actually happened (Golden 1992). They can also be tainted by the version of the past one wants to promote, to push for one vision of the organization over another or to defend past decisions (Lipartito 2014). In this category, eyewitness accounts are generally preferred over second-hand ones (although second-hand accounts can be exemplary in their analysis). In general, documents produced at the time focal events took place are preferred because they tend to present a high degree of authenticity (Megill 2007). Nevertheless, the disclosure of the sources of a narrative can help establish its credibility, even if one's account is produced years later (Gaddis 2002).

Archives can be a particularly valuable source of documents (e.g. meeting minutes, internal memos and position papers) for the study of how organizations manage the future. The main advantage of documents stored in archives is that they were, for the most part, intended for internal use. Moreover, many of the documents stored in archives were produced at the time that focal events were taking place. In my own research on Greenpeace, I used a variety of documents, including accounts from past Greenpeace members and historians. The Greenpeace archives, however, remained the most important source of documents because the documents stored in the archives were illustrative of the main concerns of actors within the organization at different points in time. They also helped me get a sense of the knowledge available to Greenpeace members back then. Other documents proved to be valuable, such as histories of the organization. Yet, some memoirs were clearly revisionist accounts of the organization's history, going against other evidence found in the archives. This is where the next principle becomes important.

Principle #2: Triangulation

The second principle refers to triangulation, which consists of drawing from multiple sources from a variety of actors to interpret the past (Kipping et al. 2014). The purpose of using multiple sources is to reduce bias, to increase confidence in one's interpretation and to decide which account to use and why when valid and credible sources contradict one another (Howell and Prevenier 2001). Triangulation is based on the sources identified above, and is particularly important because of the challenge of dealing with often incomplete data to reconstruct the past.

When it comes to studying how organizations manage the future, triangulation allows for validating what happened, when and with what impact. It is closely linked with the first principle of source criticism. The most important documents are not always private or internal. Some of these documents can simply reveal one actor's perspective or one part of the larger whole. Some documents can be ideas that never saw the light of day, programmes that were started or plans that were initiated but stopped before they led to a more formal commitment. The absence of documents concerning one issue or topic, or what Decker (2013) calls 'silences', can also provide important information as to what an organization did not consider as possible futures worth debating. The key point here is that not all documents are relevant, and the absence of documents can also provide information about an organization's view of the future.

Principle #3: Hermeneutic Circle

The third principle is the hermeneutic circle. The hermeneutic circle is an iterative process where the researcher attempts to situate text within its historical context and in relation to other texts (Kipping et al. 2014). Because historical sources were produced at a different time and for a specific use, their meaning can be misinterpreted. The risk is to impose 'categories and methods of thought from the present onto the past' (Kipping et al. 2014, p. 320) that could distort one's understanding of past events, actions or communications. For this reason, sources have to be historically contextualized. As such, the researcher needs 'to understand historical actors' own ways of sense-making and sense-giving in order to analyse the sources they produced' (Kipping et al. 2014, p. 320). For this, one must be mindful of the information that was available to historical actors at that time. What was known/unknown then? Were the focal actors aware of the available information at that time? How could having access to that information have changed their actions or impacted their reading of a situation?

In practice, the hermeneutics circle is ensured by interpreting a primary source in relation to other sources that establish the context for its interpretation, and by using this context to understand the author's intention or point of view in producing the source (Kipping et al. 2014). Documents serve a specific function in organizations, and this function can change across organizations and across time within the same organization. One must understand these functions if one is to understand the meaning of the texts being studied (for an illustration of this process, see Wright 2011). It is also important that the documents and their content are analysed in relation to what was going on in the field, or in the world more generally, at a given time. Here, secondary sources and quantitative data can come in handy, as both can provide information about the context. In one of my projects focusing on Greenpeace's sense-making as regards the impact GMOs could have on the future, secondary sources (e.g. histories of science and agriculture) and quantitative data (e.g. on the acceptance of GMOs and the diffusion of the technology) provided information about the historical context and how it impacted Greenpeace's internal debates on the topic. In another project, where I tracked Greenpeace's structures and practices over the course of its history, graphs on declining membership and revenues provided a sense of how the organization was doing at different times. This data shed new light on the communications between members and raised questions about why the topic was discussed only when the problem related to Greenpeace financials had become too important to ignore. The central point here is that historical documentation cannot be looked at in isolation from its historical context, and efforts must be made to understand that context in order to understand the meaning of the texts under investigation.

Discussion and Conclusion

In this chapter, I made the case for the use of historical methods to study how organizations manage the future. Future studies have long made use of the past to evaluate the plausibility of an event or its probability (Wiek et al. 2013). Methods such as forecasting (e.g. Cuhls 2003), backcasting (e.g. Robinson 1988; Dreborg 1996) and scenario planning (e.g. Sarpong

2011) all draw on the past in one way or another to anticipate what might happen in the future. In contrast, the use of the past proposed in this chapter focuses on examining the future from the past to investigate how historical actors managed the future. A historical approach has its limitations. Not all organizations maintain archives, and information can be incomplete. Nevertheless, a focus on the past provides the benefit of hindsight, which allows us to see the interplay of the future and organizing while being knowledgeable about the outcome of this interplay.

The project presented in this chapter to illustrate different applications of historical methods for the study of how organizations manage the future concerned a single organization (i.e. Greenpeace). Other organizations have been the focus of similar investigations, including General Electric (e.g. Joseph and Ocasio 2012), SmithCorona (e.g. Danneels 2011), Kodak (e.g. Tripsas and Gavetti 2000) and Intel (e.g. Burgelman 2001). In each of these cases, the benefits of using a historical approach included seeing how historical actors approached the future, what changes they favoured and with what impact (positive or negative). Single cases are not the only alternative, and similar investigations could be done using different approaches. For instance, comparative histories, where the researcher 'engages in systematic and contextualized comparisons of similar and contrasting cases' (Mahoney and Rueschemeyer 2003, p. 48) could enrich our understanding of why some organizations are more successful than others at preparing for the future. Historical methods could also be used to study outliers, to investigate the role of different practices in predicting the future and to explore the effectiveness of different methods of 'making sense of the future'. Historical methods offer plenty of ways to learn more about past enactments of the future: it is up to researchers to think creatively about how we can use the past to inform current practices.

In conclusion, studying the future from the past can be a useful way to explore how organizations manage the future. We should not forget that decades old organizations, such as Alcoa in the aluminium industry or Monsanto in agriculture, have also had a lasting influence on the recent past. For these organizations, our past was their future. Historical actors that were part of that past faced many of the same challenges that we face today when we try to forecast the future: they might have thought in terms of future-perfect thinking, built scenarios or used backcasting techniques to inform their own actions to shape or prepare for the future. A focus on the past can, thus, help uncover and unpack how actors were thinking about possible futures, as we draw on what is now known in order to seek explanations as to why some organizations and/or actors were able to sense cues that others missed.

References

Burgelman, Robert A. 2001. *Strategy Is Destiny: How Strategy-Making Shapes a Company's Future*. New York: The Free Press New York.

———. 2011. Bridging History and Reductionism: A Key Role for Longitudinal Qualitative Research. *Journal of International Business Studies* 42 (5): 591–601.

Cuhls, Kerstin. 2003. From Forecasting to Foresight Processes – New Participative Foresight Activities in Germany. *Journal of Forecasting* 22 (2–3): 93–111.

Danneels, Erwin. 2011. Trying to Become a Different Type of Company: Dynamic Capability at Smith Corona. *Strategic Management Journal* 32 (1): 1–31.

Decker, Stephanie. 2013. The Silence of the Archives: Business History, Postcolonialism and Archival Ethnography. *Management & Organizational History* 8 (2): 155–173.

Donnelly, Mark, and Claire Norton. 2011. *Doing History*. London: Routledge.

Dreborg, Karl H. 1996. Essence of Backcasting. *Futures* 28 (9): 813–828.

Fear, Jeffrey. 2014. Mining the Past: Historicizing Organizational Learning and Change. In *Organizations in Time: History, Theory, Methods*, ed. Marcelo Bucheli and R. Daniel Wadhwani, 169–191. Oxford: Oxford University Press.

Gaddis, John Lewis. 2002. *The Landscape of History: How Historians Map the Past*. Oxford: Oxford University Press.

Godfrey, Paul C., John Hassard, Ellen S. O'Connor, Michael Rowlinson, and Martin Ruef. 2016. What Is Organizational History? Toward a Creative Synthesis of History and Organization Studies. *Academy of Management Review* 41 (4): 590–608.

Golden, Brian R. 1992. The Past Is the Past – Or Is It? The Use of Retrospective Accounts as Indicators of Past Strategy. *Academy of Management Journal* 35 (4): 848–860.

Gottschalk, Louis Reichenthal. 1969. *Understanding History: A Primer of Historical Method*. New York: Random House Inc..

Howell, Martha, and Walter Prevenier. 2001. *From Reliable Sources: An Introduction to Historical Methods*. Ithaca: Cornell University Press.

Joseph, John, and William Ocasio. 2012. Architecture, Attention, and Adaptation in the Multibusiness Firm: General Electric from 1951 to 2001. *Strategic Management Journal* 33 (6): 633–660.

Kipping, Matthias, R. Daniel Wadhwani, and Marcelo Bucheli. 2014. Analyzing and Interpreting Historical Sources: A Basic Methodology. In *Organizations in Time: History, Theory, Methods*, ed. Marcelo Bucheli and R. Daniel Wadhwani, 305–329. Oxford: Oxford University Press.

Levi, Giovanni. 2001. On Microhistory. In *New Perspectives on Historical Writing*, ed. Peter Burke, 97–119. Cambridge: Polity Press.

Lipartito, Kenneth. 2014. Historical Sources and Data. In *Organizations in Time: History, Theory, Methods*, ed. Marcelo Bucheli and R. Daniel Wadhwani, 284–304. Oxford: Oxford University Press.

Magnússon, Sigurður Gylfi, and István M. Szijártó. 2013. *What Is Micro History? Theory and Practice*. London: Routledge.

Mahoney, James, and Dietrich Rueschemeyer. 2003. *Comparative Historical Analysis in the Social Sciences*. Cambridge: Cambridge University Press.

Megill, Allan. 2007. *Historical Knowledge, Historical Error: A Contemporary Guide to Practice*. Chicago: University of Chicago Press.

Plourde, Yves. 2015. *Engaging with the Future: A Historical Investigation of Greenpeace*. London: Ivey Business School, University of Western Ontario.

Robinson, John B. 1988. Unlearning and Backcasting: Rethinking Some of the Questions We Ask About the Future. *Technological Forecasting and Social Change* 33 (4): 325–338.

———. 2003. Future Subjunctive: Backcasting as Social Learning. *Futures* 35 (8): 839–856.

Rowlinson, Michael. 2004. Historical Analysis of Company Documents. In *Essential Guide to Qualitative Methods in Organizational Research*, ed. Catherine Cassel and Gillian Symon, 301–311. London: Sage Publications.

Rowlinson, Michael, John Hassard, and Stephanie Decker. 2014. Research Strategies for Organizational History: A Dialogue Between Historical Theory and Organization Theory. *Academy of Management Review* 39 (3): 250–274.

Sarpong, David. 2011. Towards a Methodological Approach: Theorising Scenario Thinking as a Social Practice. *Foresight* 13 (2): 4–17.

Smircich, Linda, and Charles Stubbart. 1985. Strategic Management in an Enacted World. *Academy of Management Review* 10 (4): 724–736.

Tripsas, Mary, and Giovanni Gavetti. 2000. Capabilities, Cognition, and Inertia: Evidence from Digital Imaging. *Strategic Management Journal* 21 (10): 1147–1161.

Vaara, Eero, and Juha-Antti Lamberg. 2016. Taking Historical Embeddedness Seriously: Three Historical Approaches to Advance Strategy Process and Practice Research. *Academy of Management Review* 41 (4): 633–657.

van der Heijden, Kees. 2004. Afterword: Insights into Foresight. In *Managing the Future: Strategic Foresight in the Knowledge Economy*, ed. Hardimos Tsoukas and Jill Shepherd, 204–211. Malden: Blackwell Publishing.

Wadhwani, R. Daniel, and Marcelo Bucheli. 2014. The Future of the Past in Management and Organization Studies. In *Organizations in Time: History, Theory, Methods*, ed. Marcelo Bucheli and R. Daniel Wadhwani, 3–32. Oxford: Oxford University Press.

White, Hayden V. 1987. *The Content of the Form: Narrative Discourse and Historical Representation*. Baltimore: John Hopkins University Press.

Wiek, Arnim, Lauren Withycombe Keeler, Vanessa Schweizer, and Daniel J. Lang. 2013. Plausibility Indications in Future Scenarios. *International Journal of Foresight and Innovation Policy* 9 (2/3/4): 133–147.

Wright, April. 2011. Watch What I Do, Not What I Say: New Questions for Documents in International Business Case Research. In *Rethinking the Case Study in International Business and Management Research*, ed. Rebekka Piekkari and Catherine Welch, 361–382. Cheltenham/Northampton: Edward Elgar Publishing.

Yates, JoAnne. 2014. Understanding Historical Methods in Organization Studies. In *Organizations in Time: History, Theory, Methods*, ed. Marcelo Bucheli and R. Daniel Wadhwani, 265–283. Oxford: Oxford University Press.

Part III

Empirical Insights

10

In the Wake of Disaster: Resilient Organizing and a New Path for the Future

A. Erin Bass and Ivana Milosevic

Introduction

Increased environmental complexity has led some to argue that organizations exist in a perpetual state of crisis (Davis et al. 2009; Hannah et al. 2009). Indeed, in addition to institutional and competitive dynamics (Chen and Miller 2015; Gnyawali and Madhavan 2001), organizations today face natural as well as manmade disasters (Van Der Vegt et al. 2015). From the financial crisis that shocked the world to near-annual natural disasters, to the British Petroleum (BP) oil spill and the GM and Volkswagen recalls, it seems that corporate crises are an ongoing concern. Understanding how organizations experience and recover from a disaster may be needed now more than ever.

A. Erin Bass (✉)
University of Nebraska Omaha, Omaha, NE, USA

I. Milosevic
College of Charleston, Charleston, SC, USA

Previous research has suggested that when faced with an uncertain future and a high probability for disaster, organizations should either shield their core via emphasis on activities that maintain equilibrium (Meyer et al. 2005; Voss et al. 2008) or, alternatively, embrace an uncertain future through complex organizing and careful interweaving of administrative and innovative practices (Uhl-Bien and Marion 2009). The former perspective—focused on maintaining equilibrium—suggests that organizations develop slack resources (Daniel et al. 2004; Wang et al. 2016) and boundary-spanning departments (Aldrich and Herker 1977; Foss et al. 2013) to buffer the organization from uncertainty. The latter perspective—focused on complex organizing—suggests that organizations develop dynamic capabilities (Barreto 2010; Helfat and Martin 2015; Schilke 2014), entangle administrative and adaptive functions (Uhl-Bien and Marion 2009) or engage in ambidextrous organizing (Raisch et al. 2009) to embrace, rather than shield from uncertainty.

Both of these views suggest that organizing—either via equilibrium maintenance or complexity—is critical for maintaining successful performance in the face of an uncertain future. Though both literatures build on the assumption that organizations are capable of withstanding uncertainty, it is less clear how to organize when the future is punctuated by a devastating disaster, such as those mentioned above, especially when the disaster completely obliterates any opportunity for business as usual. Despite creating devastating consequences and uncertainty, the disaster may also create a new future for the organization. To this end, we utilize insights from the resilient organizing literature (Weick & Sutcliffe, 2011) to explore how organizations bounce back and even beyond post-disaster to chart a new path for the future.

Resilient Organizing

Resilient organizing is critical for a contemporary organization's ability to confront, absorb and adapt to unplanned organizational events (Meyer 1982; Williams et al. 2017; Weick and Sutcliffe 2011). It embodies 'the process by which an actor (i.e. individual, organization or community) builds and uses its capability endowments to interact with the environment in a way that positively adjusts and maintains functioning prior to, during, and following adversity' (Williams et al. 2017, p. 742). Resilient organizing is characterized by three key elements. First, resilient organizing involves positive adjustments under difficult conditions (Lengnick-Hall et al. 2011; Luthans et al. 2007). These positive adjustments entail confidence in the organization's ability to bounce back and optimism that a new path for the future can be uncovered and pursued. Second, resilient organizing involves redefining success based on the new reality that the disaster creates (Lengnick-Hall et al. 2011). The effort here is on reestablishing a fit between the organization and the new environment through focusing on behaviors and activities that strengthen this fit, and shedding behaviors and activities that detract from it (Quinn and Worline 2008). Third, resilient organizing involves hardiness, or the organization's ability to experience and navigate the disaster (Mamouni Limnios et al. 2014; Kobasa et al. 1982). In this vein, resilient organizing compels organizations to experience the disaster (Weick and Sutcliffe 2011) and find resolution in achieving organization–environment fit in the new, post-disaster reality (Williams et al. 2017).

Although literature on resilient organizing implies that organizations will build a new future post-disaster when they embody resilient organizing (Weick and Sutcliffe 2011), the relation between resilient organizing and organizing for the future has not been systematically explored. Building on the previous literature (Lengnick-Hall et al. 2011; Mamouni Limnios et al. 2014; Weick and Sutcliffe 2011), we endeavor to uncover how resilient organizing in the wake of a disaster enabled a high-hazard organization to build a new future. In the subsequent section, we present an instrumental case study of BP's post-disaster activities following the Deepwater Horizon oil spill in 2010 to explicate how BP embodied resilient organizing to create a new future. We describe BP as a high-hazard (Perrow 1984), rather than a high-reliability (Weick and Roberts 1993) organization because, in the period before the disaster, BP did not embody the key elements of high-reliability: a preoccupation with failure, system-wide processes focused on reliability and a strong focus on learning (La Porte and Cansolini 1991; Milosevic et al. 2016; Roberts 1989).

Research Methods

The research context for this study is BP's post-disaster activities following the 2010 Deepwater Horizon oil spill. BP is a 'high-hazard organization' because it engages in 'potent activities with the power to kill or maim' (Gaba 2000, p. 85). These potent activities can create catastrophic events (Carroll 1998), which often arise because of (1) the unpredictability or unusual circumstances created by individuals and/or machines, (2) poor training or (3) management carelessness, all of which can produce disasters coupled with performance failures (Perrow 1984). High-hazard organizations often operate in demanding contexts, including extractive industries such as the petroleum industry; technology-intensive industries such as the aeronautic industry; or highly coordinated industries such as the transportation industry (Roberts 1989). Given our focus on resilient organizing post-disruptive and hazardous events, BP's activities following the Deepwater Horizon oil spill is an appropriate context for the study.

On April 20, 2010, an explosion, or blowout, occurred on BP's Deepwater Horizon rig. Workers, in an attempt to save their lives, abandoned the burning rig and jumped into the flaming ocean. Eleven workers were killed by the explosion and an additional 17 were injured (Ingersoll et al. 2012). A series of response efforts to find and treat workers on the rig and contain the spill ensued. The spill was contained in September 2010, after an estimated 4.9 million barrels of oil was discharged into the area. The oil spill reached the shoreline of all five states on the Gulf coast (Texas, Louisiana, Alabama, Mississippi and Florida), resulting in contamination of over 55 miles of shoreline (Lozano 2010). Given the large-scale nature of this disaster, many questioned whether BP could survive the disaster and ever return to its previous operational and financial performance.

To better understand how organizations that embody resilient organizing build a new future post-disaster, we collected conference call and presentation transcript data of BP executives following the spill, from 2010 to 2012 inclusively, in addition to other archival documents (see Table 10.1 for additional information on data sources and Fig. 10.1 for the data collection and analysis procedures). We followed previous research that emphasizes the critical role of human capital and especially

Table 10.1 Data sources

Data source	Title	Date	Source	Pages
Conference call	BP 2010 Q1 Earnings	2010	BP	20
Conference call	BP 2010 Q2 Earnings Q&A	2010	BP	23
Conference call	BP 2010 Q3 Earnings Q&A	2010	BP	15
Conference call	BP 2010 Q4 Earnings	2010	BP	32
Presentation	BP 2010 Strategy Presentation	2010	BP	27
Presentation	BP 2010 Results and Investor Presentation	2010	BP	32
Presentation	BP Strategy Presentation	2010	BP	4
Interview	In His Own Words: Forbes Q&A	2010	Forbes	11
Interview	Interview with BP CEO Tony Hayward	2010	Fox News	3
Interview	BP CEO Tony Hayward on Deepwater Horizon	2010	Der Spiegel	2
Interview	We will stop the leak	2010	BBC News	9
Article	BP oil spill: testing begins after installation of new containment cap	2010	The Guardian	2
Conference call	BP 2011 Q1 Earnings	2011	BP	7
Conference call	BP 2011 Q2 Earnings	2011	BP	16
Conference call	BP 2011 Q3 Earnings Q&A	2011	BP	34
Conference call	BP 2011 Q4 Earnings	2011	BP	20
Presentation	BP 2011 Results and Strategy	2011	BP	12
Presentation	BP 4Q11 Results and 2012 Strategy	2011	BP	72
Article	BP Oil Spill, One Year Later	2011	The Destin Log	1
Conference call	BP 2012 Q1 Earnings Q&A	2012	BP	19
Conference call	BP 2012 Q2 Earnings	2012	BP	23
Conference call	BP 2012 Q3 Earnings	2012	BP	20
Conference call	BP 2012 Q4 Earnings	2012	BP	28
Presentation	Upstream Investor Day	2012	BP	33
Presentation	Upstream Break-out	2012	BP	13
Presentation	2Q 2012 Results Presentation	2012	BP	2
Article	BP's oil spill setback	2012	The Times	1
Article	Trial to put BP oil spill in perspective; Also will hold magnifying glass on key players	2012	USA Today	2

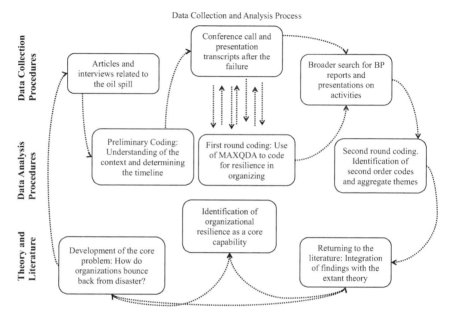

Fig. 10.1 Data collection and analysis process

senior managers in resilient organizing (Lengnick-Hall et al. 2011) and focused the analysis on how executives at BP organized for the future. We utilized MAXQDA software to analyze transcripts. We coded the data following inductive thematic analysis of both the semi-scripted and unscripted portions of the transcripts (Creswell 2012; Strauss and Corbin 1994). We adopted a categorical aggregation approach to data analysis (Creswell 2012; Stake 1995), identifying a collection of similar strands of data and allowing elevated themes to emerge.

Resilient Organizing and a New Path for the Future

In this study, we uncovered four related themes embodied in resilient organizing—the process that created a space for BP to chart a path for a new and different future: learning from the disaster, finding resolve, refocusing efforts and experiencing transformation through action. Evidence of these themes is interwoven in the subsequent paragraphs as well as being provided in Table 10.2. Learning from the disaster was the most salient and overarching finding, because it demonstrated the organization's ability to use the disaster as a learning opportunity through which it moved forward renewed. Finding resolve enabled BP to reconcile its internal and external relationships following the disaster. BP created a sense of urgency in order to refocus on its strengths and identify how to proceed toward a new future. Enacting resilience enabled BP to identify and serve stakeholders, and in doing so discover new opportunities for future success. Through these activities embodied in resilient organizing, BP was able to navigate the disaster, but also bounce back and beyond toward a new future. We depict our findings in Fig. 10.2.

Preparing for the New Future: Learning from the Disaster Through Resilient Organizing

Experiencing and navigating a disaster requires the organization to recognize that what's been done in the past cannot be acceptable when preparing for a new future (Weick 2010). In this vein, the organization must use the disaster as a learning opportunity to foster renewal (Carroll et al. 2002; Madsen 2008). For example, Madsen (2008) explored accidents in coal mining and proposed that individuals create new knowledge as they gain both direct and vicarious experience with minor accidents and major disasters—new knowledge that enables them to handle future obstacles. This is in line with research that suggests that changes in internal and/or external environments, such as disasters, represent chances for organizational renewal, which 'requires managers to change their mental models in response to environmental changes' (Barr et al. 1993, p. 16).

As depicted in Table 10.2 and Fig. 10.2, we discover that learning was manifested in the way the executives experienced and navigated the disaster. The oil spill appeared to humble BP because, especially during the Q&A sessions, the executives used statements like 'we don't know' or 'we're not sure' to temper responses to questions about the organization's operations, the environment or the market. In other words, we show that

Table 10.2 Aggregate themes and evidence of resilient organizing and a new path for the future

Aggregate theme	Embodiment of resilient organizing	Evidence from data
Preparing for the new future	To learn from the disaster	'There are many lessons to be learned for the industry from the Gulf of Mexico oil spill. We're committed to be at the forefront in sharing these lessons and building capability for the future. For example; in the course of mounting the largest surface spill response in history, we've made significant advances in skimming technology. We'll share these with the industry.' (BP 2010 Q2 Earnings Q&A)
		'We are the largest deepwater producer amongst the major international oil companies and are determined to take the lessons of the last year around the world and build on our know how and capability. I think we have a responsibility to do this.' (BP 2010 Q4 Earnings)
		'That integrity has included looking deep into the event and publically spreading the lessons learned. Last year's events were never going to be something that any company could recover from overnight. We have taken the event very seriously and embedded change in a serious way throughout the organisation.' (BP 2011 Q2 Earnings)
		'These voluntary performance standards go beyond existing regulatory obligations and reflect the Company's determination to apply the lessons learned from the incident.' (BP 2011 Q2 Earnings)
		'We're also committed to sharing what we have learned with the industry, regulators and governments worldwide and our teams have travelled to 20 countries to explain what we have learned.' (BP 2011 Q2 Earnings)

Building the new future	To find resolve	'BP's commitments run deep and we will fulfill the promises we have made to the Gulf States and Federal Government.' (BP 2010 Q2 Earnings Q&A)
		'I have the greatest admiration for Tony and what he's done as a Chief Executive of BP and how he transformed the Company over the last three years and for his unwavering dedication to ensuring BP will meet its commitments to the people of the American Gulf Coast.' (BP 2010 Q2 Earnings Q&A)
		'My final thoughts are with the families and friends of those who died on the 20 of April. We can and will compensate those financially affected by the spill and in the long run, we can restore the environmental impact on the Gulf Coast. But nothing can bring back the 11 people who lost their lives, and let's never forget them and it is important that everyone remembers them on days like today.' (BP 2010 Q2 Earnings Q&A)
		'We recognize the importance of rebuilding trust with those around us. This involves meeting our commitments in the US and resolving the uncertainties we face.' (BP 2011 Q2 Earnings)
		'We are meeting our commitments in the Gulf. We have already paid half of the $20 billion we committed for the Trust Fund to meet the costs of the Deepwater Horizon incident. We've reached settlements with Mitsui and Weatherford, and just last week announced settlement with Anadarko.' (BP 2011 Q3 Earnings Q&A)
Cultivating the new future	To refocus	'These results demonstrate both the strength of our underlying businesses and assets, and the determination of our employees to move the company forward.' (BP 2010 Q3 Earnings Q&A)
		'We plan to extend our footprint within these businesses with a focus on growth markets. All of this will continue to be achieved within a disciplined financial framework.' (BP 2011 Q3 Earnings Q&A)
		'All of this must be within a disciplined financial framework with active portfolio management to ensure a tight focus on quality positions.' (BP 2011 Q4 Earnings)
		'The 10-point plan will continue to provide the background, backbone for our program for value creation of what you can expect and what you can measure.' (BP 2011 Q4 Earnings)
		'Now, the move from a decentralized asset structure to a fully functional organization has been the biggest organizational change, we've taken on in the last 20 years. It's hard work, but it's going well. We now have the functional organization lined up with every dimension of operational delivery and with full-line accountability from our global approach to exploration and appraisal to a global approach to our major projects. This allows us to optimize activity choices effectively and execute them more reliably and efficiently.' (BP 2011 Q4 Earnings)

(continued)

Table 10.2 (continued)

Committing to the new future	To experience transformation through action	'All in all, we intend to focus on continuous reduction in risk, value as much as volume, and quality over quantity. It's about choices for the future rather than the legacy of the past.' (BP 2010 Q4 Earnings) 'So let's look more specifically at the events of 2010 and our response. Following the accident we acted rapidly to fulfil our commitments as a responsible party—to stop the oil flow and clean up the water and shoreline.' (BP 2010 Q4 Earnings) 'We have clear priorities and a programme of action. The main priority is to strengthen process safety and reduce operating risks. This requires the alignment of the organisation from top to bottom with a consistent set of standards and behaviours.' (BP 2010 Q4 Earnings) 'Our Safety and Operational Risk organization—or "S&OR"—is now in action to drive safe, reliable and compliant operations across BP. Its leader reports directly to me. S&OR has a highly experienced central team which maintains our global standards. It also has several hundred representatives who are deployed at the operating level in both the upstream and downstream businesses to drive the systematic and disciplined application of those standards. S&OR's work includes a strengthened audit function and we continue to build programs to develop capability.' (BP 2011 Q2 Earnings) 'Leadership determines the safety culture of the firm—and our action plan here includes requiring leaders to spend time in the field, observing and inspecting.' (BP 2011 Q4 Earnings)

In the Wake of Disaster: Resilient Organizing and a New Path... 203

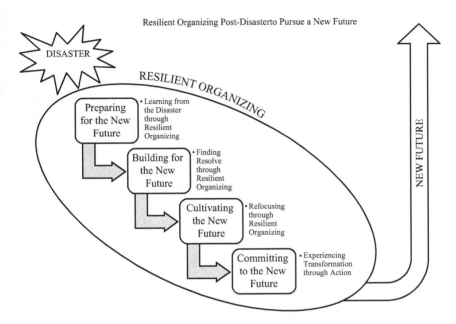

Fig. 10.2 Resilient organizing post-disaster to pursue a new future

resilient organizing involves tempered confidence (Radzevick and Moore 2011, p. 103) in which confidence is 'more muted, marked by lower peak confidence levels and wider distributions'. Tempered confidence is different from loss of confidence because BP believed it had a future post-disaster, but that future would be different. BP acknowledged that its operations had faltered, resulting in disaster. It demonstrated humility on the part of the organization, that it didn't have all the answers, and that, despite its best efforts, it was not invincible. This introduced a human, imperfect element to the organization that was a necessary part of learning from the disaster to prepare for a new future.

Executives often discussed 'finding the silver lining in the disaster and using it as a learning opportunity', to build the resilience needed for the future. Learning from mistakes embodied in resilient organizing enabled BP to address questions with regard to its ability to survive the disaster in the period between the blowout in April 2010 and when the well was capped in September 2010. Once BP survived the blowout, it turned its attention toward recovery from the disastrous oil spill via opportunities to learn (Bandura 1990; Bohn 2002). This was evident not just in the recognition executives paid toward the recovery efforts, but also in the consistent message that BP had the ability to learn and make improvements as a result of the Deepwater Horizon oil spill, and that it could leverage and apply these improvements to other global locations, positively impacting the future of the organization's operations as a whole:

What people have done in the Company, has worked incredibly hard to take a step back from drilling, how we manage our own activities, how we interact with contractors, have developed a new set of voluntary drilling standards in the Gulf which will adopt much of that and use it globally, and getting ready, and then approaching the authorities who I think value the work that we're doing and they see the changes and the commitment to it, and as a result of that we are step-by-step going back to work in the Gulf (BP 2011 Q3 Earnings).

To prepare for a new future, the conversation moved away from what went wrong to what could be gained and leveraged for a new future. This discussion encompassed not just learning from the spill, but also how the spill fostered new relationships between BP and other organizations in the industry, the government, and even seemingly unrelated industries, such as tourism and fishing. Indeed, BP executives recognized that: 'there is always more to do and in every crisis there is an opportunity' (BP 2010 Q2 Earnings). Thus, executives positively described how the oil spill fostered a platform for change in the organization—change that can prepare the organization for a new future through relationships with others:

> BP is a company that has been tested to the utmost, but we have resilient committed people. I believe we are equal to the test we face in this event that will simply underscore our determination to run our operations that are safe, secure, enabled to delivery energy for customers and value for shareholders. (BP 2012 Q4 Earnings)

Building the New Future: Finding Resolve Through Resilient Organizing

A large part of navigating the oil spill required BP to find resolve not only within the organization but also in its relationships with affected entities external to the organization. Finding resolve encapsulates organizational efforts to reconcile wrongdoing in order to generate a new future. Indeed, an important facet of resilience is being able to right a wrong. This search for resolution was consistently conveyed by the BP executives:

> We deeply regret the impact of this incident, and we are committed to healing and restoring the communities of the Gulf of Mexico, to finish immediate cleanup, to mitigate the long-term environmental impacts and to make whole those whose livelihood has been damaged. (BP 2010 Q2 Earnings Q&A)

We provide evidence for this theme in Table 10.2, and depict its role in the process embodied in resilient organizing in Fig. 10.2.

The executives often referred to finding resolve as making commitments: internally to operations or employees and externally to stakeholders and the environment. Internally, BP sought to find resolve by making changes to its operations and searching for ways to make the organization a better place for employees. The main contributors to the blowout on the Deepwater Horizon rig and the subsequent oil spill was a lack of maintenance and upgrades to the rig and its support systems, lack of procedural control and human error. As an organization, BP incurred debilitating costs from the blown rig: amassing approximately $374 million in lost revenues and the loss of 11 workers' lives. Resilient organizing through finding resolve with individuals working for BP enabled the organization to enact radical change in operations so that the failures that contributed to the blowout on the Deepwater Horizon rig would not be repeated. As indicated by one BP executive: 'we're fundamentally a different company in about how we manage risk and how the care that we take with our decisions. If you spend time with any of our management team and employees, I know you'll feel that' (BP 2011 Q3 Earnings Q&A).

Externally, BP sought to find resolve through commitments to stakeholders. In addition to lost revenues and the loss of 11 lives, the oil spill deeply impacted the gulf coast ecosystem, from fisheries to wetland wildlife to tourism (Ingersoll et al. 2012). Finding resolve by deepening its commitment to impacted external stakeholders was a common theme expressed by BP executives throughout the data: 'Following the accident we acted rapidly to fulfill our commitments as a responsible party' (BP 2010 Q4 Earnings). Resilience was important to finding resolve because, at the time of the disaster and especially in the months following its occurrence, BP came under scrutiny by many stakeholders. Resilience was critical to help the organization stay committed to finding resolve by 'righting the wrong' created by the oil spill with external and internal stakeholders.

Cultivating the New Future: Refocusing Through Resilient Organizing

In order for BP to cultivate the new future post-disaster, a sense of urgency emerged to refocus on the organization's strengths and on where it excels (see Fig. 10.2 and Table 10.2). In this effort, BP funneled resources back to its core, refocusing on where it found success in the past to cultivate its new future. Previous literature describes refocusing as realigning operations after disaster and participating in '"active" thinking about how best to respond, asking themselves what aspects they can control, what impact they can have, and how the breadth and duration of the crisis might be contained' (Margolis and Stoltz 2010, p. 4). We build on this insight and illustrate how BP refocused on its strengths as a global organization and recommitted itself as an industry leader with a new future. An executive described this as recommitment to quality: 'we are not focused on being the largest player in any of our businesses, but of holding the highest quality portfolio and operating it well. I believe this is beginning to show through in our competitive results' (BP 2010 Q4 Earnings).

Indeed, BP had amassed extensive experience and expertise by operating as an integrated energy company with locations across the globe and an employee base of industry experts. It subsequently leveraged this expertise and global reach as a necessary stepping stone to cultivating a new future, as described by the executive: 'BP has a portfolio of very strong businesses and great professional teams around the globe to ensure that we will be back on the on the road to recovery' (BP 2010 Q2 Earnings Q&A). The refocusing effort also encompassed the commitment to identifying and improving what, to that point, wasn't working well. High-hazard organizations, like BP, should be preoccupied with safety (Weick and Roberts 1993) and achieve a state of high-reliability—something BP lacked before the disaster occurred. Thus, a large part of the refocusing effort entailed reemphasizing safety and how instilling mistake-free operations would help cultivate a new future for the organization. By refocusing on what the organization hadn't done well and improving its areas of weakness, it could be repositioned to leverage its successes and recommit as an industry leader: '[operations] must be safe and reliable. Across BP, safety remains our number one priority' (BP 2010 Q1 Earnings).

This refocusing effort fundamentally changed 'business as usual' for BP. The disaster required BP to prepare for and build a new future. Through resilient organizing and by refocusing its efforts via organizational changes such as 10-point plans, new safety measures and improved documentation of operational processes, it could cultivate a new future that was markedly different than the one pursued prior to the disaster. As described by a BP executive: 'Our 10-point plan provides the roadmap, how we will play to our strengths and be safer, stronger, and simpler and more standardized' (BP 2011 Q4 Earnings).

Committing to the New Future: Experiencing Transformation Through Action

In order for BP to pursue a new future, it had to experience transformation by not just speaking of a new future, but acting upon it. This required executives at BP to see the disaster as a way to move forward renewed. Seeing the disaster as a way to move forward renewed helped BP recognize that it could bounce back to be something greater than it was before (Youssef and Luthans 2007). It wasn't just about coming back or surviving but, rather, the executives saw BP as a 'phoenix rising from the ashes': 'I believe strongly that the strength of this team is the way we see the opportunity to instill those lessons deeply into the fabric of our company, this will make BP a safer, stronger and more resilient company. And this is good business' (BP 2010 Q4 Earnings).

As depicted in Fig. 10.2 and Table 10.2, BP was confident that it could commit to a new future by acting on its obligations to others. That is, rather than just emphasizing the commitment in this stage of resilient organizing, the organization actualized its commitment through actions: 'This program will reset our position and create a stronger performing portfolio, while at the same time remove any worry about our financial strength' (BP 2010 Q2 Earnings). This sentiment—that transformation could only occur through action—was echoed by a BP executive: 'BP is a changing company as a result of what happened in 2010. I believe the changes will be for the better. These are not just words: you can see that from our actions' (BP 2010 Q4 Earnings).

Given its focus on actions that contributed to its commitment to a new future, BP executives looked for and emphasized promising signs of resilient organizing to signify that the transformation for the future was in fact taking place. One of the executives explained: 'The lubricants business … continued to deliver resilient profitability both year-on-year and compared with last' (BP 2012 Q2 Earnings). These signs led to BP distancing itself from the disaster on one hand, and painting a picture for the renewed future via transformation on the other. In other words, these turning points indicated that BP was purposefully committing to a new path for the future. A BP executive described the critical nature of turning points:

> So, we will have taken major steps forward on many fronts in a relatively short space of time. Of course, as we said upfront this has increased some costs and reduced some volumes, but these were short-term effects as we laid stronger foundations for the future. This has brought us to a clear turning point. (BP 2011 Q3 Earnings Q&A)

Resilient Organizing for the Future: Implications and Future Directions

The experience and actions of BP executives post-disaster show that resilient organizing may enable organizations to bounce back from a disaster and chart a path for a new future—a process that has not been systematically explored to date. Our findings build on previous work that points to the importance of learning (Weick and Sutcliffe 2011), leadership (Williams et al. 2017) and resolution (Lengnick-Hall et al. 2011) for organizing post-disaster and enabling the organization to navigate it. We contribute to this area of research by developing a process model embodied in resilient organizing that enables the organization to prepare for, build, cultivate and commit to a new future. In doing so, we extend the literature in three important ways. First, we illustrate the nature of resilient organizing in organizations in high-hazard contexts. Unlike other industries, organizations operating in these contexts embody two important differentiating characteristics: (1) they are often vital for the region they operate in due to the resources they possess as well as the services they provide (Milosevic et al. 2016) and (2) they are capable of experiencing disasters that can have far-reaching consequences (such as the oil spill discussed here) (LaPorte and Consolini 1991). Consequently, many of these organizations build dynamic structures that enable tight control on one hand, and responsive locales on the other (Milosevic et al. 2016; Weick and Roberts 1993) that enable them to minimize opportunities for disaster to occur. We contribute to this line of research by illustrating how organizations may bounce back and beyond when disasters do occur via embodying resilient organizing. We emphasize learning, resolution, resolve and transformation as key to the process embodied in resilient organizing. Although we provide insights on resilient organizing in high-hazard contexts, one of the key research questions emerging from our study is how does resilient organizing manifest in more mainstream (i.e. non-hazardous) organizations? Understanding this may be particularly important today when even failure-tolerant organizations experience constrained opportunities to learn from mistakes when faced with relentless competitive pressures and increasing customer expectations.

Second, we show how resilient organizing enables the organization to create a path for a new future by recognizing the organizational shortcomings that might have contributed to creating the disaster. By viewing the disaster as a learning opportunity, organizations can bounce back and beyond to experience transformation and commit to a new future. We show the process embodied in resilient organizing as BP was grappling with the devastating consequences of its own misjudgments—trying to make sense of what transpired while searching for ways to move forward. Our process model demonstrates resilient organizing and how a disaster triggers an organization to prepare for, build, cultivate and commit to a new future. However, given the importance of resilient organizing, both in terms of avoidance of errors (Weick et al. 2008) and bouncing back and beyond once those do occur, it may be important to explore the process embodied in resilient organizing a priori rather than in the wake of the disaster. This may be particularly important for organizations in high-hazard contexts where errors may have devastating consequences for all involved.

Finally, we show how resilient organizing enables organizations to leverage and recombine scarce resources when faced with a changing context (Rouse and Zietsma 2008). More specifically, we show that resilient organizing creates a space where organizations are able to identify which resources to use and how to leverage positive attributes to experience and overcome the disaster. To this end, resilient organizing may enable the organization to not just withstand the disaster but also prepare for a future renewed. Thus, we emphasize that resilient organizing enables organizations to experience, rather than fix, a disaster. In doing so, the organization can use the disaster to bounce back and beyond to a new future. However, given our focus on resilience in times of disaster, we have provided limited insight into the nature of resilience once the organization has been renewed. To this end, a final research question we suggest is: How do organizations leverage resilience for the future? More specifically, is resilient organizing relevant only in disaster situations, or is it relevant in times of relative stability (i.e. positive future) (Osborn et al. 2002)? We hope that future studies will address these questions and provide additional insight into the nature of resilient organizing.

References

Aldrich, Howard, and Diane Herker. 1977. Boundary Spanning Roles and Organization Structure. *Academy of Management Review* 2 (2): 217–230.
Bandura, Albert. 1990. Perceived Self-Efficacy in the Exercise of Control over AIDS Infection. *Evaluation and Program Planning* 13: 9–17.
Barr, Pamela S., J.L. Stimpert, and Anne S. Huff. 1993. Cognitive Change, Strategic Action and Organizational Renewal. *Strategic Management Journal* 13 (S1): 15–36.
Barreto, Ilídio. 2010. Dynamic Capabilities: A Review of Past Research and an Agenda for the Future. *Journal of Management* 36 (1): 256–280.
Bohn, James G. 2002. The Relationship of Perceived Leadership Behaviors to Organizational Efficacy. *Journal of Leadership & Organizational Studies* 9 (2): 65–79.
Carroll, John S. 1998. Organizational Learning Activities in High-Hazard Industries: The Logics Underlying Self-Analysis. *Journal of Management Studies* 35 (6): 699–717.
Carroll, John S., Jenny W. Rudolph, and Sachi Hatakenaka. 2002. Learning from Experience in High-Hazard Organizations. *Research in Organizational Behavior* 24: 87–137.
Chen, Ming-Jer, and Danny Miller. 2015. Reconceptualizing Competitive Dynamics: A Multidimensional Framework. *Strategic Management Journal* 36 (5): 758–775.
Creswell, John W. 2012. *Qualitative Inquiry and Research Design: Choosing Among Five Approaches*. 3rd ed. Thousand Oaks: Sage.
Daniel, Francis, Franz T. Lohrke, Charles J. Fornaciari, and R. Andrew Turner. 2004. Slack Resources and Firm Performance: A Meta-Analysis. *Journal of Business Research* 57 (6): 565–574.
Davis, Jason P., Kathleen M. Eisenhardt, and Christopher B. Bingham. 2009. Optimal Structure, Market Dynamism, and the Strategy of Simple Rules. *Administrative Science Quarterly* 54 (3): 413–452.
Foss, Nicolai J., Jacob Lyngsie, and Shaker A. Zahra. 2013. The Role of External Knowledge Sources and Organizational Design in the Process of Opportunity Exploitation. *Strategic Management Journal* 34 (12): 1453–1471.
Gaba, David M. 2000. Structural and Organizational Issues in Patient Safety: A Comparison of Health Care to Other High-Hazard Industries. *California Management Review* 43 (1): 83–102.

Gnyawali, Devi R., and Ravindranath Madhavan. 2001. Cooperative Networks and Competitive Dynamics: A Structural Embeddedness Perspective. *Academy of Management Review* 26: 431–445.

Hannah, Sean T., Mary Uhl-Bien, Bruce J. Avolio, and Fabrice L. Cavarretta. 2009. A Framework for Examining Leadership in Extreme Contexts. *The Leadership Quarterly* 20 (6): 897–919.

Helfat, Constance E., and Jeffrey A. Martin. 2015. Dynamic Managerial Capabilities: Review and Assessment of Managerial Impact on Strategic Change. *Journal of Management* 41 (5): 1281–1312.

Ingersoll, Christina, Richard M. Locke, and Cate Reavis. 2012. BP and the Deepwater Horizon Disaster of 2010. *MIT Sloan Management Case Collection* 10 (110): 1–28.

Kobasa, Suzanne C., Salvatore R. Maddi, and Stephen Kahn. 1982. Hardiness and Health: A Prospective Study. *Journal of Personality and Social Psychology* 42 (1): 168–177.

LaPorte, Todd R., and Paula M. Consolini. 1991. Working in Practice but Not in Theory: Theoretical Challenges of 'High-Reliability Organizations. *Journal of Public Administration Research and Theory: J-PART* 1 (1): 19–48.

Lengnick-Hall, Cynthia A., Tammy E. Beck, and Mark L. Lengnick-Hall. 2011. Developing a Capacity for Organizational Resilience Through Strategic Human Resource Management. *Human Resource Management Review* 21 (3): 243–255.

Limnios, Mamouni, Elena Alexandra, Tim Mazzarol, Anas Ghadouani, and Steven G.M. Schilizzi. 2014. The Resilience Architecture Framework: Four Organizational Archetypes. *European Management Journal* 32 (1): 104–116.

Lozano, Juan A. 2010. Tar Balls in Texas Mean Oil Hits All 5 Gulf States. *The Associated Press*, July 6. http://usatoday30.usatoday.com/news/nation/2010-07-05-Texas-oil-spill_N.htm.

Luthans, Fred, Carolyn M. Youssef, and Bruce J. Avolio. 2007. Psychological Capital: Investing and Developing Positive Organizational Behavior. In *Positive Organizational Behaviour*, ed. D. Nelson and C. Cooper. Thousand Oaks: Sage.

Madsen, Peter M. 2008. These Lives Will Not Be Lost in Vain: Organizational Learning from Disaster in U.S. Coal Mining. *Organization Science* 20 (5): 861–875.

Margolis, Joshua D., and Paul G. Stoltz. 2010. How to Bounce Back from Adversity. *Harvard Business Review* 88 (1–2): 86–92.

Meyer, Alan D. 1982. Adapting to Environmental Jolts. *Administrative Science Quarterly* 27 (4): 515–537.

Meyer, Alan D., Vibha Gaba, and Kenneth A. Colwell. 2005. Organizing far from Equilibrium: Nonlinear Change in Organizational Fields. *Organization Science* 16 (5): 456–473.

Milosevic, Ivana, A. Erin Bass, and Gwendolyn Combs. 2016. The Paradox of Knowledge Creation in a High-Reliability Organization: A Case Study. *Journal of Management* doi: 0149206315599215.

Osborn, Richard N., James G. Hunt, and Lawrence R. Jauch. 2002. Toward a Contextual Theory of Leadership. *The Leadership Quarterly* 13 (6): 797–837.

Perrow, Charles. 1984. *Normal Accidents: Living with High-Risk Technologies.* New York: Basic Books.

Quinn, Ryan W., and Monica C. Worline. 2008. Enabling Courageous Collective Action: Conversations from United Airlines Flight 93. *Organization Science* 19 (4): 497–516.

Radzevick, Joseph R., and Don A. Moore. 2011. Competing to Be Certain (But Wrong): Market Dynamics and Excessive Confidence in Judgment. *Management Science* 57 (1): 93–106.

Raisch, Sebastian, Julian Birkinshaw, Gilbert Probst, and Michael L. Tushman. 2009. Organizational Ambidexterity: Balancing Exploitation and Exploration for Sustained Performance. *Organization Science* 20 (4): 685–695.

Roberts, Karlene H. 1989. New Challenges in Organizational Research: High Reliability Organizations. *Organization & Environment* 3 (2): 111–125.

Rouse, Michael J, and Charlene Zietsma. 2008. *Responding to Weak Signals: An Empirical Investigation of Emergent Adaptive Capabilities.* OLKC 2008, The International Conference on Organizational Learning, Knowledge and Capabilities. Copenhagen, Denmark.

Schilke, Oliver. 2014. On the Contingent Value of Dynamic Capabilities for Competitive Advantage: The Nonlinear Moderating Effect of Environmental Dynamism. *Strategic Management Journal* 35 (2): 179–203.

Stake, Robert E. 1995. *The Art of Case Study Research.* Thousand Oaks: Sage.

Strauss, Anselm, and Juliet Corbin. 1994. Grounded Theory Methodology. *Handbook of Qualitative Research* 17: 273–285.

Uhl-Bien, Mary, and Russ Marion. 2009. Complexity Leadership in Bureaucratic Forms of Organizing: A Meso Model. *The Leadership Quarterly* 20 (4): 631–650.

Van Der Vegt, Gerben S., Peter Essens, Margareta Wahlström, and Gerard George. 2015. Managing Risk and Resilience. *Academy of Management Journal* 58 (4): 971–980.

Voss, Glenn B., Deepak Sirdeshmukh, and Zannie Giraud Voss. 2008. The Effects of Slack Resources and Environmental Threat on Product Exploration and Exploitation. *Academy of Management Journal* 51 (1): 147–164.

Wang, Heli, Jaepil Choi, Guoguang Wan, and John Qi Dong. 2016. Slack Resources and the Rent-Generating Potential of Firm-Specific Knowledge. *Journal of Management* 42 (2): 500–523.

Weick, Karl E. 2010. Reflections on Enacted Sensemaking in the Bhopal Disaster. *Journal of Management Studies* 47: 537–550.

Weick, Karl E., and Karlene H. Roberts. 1993. Collective Mind in Organizations: Heedful Interrelating on Flight Decks. *Administrative Science Quarterly* 38 (3): 357–381.

Weick, Karl E., and Kathleen M. Sutcliffe. 2011. *Managing the Unexpected: Resilient Performance in an Age of Uncertainty*. Vol. 8. New York: Wiley.

Weick, Karl E., Kathleen M. Sutcliffe, and Davide Obstfeld. 2008. Organizing for High Reliability: Processes of Collective Mindfulness. *Crisis Management* 3 (1): 81–123.

Williams, Trenton A., Daniel A. Gruber, Kathleen M. Sutcliffe, Dean A. Shepherd, and Eric Yanfei Zhao. 2017. Organizational Response to Adversity: Fusing Crisis Management and Resilience Research Streams. *Academy of Management Annals* 11 (2): 733–769.

Youssef, Carolyn M., and Fred Luthans. 2007. Positive Organizational Behavior in the Workplace. *Journal of Management* 33 (5): 774–800.

11

The Darkened Horizon: Two Modes of Organizing Pandemics

Matthias Leanza

Introduction

The horizon has darkened. The future no longer seems like an open space full of opportunities and risks. Rather, what is in store appears to be deeply threatening. Whether one thinks of global warming, terrorism or the continuing instability of the banking and finance sector, our expectations for the future in many areas of public life exemplify what Craig Calhoun (2004, p. 376) calls an 'emergency imaginary': 'A discourse of emergencies is now', as he wrote more than 10 years ago in a diagnosis that is even more applicable today, 'central to international affairs. It shapes not only humanitarian assistance, but also military intervention and the pursuit of public health.' Due to this emergency imaginary, we feel that our social institutions, our health and well-being, and even, as in the case of global warming, the future of mankind as such are deeply endangered.

M. Leanza (✉)
Sociology Department, University of Basel, Basel, Switzerland

This chapter deals with the recent darkening of the future horizon in the global fight against pandemics. Around the year 2000, the World Health Organization (WHO) started collaborating with a large number of local actors and made a concentrated effort to protect the world's population against emerging infectious diseases such as severe acute respiratory syndrome (SARS), swine flu, Ebola and Zika. Although efforts have been made so that the spread of future infectious diseases will be contained through early intervention, the actors in charge expect the extant measures to fail to some degree. They believe it is simply impossible to prevent all pandemics from happening. But steps can and should be taken through emergency preparation to lessen an unavoidable pandemic's impact. As Andrew Lakoff (2007, pp. 253–254) summarizes:

> Preparedness assumes the disruptive, potentially catastrophic nature of certain events. Since the probability and severity of such events cannot be calculated, the only way to avert catastrophes is to have plans to address them already in place and to have exercised for their eventuality—in other words, to maintain an ongoing capability to respond appropriately.

In recent years, scholars of security studies, cultural studies and other research areas have paid much attention to these developments in emergency preparedness, which, it is worth noting, are not limited to the domain of public health. This issue has primarily been addressed at two levels: first, by changing global security policies after the 9/11 attacks, and, second, by scrutinizing the narratives and rhetorical strategies through which the emergency imaginary is constructed and gains plausibility (e.g. Massumi 2005; Aradau and van Munster 2011; Horn 2014). In this chapter, I will focus on *organizations* as key actors in these processes of emergency planning. Without the capacity of organizations to produce binding decisions for their members, which allows them to plan for an uncertain future, pandemic preparedness would not be feasible—especially not on a global scale.

I will unfold my argument in four steps. With regard to the WHO, which was established in 1948, I will discuss the question of how supranational coordination and planning for the future is rendered possible by building formal organizations and organizational networks at a global level. I will then highlight some aspects of the attempts undertaken by the WHO and its partners after the year 2000 to fight pandemics on a global scale. My analysis of relevant policy papers, legal norms and manuals shows that two different though complementary strategies are applied: early intervention and emergency planning.[1] These are, as I will discuss more explicitly in the final section, two different kinds of organizing (for) the future or, to put it differently, two modes of how organizations manage pandemics. The overall aim of the empirical analysis offered in this chapter is to reconstruct organizational programmes and rationales rather than to give an account of the actual operations of these systems. The focus lies on public discourses and normative texts and not so much on the 'inside' of these organizations, meaning their day-to-day routines and practices.

Organizing Global Public Health

Contagious diseases do not stop at state borders. Pathogens circulate without regard for political and administrative spheres of influence. What Gilles Deleuze and Félix Guattari (2005, introduction) establish for rhizomes in general also applies to infection chains in particular: by growing rampantly, they produce a 'deterritorializing effect'. Pathogens connect distant regions and different kinds of people; zoonoses even trespass the boundary between animals and humans. By doing so, communicable diseases create spaces and communalities that did not exist before. This is also the reason why every epidemic requires new maps (e.g. Koch 2015).

Even though pathogens do not stop at state borders, sovereignty ends there, and the difficult terrain of diplomacy begins. The International Sanitary Conferences, which took place between 1851 and 1938, made a first step towards creating a global field of public health (Howard-Jones 1975; Bynum 1993). While the first couple of these conferences—there were 14 in all—dealt primarily, though not exclusively, with cholera, further diseases and topics were discussed and negotiated beginning in the 1880s. Laborious agreements regarding quarantine, inspection and surveillance measures were worked out and in some cases ratified.

But the field of global health diplomacy did not receive a coordination and control unit until 1948 with the establishment of the WHO as a specialized agency of the United Nations (Zimmer 2017). In passing the International Health Regulations (IHR) of 1969, which superseded the International Sanitation Regulations of 1951, the WHO established standards and norms with a legally binding character for its signatory states. The primary goal of these regulations was to provide 'maximum security against the international spread of disease with the minimum interference with world traffic' (WHO 1962, p. 5). To this end, epidemiological surveillance and alarm systems were installed in signatory states, or already existing structures were expanded. In addition, the WHO made more specific efforts to combat infectious diseases. One of the first large projects was the Global Malaria Eradication Program (1955–1969). In order to defeat the dangerous tropical disease, the insecticide DDT (dichloro-diphenyl-trichloroethane) was used liberally and repeatedly in over 60 countries. Even though certain regions profited from this measure, the actors in charge had to accept in the end that this goal was, on the whole, too ambitious (Zimmer 2017, pp. 198–362). More successful, however, was the vaccination programme against smallpox, which was enacted in 1959 and intensified in 1966 (Fenner et al. 1988, pp. 365–592, 1103–48). After roughly 20 years, it finally reached its goal. In 1980, the WHO announced: 'smallpox is dead!' (ibid., p. 1106).

Sovereign nation states use the mechanism of formal organization to cooperate in this and further policy areas of international concern. While 'leagues of subjects' within a state 'savour of unlawful design', as Thomas Hobbes (1651, p. 145) famously wrote in *Leviathan*, 'leagues between Commonwealths, over whom there is no human power established to keep them all in awe, are not only lawful, but also profitable for the time they last'. As well as mutual agreements and legally binding contracts, inter- or supranational organizations are a specific form taken by such leagues today. Drawing on Niklas Luhmann (1964), organizations can be perceived as a type of social system that is defined by formal membership roles and processes of decision-making. As inter- or supranational organizations demonstrate, not only natural but also legal persons, such as states, can become members of organizations. By entering an organization, sovereign nation states are, in principle, capable of producing collectively binding decisions on a global level, without losing their autonomy to a sovereign world state.

Today, a wide range of organizations constitute the global field of public health and disease control (Youde 2012, part 2). Besides the WHO, they include the World Bank, UNAIDS (which was established in 1996) and governmental and nongovernmental organizations. These organizations are the main action centres within the field of global public health. They deliver expertise, develop policies, launch programmes and mobilize the global community. To achieve their goals, they regularly ally with other organizations and build networks that can be activated when necessary. This especially holds true for the global fight against pandemics. In certain respects, in order to deal with an unfolding threat, organizational networks have to spread as rampantly as the pathogens themselves. Otherwise they will be unable to prevent further harm.

Early Intervention

In 2000, and thus very much in the shadow of the global AIDS crisis, the WHO laid the foundation for a new regime in the global fight against pandemics by setting up the Global Outbreak Alert and Response Network (GOARN). Since then it has acted in more than 130 cases (Mackenzie et al. 2014). Through 'rapid identification, verification and communication of threats' (WHO 2000, p. 2), GOARN seeks to contain the spread of infectious diseases, especially highly infectious ones. 'No single institution or country', so the main argument for this international cooperation goes, 'has all of the capacities to respond to international public health emergencies caused by epidemics and by new and emerging infectious diseases' (WHO n.d.). In 2002–2003, the SARS pandemic, which resulted in nearly 800 registered deaths, triggered a global health alarm due to GOARN, though the communication of this risk kindled by the predicted future *potential* of the pandemic outstripped, in certain respects, its *actual* impact (Smith 2006; Ong 2009).

The thoroughly redesigned IHR from 2005, which came into force in 2007, further developed and shaped this process. In contrast to the regulations it replaced—the International Sanitation and Health Regulations of 1951 and 1969, which, in comparison, were quite static since they only applied to a specific catalogue of communicable disease—the IHR now includes an early warning system that seeks to detect every potential 'Public Health Emergency of International Concern' (PHEIC) (Fidler 2005). The focus is on so-called points of entry, especially sea- and airports (WHO 2005a, pp. 11–15, 18–20). The member states of the WHO are responsible for implementing this global safety net at the local level; they must establish surveillance, contact and coordination units. In Germany, for instance, the Federal Office of Civil Protection and Disaster Assistance coordinates and oversees this implementation process in cooperation with the Robert Koch Institute.[2] The Robert Koch Institute, in turn, works with the European Centre for Disease Prevention and Control, which is an important partner of GOARN.[3]

Because many different kinds of organizations across a wide range of countries are connected in this network, it is necessary to standardize decision-making. Without the 'structural coupling' (Maturana and Varela 1987, pp. 75–80) of a shared decision process, cooperation and coordination between the participating organizations would not be feasible. Decisions would simply not be able to circulate within the network. Instead, they would have to be re-evaluated at every nodal point. For this reason, the IHR (WHO 2005a, pp. 43–46; see also WHO 2012) stipulates a risk-assessment matrix for signatory countries: after a local surveillance unit has detected an event 'that may constitute a Public Health Emergency of International Concern' (WHO 2005a, p. 43), three yes/no questions regarding its actual and potential impact must be answered. Then, it is determined whether the event should be rated as unusual or unexpected. If the answers are all positive, the WHO must be notified within 24 hours. If they are not all positive, there are two further levels of such yes/no questions, which address the risk of international spread and, in a final step, the possibility that countries or other entities would impose international travel or trade restrictions in response to the outbreak. The answers to these questions then determine whether notifying the WHO is required or not.

This decision-making tool can be understood as an 'attention filter'. Since there are now many globally connected surveillance units, mechanisms have to be installed that not only allow and trigger but also suppress communication between them. Otherwise, the network would be flooded with more information than it can process. In other words, the elements within this structure would be too closely connected. Nonetheless, the goal is to set the attention thresholds as low as possible. Even if notifying the WHO is not required at one point, the event in question has to be kept under surveillance. This, of course, does not prevent the situation from being evaluated incorrectly. The 2014–2015 Ebola outbreak, for instance, was declared a PHEIC relatively late because the actors in charge initially viewed it as only a local problem of a poor region in West Africa (Lakoff et al. 2015).

Together with the attention thresholds, the reaction times of the relevant public health organizations are also to be lowered. While the decentralized structure of networks improves the alarm function, since attention is widely distributed, a missing or weakly developed action centre has an adverse effect on the intervention function. In defiance of all network rhetoric, the global fight against pandemics cannot proceed without the structural principles of hierarchy and the distribution of tasks. According to the IHR, after being informed of a positive risk assessment by local organizations, the WHO has to provide them with further information and instructions and send experts to the affected regions (WHO 2005a, pp. 11–15, 31–34, 40–42). The WHO is the 'obligatory passage point' (Callon 1984) for this process. A combination of the network, hierarchy and the distribution of tasks aims to make rapid intervention possible.

Even though the WHO wants, in principle, global traffic to flow without any hindrance, in some cases a temporary interruption of the circulation of goods and people may be considered necessary to protect global public health (Stephenson 2011; Opitz 2015). The IHR and national regulations therefore stipulate travel restrictions on certain people and allow measures like quarantine and isolation to be imposed.[4] In an age of global flows and a greater awareness of fundamental rights, this specific kind of intervention has to some extent become problematic. As the first principle of the IHR states 'The implementation of these

Regulations shall be with full respect for the dignity, human rights and fundamental freedoms of persons' (WHO 2005a, p. 10). Similarly, the WHO (2013, p. 47) explained in 2013: 'In emergency situations, the enjoyment of individual human rights and civil liberties may have to be limited in the public interest. However, efforts to protect individual rights should be part of any policy. Measures that limit individual rights and civil liberties must be necessary, reasonable, proportional, equitable, non-discriminatory and in full compliance with national and international laws.' Besides these reservations, the global fight against pandemics cannot proceed without restrictive measures, as the SARS pandemic and Ebola outbreak have shown.

Emergency Planning

Although a concentrated global effort has been made to prevent pandemics via early detection and rapid response, the actors in charge expect them to happen. It is only a matter of time, they believe, until the next health emergency occurs. 'Influenza experts agree', the WHO (2005b, pp. vi–vii) warned in 2005, 'that another pandemic is likely to happen but are unable to say when. The specific characteristics of a future pandemic virus cannot be predicted. Nobody knows how pathogenic a new virus would be, and which age groups it would affect.' Although its exact time of emergence, etiological nature and epidemiological distribution pattern may be unpredictable, it is considered a fact that the next pandemic will occur in the near or not so distant future (see also MacPhil 2010). A glossy brochure on pandemic planning by the US Department of Homeland Security (2006, p. 10) presented a similar way of looking at things. In a quotation in the brochure, the US Secretary of Health and Human Services, Mike Leavitt, states: 'Some will say this discussion of the Avian Flu is an overreaction. Some may say, "Did we cry the wolf?" The reality is that if the H5N1 virus does not trigger pandemic flu, there will be another virus that will.'

This statement demonstrates that the general trend of thinking about emergencies and accidents as 'normal' has permeated the field of global public health (Calhoun 2004; Lakoff 2007). In the 1970s, in many areas of public life, the future was already perceived as unsafe and potentially catastrophic, and this view was intensified after the year 2000 (Aradau and van Munster 2011; Horn 2014). Although the future horizon has darkened with the looming prospect of ecological, political and economic crises, not all hope is lost. The occurrence of (massive) harm might be inevitable, but what can yet be prevented is the worst-case scenario. It is assumed that through emergency planning, the severity of the potential damage can be lessened. This is what 'preparedness' means: acting, deciding and governing under conditions of insecurity (Lentzos and Rose 2009; Anderson 2010). As the WHO explained in 2005: 'Although it is not considered feasible to halt the spread of a pandemic virus, it should be possible to minimize its consequences through advance preparation to meet the challenge' (WHO 2005c, p. 3). In his address to the 62nd World Health Assembly in 2009, the UN Secretary-General, Ban Ki-moon, posed the same question: 'How do we build resilience in an age of unpredictability and interconnection?' Through emergency planning is his answer. 'This is how we will make the global community more resilient. This is how we ensure that wherever the next threat to health, peace or economic stability may emerge, we will be ready.'

Of special interest in this regard are critical infrastructures, such as water supply, that might be affected by a severe disease outbreak.[5] Local public health emergency centres, which the WHO (2015) assembled as a global network (EOC-Net) in 2012, are responsible for the planning process. As well as taking stock of the available resources and contingents in a country or region, scenario planning and agent-based computer simulations are of fundamental importance[6]; they enable us to imagine possible scenarios via enactment and visualization without the necessity of making any probability assumptions. It is believed that in order to be prepared for future emergencies, the organizational imagination must to some extent be liberated from restrictions imposed by past experiences.

Organizations are of crucial importance for the planning process. For instance, the WHO guidelines, *Whole-of-Society Pandemic Readiness*, aim 'to support integrated planning and preparations for pandemic influenza across all sectors of society, including public and private sector organizations and essential services' (WHO 2009, p. 5). To strengthen organizational resiliency against the stresses and strains that may result from a pandemic, thorough preparation is required. 'In the absence of early and effective planning, countries may face wider social and economic disruption, significant threats to the continuity of essential services, lower production levels, distribution difficulties, and shortages of supplies' (p. 5). Emergency planning is furthermore imperative since '[t]he failure of businesses to sustain operations would add to the economic consequences of a pandemic. Some business sectors will be especially vulnerable (e.g. those dependent on tourism and travel), and certain groups in society are likely to suffer more than others' (p. 5). The 'Readiness Framework' therefore asks all organizations that provide basic services such as food, water, health, defence, law and order, finance, transportation, telecommunications and energy to prepare for pandemics via simulation exercises and drills based on different scenarios. Furthermore, business continuity plans have to be developed. For this purpose, a pandemic coordinator should be assigned to oversee the planning process. All organizations that are crucial for public life are strongly advised to prepare themselves for the next pandemic. Given the interdependencies between these organizations, general preparedness is the only way to prevent a complete breakdown. Or, as the guidelines put it: 'It is prudent to plan for the worst, while hoping for the best' (p. 8).

Pandemics in a Society of Organizations

According to Lakoff (2010), today's highly differentiated field of global health is characterized by, among other things, the juxtaposition of two regimes: global health security and humanitarian biomedicine. 'Each of these regimes', he elaborates, 'combines normative and technical elements to provide a rationale for managing infectious disease on a global scale. They each envision a form of social life that requires the fulfillment of an innovative technological project. However, the two regimes rest on very different visions of both the social order that is at stake in global health and the most appropriate technical means of achieving it' (p. 59). While global health security turns its attention to emerging infectious diseases, 'which are seen to threaten wealthy countries, and which typically (though not always) emanate from Asia, sub-Saharan Africa, Latin

America', humanitarian biomedicine deals with 'diseases that currently afflict the poorer nations of the world, such as malaria, tuberculosis, and HIV/AIDS' (p. 60).

In addition to Lakoff's (2010, see also 2007) distinction between the two regimes of global health, my analysis highlights two layers that are encompassed by one of these regimes, the global fight against emerging infectious diseases. The two modes of organizing of such pandemics are not organizations themselves. They are programmes that structure the organizational decision-making and the corresponding membership roles. In analysing these programmes, the focus lies not so much on the actual operation of the system—since it is always a creative translation of cognitive and normative schemes into concrete practice—but rather on the intended actions of the system. A first line of defence is defined through early intervention. For this purpose, a wide and ramified organizational network is put in place. It allows pandemics to be detected while they are still emerging, and this makes it possible to limit the potential scope of their spread. Because the goal is to prevent a further unfolding of potential threats into actual damages, time is of the essence in detection. The organizations must react quickly while ensuring, at same time, that the information they generate, process and communicate to others is reliable. The strategies they decide to follow also have to be effective. Otherwise the primary goal is not achieved: preventing pandemics from happening.

In reality, this highly ambitious goal cannot always be met. But the organizations in charge know their limitations and are therefore requested to install a second line of defence: emergency planning. All organizations that are critical for society are asked to have emergency plans in place so that, in the case of a pandemic, they would still be able to react. The goal here shifts from preventing the spread of disease towards securing the 'autopoiesis' (Maturana and Varela 1987, pp. 47–52) of the system, meaning its ability to reproduce itself even under enormous environmental pressures. While early intervention requires organizations to be capable of acting quickly, pandemic preparedness aims to produce robust systems that are immune to breakdown.

Despite operating from different angles, these two modes of organizing pandemics are complementary. Early intervention relates to preventable damages. The underlying assumption is that pandemics can be avoided through early detection and rapid response. The future scenario of early intervention is therefore an altogether positive one, in which organizations are capable of doing their job in the face of danger, namely containing infectious diseases. Pandemic preparedness, in contrast, works not with one but with two kinds of damages: *primary damages*, which cannot be prevented, and *preventable consequential damages*, which pose an existential threat. The aim is still to prevent harm, but preparedness does not focus on the pandemics per se but on the fatal repercussions that they might have for societies. This is a minimal form of prevention, and it is no longer believed that it is possible to escape such a pandemic unscathed. Both modes of relating to the future do not exclude but rather complement each other. If early intervention does not work in a specific scenario, there is still a second prevention strategy, which, of course, can only partially contain the effects of the pandemic since (massive) harm will have already occurred. But by strengthening the resilience of organizations and societies, pandemic preparedness aims to preserve existential functions and operations.

In his by now classic essay from 1991, Charles Perrow describes organizations, especially large ones, as a key element of modern societies. According to Perrow, fundamental social functions are maintained by private and public organizations. This also holds true for responding to pandemics. In a 'society of organizations' (Perrow 1991), it is organizations and their professionals who manage pandemics. But two kinds of organizations have to be distinguished which correspond to the two modes or programmes for managing emerging infectious diseases: first, organizations and professionals in the public health sector try to prevent pandemics through early intervention (and further preventative measures, such as vaccination programmes). It is their job to protect the general public from health risks; this is the purpose of these specialized organizations and the goal of their corresponding professional activities. Second, and in contrast, all organizations that provide basic services for society are asked to make emergency plans and prepare themselves for the next pandemic. This includes public health organizations but is also addressed to, first and foremost, private and public organizations that provide food, water, defence, law and order, finance, transportation, telecommunications and energy.

The second programme is no less ambitious than the first. Organizations and professionals in the public health sector may not always succeed in preventing pandemics: as we have seen, they are well aware of this fact, and that is why emergency plans are developed in the first place. But this implies that, in principle, all organizations that provide basic services for society have to professionalize themselves in this specific area. One could describe this as a 'colonization' of non-health organizations through public health imperatives. This is, of course, not a completely new development if one considers, for instance, company doctors or health and safety officers. Furthermore, many large organizations have undergone a professionalization in areas that do not traditionally belong to their core activities, such as when they maintain legal, public relations or research departments, or when they offer childcare or psychological counselling to their employees. To some extent, this is a likely consequence of the 'functional differentiation of modern societies' (Luhmann 1997): even if organizations are typically specialized in providing only one or two services, they have to take further social functions into account. What is new here is the kind of task, that is, preparing for pandemics in order to prevent the worst-case scenario—a complete breakdown of the system that would result from the absence of employees due to illness. In a society of organizations, the autopoiesis of society as whole cannot be separated from the autopoiesis of its organizations. Preserving society in a public health emergency depends on keeping organizations functional.

Notes

1. In the empirical reconstruction of these strategies I use material and passages from my book *Die Zeit der Prävention* (2017, pp. 258–264).
2. The implementation of the IHR in Germany is regulated by the following laws: the 'Gesetz zu den Internationalen Gesundheitsvorschriften (2005) (IGV)' of 2007 and the 'Gesetz zur Durchführung der Internationalen Gesundheitsvorschriften (2005) und zur Änderung weiterer Gesetze' of 2013.
3. For a list of the so-called coordinating competent bodies of each member state, see European Centre for Disease Prevention and Control (n.d.).

4. For measures of disease assessment and control in Germany, see the 'Gesetz zur Neuordnung seuchenrechtlicher Vorschriften' of 2000.
5. For a discussion of how biosecurity intertwines the field of public health with the security sector, see also Fidler and Gostin (2008).
6. See, for example, Orbann et al. (2017).

References

Anderson, Ben. 2010. Preemption, Precaution, Preparedness: Anticipatory Action and Future Geographies. *Progress in Human Geography* 34: 777–798.
Aradau, Claudia, and Rens van Munster. 2011. *Politics of Catastrophe: Genealogies of the Unknown*. London: Routledge.
Bynum, William F. 1993. Policing Hearts of Darkness: Aspects of the International Sanitary Conferences. *History and Philosophy of the Life Sciences* 15: 421–434.
Calhoun, Craig. 2004. A World of Emergencies: Fear, Intervention, and the Limits of Cosmopolitan Order. *Canadian Review of Sociology/Revue canadienne de Sociologie* 41: 373–395.
Callon, Michel. 1984. Some Elements of a Sociology of Translation: Domestication of the Scallops and the Fishermen of St Brieuc Bay. *The Sociological Review* 32: 196–233.
Deleuze, Gilles, and Félix Guattari. 2005. *A Thousand Plateaus: Capitalism and Schizophrenia*. Minneapolis: University of Minnesota Press.
Department of Homeland Security. 2006. *Pandemic Influenza: Preparedness, Response, and Recovery; Guide for Critical Infrastructure and Key Resources*. Washington, DC: Department of Homeland Security.
European Centre for Disease Prevention and Control. n.d. Competent Bodies. https://ecdc.europa.eu/en/about-us/governance/competent-bodies. Accessed 31 July 2017.
Fenner, Frank, Donald Ainslie Hendemon, Isao Arita, Zdeněk Ježek, and Ivan Danilovich Ladnyi. 1988. *Smallpox and Its Eradication*. Geneva: WHO.
Fidler, David P. 2005. From International Sanitary Conventions to Global Health Security: The New International Health Regulations. *Chinese Journal of International Law* (2): 325–392.
Fidler, David P., and Lawrence O. Gostin. 2008. *Biosecurity in the Global Age: Biological Weapons, Public Health, and the Rule of Law*. Stanford: Stanford Law and Politics.

Hobbes, Thomas. 1651. *Leviathan or the Matter, Forme & Power of a Common-Wealth Ecclesiasticall and Civil*. London: Crooke.
Horn, Eva. 2014. *Zukunft als Katastrophe*. Frankfurt am Main: Fischer.
Howard-Jones, Norman. 1975. *The Scientific Background of the International Sanitary Conferences 1851–1938*. Geneva: WHO.
Ki-moon, Ban. 2009. Resilience and Solidarity: Our Best Response to Crisis. Address to the 62nd World Health Assembly, May 19, 2009. http://www.who.int/mediacentre/events/2009/wha62/secretary_general_speech_20090519/en/. Accessed 31 July 2017.
Koch, Tom. 2015. Mapping Medical Disasters: Ebola Makes Old Lessons, New. *Disaster Medicine and Public Health Preparedness* 9: 66–73.
Lakoff, Andrew. 2007. Preparing for the Next Emergency. *Public Culture* 19 (2): 247–271.
Lakoff, Andrew. 2010. Two Regimes of Global Health. *Humanity* 1: 59–79.
Lakoff, Andrew, Stephen J. Collier, and Christopher Kelty, eds. 2015. Ebola's Ecologies. *Limn* 5, Special issue.
Leanza, Matthias. 2017. Die Zeit der Prävention. *Eine Genealogie*. Weilerswist: Velbrück.
Lentzos, Filippa, and Nikolas Rose. 2009. Governing Insecurity: Contingency Planning, Protection, Resilience. *Economy and Society* 38: 230–254.
Luhmann, Niklas. 1964. *Funktionen und Folgen formaler Organisation*. Berlin: Duncker & Humblot.
———. 1997. *Die Gesellschaft der Gesellschaft*. Frankfurt am Main: Suhrkamp.
Mackenzie, John S., Patrick Dury, Ray R. Arthur, Michael J. Ryan, Thomas Grein, Raphel Slattery, Sameera Suri, Christine Tiffany Domingo, and Armand Bejtullahu. 2014. The Global Outbreak Alert and Response Network. *Global Public Health* 9: 1023–1039.
MacPhil, Theresa. 2010. A Predictable Unpredictability: The 2009 H1N1 Pandemic and the Concept of 'Strategic Uncertainty' Within Global Public Health. *Behemoth* 3 (3): 57–77.
Massumi, Brian. 2005. Fear (The Spectrum Said). *Positions: East Asia Cultures Critique* 13: 31–48.
Maturana, Humberto R., and Francisco J. Varela. 1987. *The Tree of Knowledge: The Biological Roots of Human Understanding*. Boston: Shambhala.
Ong, Aihwa. 2009. Assembling Around SARS: Technology, Body Heat, and Political Fever in Risk Society. In *Ulrich Becks kosmopolitisches Projekt: Auf dem Weg in eine andere Soziologie*, ed. Angelika Poferl and Nathan Snaider, 81–89. Baden-Baden: Nomos.

Opitz, Sven. 2015. Regulating Epidemic Space: The *nomos* of Global Circulation. *Journal of International Relations and Development* 18 (1): 1–22.
Orbann, Carolyn, Lisa Sattenspiel, Erin Miller, and Jessica Dimka. 2017. Defining Epidemics in Computer Simulation Models: How Do Definitions Influence Conclusions? *Epidemics* 19: 24–32.
Perrow, Charles. 1991. A Society of Organizations. *Theory and Society* 20: 725–762.
Smith, Richard D. 2006. Responding to Global Infectious Disease Outbreaks: Lessons from SARS on the Role of Risk Perception, Communication and Management. *Social Science & Medicine* 63: 3113–3123.
Stephenson, Niamh. 2011. Emerging Infectious Diseases/Emerging Forms of Biological Sovereignty. *Science, Technology, & Human Values* 36: 616–637.
WHO. 1962. International Sanitation Regulations. *Treaty Series* 22.
———. 2000. *Global Outbreak Alert and Response: Report of a WHO Meeting*. Geneva: WHO.
———. 2005a. *International Health Regulations*. Geneva: WHO.
———. 2005b. *WHO Checklist for Influenza Pandemic Preparedness Planning*. Geneva: WHO.
———. 2005c. *WHO Global Influenza Preparedness Plan: The Role of WHO and Recommendations for National Measures Before and During Pandemics*. Geneva: WHO.
———. 2009. *Whole-of-Society Pandemic Readiness*. WHO Guidelines for Pandemic Preparedness and Response in the Non-Health Sector. Geneva: WHO.
———. 2012. *Rapid Risk Assessment of Acute Public Health Events*. Geneva: WHO.
———. 2013. *Pandemic Influenza Risk Management: WHO Interim Guide*. Geneva: WHO.
———. 2015. *Framework for a Public Health Emergency Operations Centre*. Geneva: WHO.
———. n.d. Global Outbreak Alert and Response Network-GOARN: Partnership in Outbreak Response. http://www.who.int/csr/outbreaknetwork/goarnenglish.pdf. Accessed 31 July 2017.
Youde, Jeremy. 2012. *Global Health Governance*. Cambridge: Polity Press.
Zimmer, Thomas. 2017. *Welt ohne Krankheit: Geschichte der internationalen Gesundheitspolitik 1940–1970*. Göttingen: Wallstein.

12

Managing the Digital Transformation: Preparing Cities for the Future

Markus Kowalski, Anja Danner-Schröder, and Gordon Müller-Seitz

Introduction

One of the most pervasive and important challenges in today's world is how organizations should cope with and negotiate the temporal mode of the future in the light of digital transformation (March 1995; Beckert 2016; Koch et al. 2016). This uncertainty is also the reason why the future is always an 'imagined' one (Beckert 2016, p. 220), as no future state is predictable. Whereas research usually explains contemporary occurrences from actions that happened in the past (David 1985; Mahoney 2000), Beckert (2016) argues that 'the future matters just as much as history matters' (Beckert 2016, p. 58). Hence, building on this conceptual shift from analyzing the past toward the important role that the temporal mode of the future plays in exploring processes of organizing, scholars appear now to be able to observe and understand the way to deal with things to come (Beckert 2016).

M. Kowalski (✉) • A. Danner-Schröder • G. Müller-Seitz
University of Kaiserslautern, Kaiserslautern, Germany

Based on the important role of time in organizing the future, Hernes (2014) introduces 'a process theory of organization'. Therein, Hernes (2014) elucidates the role of time in terms of the relationship between past, present and future actions. According to the core message of this process theory, that the world we are living in is in a continuous flow in time, actions that happened in the past, present or future cannot be seen as distinct forms. The linkage between the flow of time can be seen in the term 'lived present' (Hernes 2014; Hussenot and Missonier 2016). Hence, actions that happened in the past need to be interpreted in the present to make sense of them so that insights of this interpretation can be projected into future actions. However, the openness of the future triggers uncertainty, so that organizing is not the result of the calculation of optimal choices. Therefore, an imagined future can be characterized as resulting from actions, shedding light on how expectations drive organizations or plunge them into a crisis when imagined futures fail to be accomplished (Beckert 2016).

Despite the importance of the temporal mode for the future (Langley et al. 2013), we still lack an understanding of which processes and practices organizations use to handle the future. To this end, one of the most pervasive challenges in today's organizational landscape—in organizing things to come—is that of coping with the issues imposed by the ever-increasing need to face digitalization (Yoo et al. 2012). Special issues in academia (e.g. Bharadwaj et al. 2013 on the topic of 'digital business strategy' in *MIS Quarterly*) or publications in popular science (e.g. Brynjolfsson and McAfee 2014) document the high level of relevance of this topic for the interplay of the future and organizing. For the purposes of our study, we comprehend digitalization in a broad sense as the use of modern information and communication technology to transform processes and services of organizations (Bharadwaj et al. 2013). Hence, digitalization requires a linkage of heterogeneous knowledge sources in terms of a precarious and unknown future (March 1995; Nonaka 1995). Beyond that, the value proposition of organizations will be influenced by the use of digital tools and therefore organizations will have to build new capabilities and practices to be responsive in terms of changes in society (Berman 2012; Fitzgerald et al. 2014).

Viewed from this perspective, and given that the need to engage with digitalization is widely acknowledged, it is astonishing that we lack a thorough understanding of how to actually engage with digitalization in this imagined future (Beckert 2016), which is commonly assumed as a tight interplay between the future and organizing. In other words, whereas the objective itself is clear (i.e. further digitalize resources and processes of almost any kind), we know little about how to actually engage in managing the digital transformation. One avenue that informs our reasoning and is evident from the empirical data, are the insights about research on interorganizational networks (Sydow et al. 2016). Managing these networks of three or more organizations is a common phenomenon across industries and fields, as actors join forces for mutual benefit (e.g. sharing financial burdens related to a planned innovation). For example, Lange et al. (2013) offer an informative account of how innovation networks in the semiconductor industry actually ideate future technological states, which are subsequently turned from fictitious states into reality.

Against this background, the present chapter is guided by the following explorative guiding research question: How can actors manage the digital transformation? This question seems particularly relevant in the highly dynamic context of digital transformation, where the future is constantly challenged by unexpected events in the form of novel technological developments that are constantly evolving (Yoo et al. 2012; Beckert 2016). We aim to address this question in this chapter by using a framework that shows the different phases in an innovation network for the management of digital transformation (Yoo et al. 2012).

Research Methodology and Data

Research Setting

To address our research question, we employed an in-depth explorative case study (Eisenhardt 1989; Yin 2013), analyzing a network of different cities in Germany, whose aim is to develop new city management concepts for the future. The objective of the network is to encourage cities to engage in transformation processes with the aim of creating more livable cities. Therefore, this kind of network initiative was designed as an enabler for new forms of collaboration. The particular network investigated in the case was venturing toward becoming a digitally transformed city. To this end, cities as research objects are intriguing, as they are the true engines of the economy, and they are where the majority of human activity has always taken place (Jacobs 1985; Neal 2013).

The traditional and static notion of an urban area is increasingly challenged by novel developments that also substantially affect cities and their management—digitalization being a prime example—and, in particular, the importance of digital technology platforms or open government initiatives developed for the purpose of encouraging collaborative approaches between different stakeholders (Doz and Kosonen 2007; Yoo et al. 2012; Müller-Seitz et al. 2016). To this end, the network we analyzed in our study supports cities in their efforts to become highly innovative and to get ready for organizing the future. Currently, the network consists of 24 industrial organizations, 11 research institutes, 14 city halls and 4 non-profit organizations. These organizations are working together to identify and develop new markets and potential within future urban systems. This kind of transdisciplinary constellation within the network has created the conditions for collaborative and innovative projects and solutions in terms of digital transformation.

The processes within the network can be divided into different phases, such as an 'initial preparatory phase', where a group of experts observed cities for a period of time, deepening their understanding on site, or a 'test city setting', to explore the potential use of digital tools in urban areas and to develop a systemic understanding of how digital transformation will influence the future of cities. Based on the findings of these in-depth analyses, dedicated 'lighthouse projects' are conceptualized with local stakeholders and the insights are disseminated both as part of a strategic roadmap for future development in the test city setting and beyond the whole network. For instance, an intermodal mobility system, developed as a lighthouse project, was tested in multiple test city settings at different locations under real conditions. An intermodal mobility hub builds upon various mobility solutions (including components such as car and bike sharing, public transport, smart parking or co-working spaces). This mobility system can optimize services in a central location via a cloud-based information and communication technology solution for the intelligent operation of shared vehicles between organizations.

This endeavor, to achieve a deep understanding of cities across different areas, was a central feature of this transdisciplinary network. Hence, it was possible for the organizations to identify the structures, processes and the most important drivers of future city development in terms of managing digital transformation. To this end, the network partners contributed complementary knowledge and competencies to develop strategies for the city of the future, as is common in more conventional interorganizational settings (Vanhaverbeke and Cloodt 2006; Sydow et al. 2016).

Data Collection

The first author collected data over a period of 25 months, starting in January 2015. To this end, our process of data collection unfolded in five steps. During the first six months, the first author participated in several meetings and conferences held by the innovation network in order to become familiar with the processes, relationships and the culture of the network (Kirk and Miller 1986). This setting allowed the first author to develop an overarching, systematic understanding in terms of how the urban area worked and what kind of relationships existed within the network. Building on this, the first author conducted seven initial interviews with the key stakeholders of the network over the next three months. Therein, he followed a semi-structured interview approach asking about their experience of engaging with digital transformation and their thoughts on its use and effects for future city development. Second, the first author participated in a test city setting as an embedded observer for almost two weeks. Within these two weeks, he participated in several meetings with key stakeholders of the city, closely observed the on-site interviews between the expert group and local key stakeholders and participated in daily roundtable discussions with the group of experts in order to discuss and reflect on the collected insights. These observations were particularly useful in understanding how relationships are actually enacted, in what kind of ways they adapt to particular situations and to identify practices and processes to actually manage the digital transformation (Feldman and Orlikowski 2011).

During and after all observations in the test city setting, as well as in the network meetings, the first author took extensive field notes. Afterward, he conducted, in a fourth step, 22 more formal interviews and participated in meetings of the innovation network (in sum: 52 meetings). These formal semi-structured interviews were of utmost importance to discuss our observations with key stakeholders in the innovation network and to deepen our understanding of how they engage with digital transformation, as well as to obtain their thoughts on its use and effects for future city development. All formal interviews were taped and transcribed, which amounted to 594 transcribed pages. Finally, we also collected and reviewed a wide range of secondary sources, for example, articles, brochures, annual reports, presentations, newspaper articles, articles and material drawn from the network and key stakeholder websites and newsletters. These documents (in sum: 2529 pages) helped us to gain a better understanding of the network context and provided us with an overview of past and current activities of the innovation network. Table 12.1 provides an overview of the data collected during the study.

Table 12.1 Data basis of the research study

Source of data	Quantity
Period of data collection	25 months
Interviews in sum	29
Initial interviews	7
Formal interviews	22
Transcripts	594 pages
Meetings	52
Test city setting	14 days of observation
Secondary sources	2529 pages

Data Analysis

The analysis of the data took place in four stages. In a first stage, we organized our collected data in terms of an event history chronology (Van de Ven and Poole 1990). This was done by chronologically ordering notes taken from the raw data (e.g. interview transcripts, field notes from the observations in the test city setting and secondary sources). Second, we started to code our data set with in-vivo codes using the language of the organizations within the network (Glaser and Strauss 1967).

In a third stage, we worked intensively with our interview transcripts, field notes and documents to undertake a more focused analysis of the three phases of an innovation network as identified below. While analyzing the collected data using an inductive approach (Miles and Huberman 1994), we were interested in the practices and processes that take place in and also between these three phases. To this end, we started to code our data again by iteratively moving from the collected data to existing theory and emerging patterns of practices (Eisenhardt 1989). This coding step, connected to the event history chronology of the first stage, helped us to categorize three different phases of an innovation network needed to manage digital transformation: (I) Understand, (II) Create and (III) Disseminate. As a final step, we discussed our results with the group of experts within the network and received feedback from them. This interactive feedback session was also an important step in checking the descriptive validity of our findings (Yin 2013).

Findings

In our study, we identified three phases in which the city organized digital transformation by making use of an innovation network. Our analysis reveals that the different phases of an innovation network produce dynamic developments. The members of the innovation network engage in the following phases: (I) Understand, (II) Create and (III) Disseminate. Building on this differentiation, we will introduce each phase in turn and provide a short description of its characteristics. We will then elucidate the practices and processes utilized in order to explore the modus operandi of organizations that are managing the digital transformation.

Phase I: Understand

In the first phase, in order to understand urban systems in general, a transdisciplinary approach was introduced by analyzing the opportunities and challenges of innovative actors in terms of digitalization in urban areas. To this end, a group of experts conducted a large-scale analysis of selected cities. This in-depth analysis included intensive on-site visits and expert interviews to identify fields of action for an open and future-oriented urban development. Anna,[1] a member of the group of experts, described the starting point of this phase as follows:

> At the beginning of the project we wanted to understand the urban system in general. It was a complex task, so we came up with the idea, that we need people and organizations of different disciplines and branches to proceed our task [...]. Within this team, we identified key sectors in the city and screened best practice examples and successful innovations that were implemented in the organizations to overcome the individual future challenges.

The group of experts therefore interviewed for-profit organizations about their current innovation projects in terms of digitalization, whereas public organizations were asked about their requirements for the development of innovative cities for the future. The main challenges of digitalization in urban areas were obtained from the results of the systematic analysis. Andreas, who is a general manager of one of the companies within the network, described the phase of getting to know each other in the network as:

> Right from the beginning, we worked together with different organizations, like city halls, research institutes and companies. All were arranged in a network, so we had a kind of an innovative form of collaboration. All were asked about their problems and all sorts of solutions they have developed until the project started [...]. During the first months, we came up with the perception, that only when organizations talk open to each other and when they were actively asked, they can get help from the network members to solve their needs.

Ben, a participating member from a research institute, made a similar argument for the stage of understanding, saying:

> An important thing is, that you need a common topic [...]. We set up also different groups with their own topic, so that we can work efficient within the group and everyone can participate.

This form of collaboration allows cities to be analyzed in a systematic way according to their opportunities, challenges and operational projects in order to shape an open future. Thereby, new and well-matched collaborations between for-profit and public organizations were enabled. For example, the movement-sensitive lighting technology developed by a multinational lighting manufacturer provided the solution to a requirement identified by a city administration to light their streets at night, providing light only when an individual walked by a particular street light. As a result, electricity consumption and its associated costs for the city administration were reduced and its citizens benefited from more secure streets at night. Gregor, a senior executive president of a manufacturing company which is part of the network, described the practices and processes he used to come up with this innovation in the network:

> We participated in conferences, talked about our core competencies and within these working groups we came up with new fields of action [...]. But you cannot organize all steps within such an innovation process, there are accidental meetings like the time we came up with the lighting technology. It happened during the dinner, because the other company listened to my talk before [...]. People who talk about subjects with different perspectives, this is what you need.

As these quotes reveal, network members had, at least retrospectively, the impression that the phase of understanding was of utmost importance, first, to closely observe the participants' competencies and fields of actions in terms of the digital transformation and, second, to understand how relationships are actually enacted within the network. Beyond that, a digital platform was implemented at the network level to support the exchange of ideas, and best-practice visits of urban areas were enabled.

Phase II: Create

In this phase, one city region was analyzed in detail in terms of its urban actors and their capabilities and requirements. Hence, structures and patterns needed to be identified and a description of the existing relationships between the various organizations of the urban area was required. Michael, the department head of a city hall, stated:

> From the viewpoint of a city hall we need a form of collaboration with the industry and research institutes. We have quite a lot of needs but we do have not the money to fulfill them [...]. Therefore, test city settings are needed as a real laboratory, where different organizations support us to manage the challenges of the digital world.

The test city setting can, hence, be used as a real-world testing ground for new ideas and technologies. Lighthouse projects, like the intermodal mobility hub, were implemented in several cities to optimize individual mobility services in central locations and new forms of collaboration were set up. Using information and communication technology, the provision of urban-related data for organizations and citizens has been identified as an important tool for organizing the future in urban areas. To this end, technological advances have led to a growing digital transformation of cities in recent years. Hence, modern information and communication technology offers a new potential for the use of data, as in the case of the intermodal mobility hub. We observed that strong alliances between research institutes, city halls and for-profit organizations were established and that the coordination of lighthouse projects became the starting point for a long-term transformation process, as Robert, a member of the group of experts, told us:

> A test city setting is the perfect opportunity to come up with different fields of actions. One important task urban areas have to accomplish in the future is to manage the digital transformation. Hence, at the beginning, not every kind of organization would agree with me that this is an important task. First, you have to explain and understand the characteristics of digitalization, but also the problems and opportunities within this field of

action [...]. Second, if you do this in an authentic way, you can establish trustworthy relationships, so that you can find solutions to overcome this challenge together.

For example, Anna recalled the following experience:

At the beginning of a test city setting, the people within the organizations are doubtful about the things we do. But when we talk to them, they are happy to tell us about their needs and are surprised that, for example, a company in the same city has a solution to their needs and that we can arrange a meeting with them, or when we explain that we had a solution to this problem in another city, they stare at us—like we were from a different world.

On the basis of these local in-depth analyses and the results thereof, potential areas for intervention, such as citizen participation, connected public spaces or a modular urban mobility system, were identified. The practice of sharing transdisciplinary expertise within the test city setting provides an opportunity to identify processes to actually manage digital transformation and to open up the network to new experts and ideas from outside the network boundaries. At the end of phase II, all projects were evaluated to identify technology and action-fields in terms of digital transformation, as well as the key drivers relevant to future urban developments.

Phase III: Disseminate

The third phase is also directly related to phases I and II. Hence, this phase is characterized by organizing and designing structures to orchestrate the network at the network level and to develop new kinds of business models to deal with the challenges of the future. Using an extensive repertoire of practices and processes used to actually manage digital transformation, which was developed and tested within numerous test city settings and organizations since the project has started, solutions for cities and enterprises were disseminated and implemented in other cities. To this end, the objective in this phase was to take advantage of the potential of cities. For example, cities can play a key role in terms of mediating the balance between energy supply and energy demand in the local city network. As Harald, a project leader in a city hall, explained:

> You have to think in systems […]. Only when you understand all the relationships and needs within such an innovation network, can you build trust between the members. We established our partnerships within and also beyond the boundaries of the network; we are now like a big family—we talk about all our problems and help each other.

In this way, network members learned how to use the digital platform or technologies for any given situation. As Anna explained:

> We had physical meetings within the test city setting but also digital meetings via Skype or other technologies to talk to organizations outside the network boundaries, from different regions or countries, who wanted to deepen their know-how in the area of digital technologies in a future-oriented urban area.

Based on the findings of the test city settings and the lighthouse projects in phase II of the innovation network, additional fields of action were developed. Hence, an urban data platform was established as a tool box to push participation and transparency through intelligent use of data. Members of the network can now pick and choose between digital technology solutions and supporting practices for their individual problems in terms of the digital transformation. Hence, the findings of the test city setting have been disseminated, for example, in business models that enable future cities to use digitalization and to establish reliable partnerships. Sebastian, who is a project leader in a research institute, explained this in the following statement:

> We all have the need to collaborate on future-oriented topics, like water or energy management or in terms of issues like the digital revolution […]. You have to be a visionary, because the future does not exist yet. Therefore, you have to divide big topics into smaller ones and do several projects with different experts to find solutions for existing or perhaps unknown problems. Learn from the past and from each other. From my point of view, this kind of learning culture would be the solution for quite a lot of our problems.

Harald, a project leader in a city hall, summed up the task of dealing with things to come as: 'The task we all have now to accomplish is to make use of the technologies. We have to do this together, because no one person has the expertise.'

Thus, in terms of the practices and processes that are associated with organizing innovative cities for the future, the three phases depicted here should not be seen as rigid, but rather as a starting point for an adaptive process in the age of digitalization for developing practices for the innovative cities for the future.

A Framework to Manage Digital Transformation Within an Innovation Network

The above findings demonstrate how a network of organizations manages the challenges of digital transformation and shed light on the practices and processes needed for self-improvement in different phases. The developed framework, as shown in Fig. 12.1, illustrates and summarizes our main findings by highlighting three phases of an innovation network, in which each phase is characterized by several tasks and objectives, which should be fulfilled by the members of the network to organize the future in urban areas within a transdisciplinary team (Pohl 2008).

Therefore, phase I was important for understanding the challenges of digitalization in urban areas, sharing a common language and building a high level of trust. Thereafter, using digital technologies, sharing ideas and mechanisms to make them fit with internal processes (Chesbrough and Appleyard 2007; Dahlander and Gann 2010) was a challenge for the network members. Right from the beginning, they developed a culture of trust so they could behave and talk openly to each other. Subsequently, the development and use of digital tools followed a path of experimentation loops. The implementation of a digital platform (Yoo et al. 2012) and the launch of lighthouse projects in phase II were the result of using these digital tools and practices. As a consequence, learning processes and a sharing of resources were encouraged.

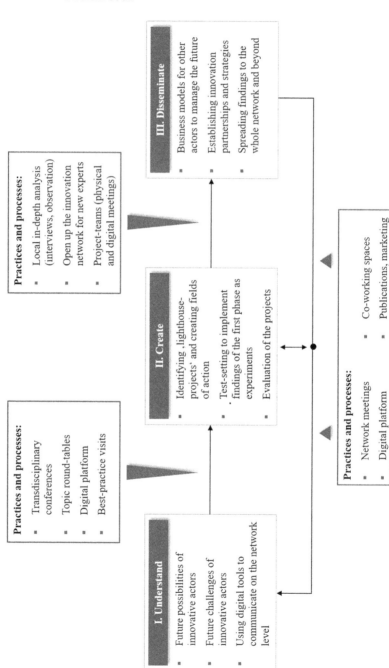

Fig. 12.1 Three phases of an innovation network to manage the challenges of the future

Having analyzed the organizations in detail in terms of their urban role and their opportunities and requirements, and using the extensive repertoire of data collected during phases I and II, phase III of the network was characterized by implementing and disseminating solutions within and beyond the network to manage digital transformation. Finally, innovation partnerships and business models for future cities were established to address future challenges and shape an open future. Overall, these findings helped network members to select specific digital tools and mechanisms that support and enhance the ability of organizations to manage digital transformation. Whereas digital technologies and tools are the basis for transdisciplinary communication beyond the boundaries of a network or organizations, the combination and balance of physical and digital practices are key for innovative activities.

Discussion

Motivated by the central debate about the crucial role that the temporal mode of the future plays in organizing (Beckert 2016), and how digital transformation as one important imagined future can be recognized and managed, our study set out to explore a framework to deal with the challenges of this important imagined future. Our findings contribute to the literature on organizing for the future by focusing on cities as informative urban test beds for engaging with digitalization.

Temporal Mode of the Future

As our findings illustrate, decision-making in society cannot be understood as the result of a rational procedure of decisions. Whereas authors interested in path dependence (David 1985; Mahoney 2000) explain contemporary occurrences from actions that happened in the past, our finding resonates with insights from the process theory of organizing by Hernes (2014) that the imagined future matters just as much as past actions (Beckert 2016). Thus, it is important to note that 'time matters'

(Hernes 2014, p. viii). Consequently, the process theory of organization offered by Hernes (2014) refers to the idea of a continuous state of flow in time.

To this end, actions that happened in the past must be interpreted to make sense of them in the present so that insights from this interpretation can be projected into future actions. Based on the important role of time in organizing the future, the temporal mode of time can be seen as a systemic loop, where the imagined future is important for understanding the present and thereby for interpreting the present as being determined through the past (Hayashi 1988; Beckert 2016). As our findings within the innovation network illustrate, it is important to understand the present in terms of knowing how to engage different actors to jointly cope with the challenges of an imagined future and manage digital transformation (Yoo et al. 2012; Beckert 2016). By sharing ideas and working together within the network, the imagined future is becoming clearer and the network's members are now better informed about how to engage with future challenges. Hence, the challenge of organizing the future becomes more specific in terms of processes required in the present. Beyond that, our study illustrates that the ability of network members to imagine the future in Beckert's (2016) sense can be a source of innovation and novelty. In terms of multiple collaborative forms within the network (Sydow et al. 2016), the members can imagine a world that is different from the existing one. Hence, in this kind of collaborative form, organizations are also involved in the creation and dissemination of technologies and in building a suitable test ground within an innovation network to solve the challenges of a complex task, like the digital transformation (Yoo 2010; Yoo et al. 2012).

For-Profit Versus a Variety of Organizations Within an Innovation Network

Previous debates on interorganizational networks concentrate primarily on for-profit organizations that are organized in the form of innovation networks to collectively share resources and knowledge, develop ideas and therefore to promote innovations (Vanhaverbeke and Cloodt 2006). As regards the literature on interorganizational networks (Sydow et al. 2016), these networks were characterized by a high level of network formality (contractual agreements) to structure the processes and knowledge flows within the interorganizational network (Simard and West 2008). Our study contributes to this network perspective by outlining why including a variety of organizations (e.g. for-profit, research and public organizations) within an innovation network is important for solving the challenges of a complex task, like digital transformation (Vanhaverbeke and Cloodt 2006; Yoo 2010; Yoo et al. 2012).

As our findings illustrate, innovation networks offer an at least partially generalizable account of how to engage different actors to jointly cope with the challenges for the future (Dahlander and Gann 2010). A network structure containing key stakeholders for knowledge generation and technology development, such as for-profit organizations or research institutes, may be referred to as an innovation system (Cooke 2001). Hence, public organizations are also involved in the creation and dissemination of technologies and in building a suitable test ground. Furthermore, geographic proximity and the external flow of knowledge are two aspects which can enhance innovation output. This finding resonates with insights from the idea of open innovation (Chesbrough 2003), which holds that organizations can increase their innovation potential by opening up their organizational boundaries and by interacting with partners (Chesbrough 2003; Dahlander and Gann 2010). Seen this way, the question is no longer whether an innovation network is an appropriate tool, but which organizations are part of the network and, moreover, how collaboration takes places within the network to organize (for) the future.

The transdisciplinary project design chosen for this study represents an enabler for new forms of collaboration in the task of transforming cities into sustainable environments for the future. In terms of dealing with an unknown future, organizations within the project develop solutions for current problems, create and establish new partnerships and try to connect relevant stakeholders at an early stage of the process. There is, however, a need for further process-based theorizing in research on strategic and future-oriented organizations. This kind of process thinking may involve consideration of the way (how and why) things (organizations, relationships, systems) act, change and evolve over time (Langley 2007).

Conclusion

Viewed from the perspective of the temporal mode of the future, the goal of our study was to deepen our understanding of how to actually engage with the temporal mode of the future and to analyze how organizations can manage things to come. In other words, whereas the objective is clear (i.e. further digitalize resources and processes of almost any kind), we know very little about how to manage digital transformation in terms of the future. This chapter is based on an explorative in-depth case study which observed how a set of innovation networks in Germany worked in a collaborative fashion to develop new city management concepts to generate an intelligent and sustainable city of the future by means of digital transformation.

With these observations in mind, the present study contributes to the existing literature on organizing for the future as follows. First, we elucidate the practices and processes of how to actually manage the digital transformation, venturing beyond accounts that merely sketch the future as a digitalized imagined state. Second, the proposed phase framework offers an at least partially generalizable account of how to engage different actors to jointly cope with the challenges of digitalization. Third, we draw—at least indirectly—attention to cities as informative urban laboratories for engagement with digitalization, offering an alternative setting to contemplate when compared to more usual settings of digitalization efforts, such as companies (e.g. von Hippel 2005) or crowds (e.g. Afuah and Tucci 2012).

Acknowledgments The authors thank the members of the research network and particularly all those members who gave up their time to be available for an interview. We would also like to thank the editors of this book, Matthias Wenzel and Hannes Krämer, for their constructive feedback which helped in shaping the contribution of this chapter.

Note

1. In terms of data privacy, pseudonyms are used for the names of the interview partners.

References

Afuah, Allan, and Christopher I. Tucci. 2012. Crowdsourcing as a Solution to Distant Search. *Academy of Management Review* 37 (3): 355–375.
Beckert, Jens. 2016. *Imagined Futures: Expectations and Capitalist Dynamics*. Cambridge, MA: Harvard University Press.
Berman, Saul J. 2012. Digital Transformation: Opportunities to Create New Business Models. *Strategy and Leadership* 40 (2): 16–24.
Bharadwaj, Anandhi, Omar A. El Sawy, Paul A. Pavlou, and N. Venkatraman. 2013. Digital Business Strategy: Toward a Next Generation of Insights. *MIS Quarterly* 37 (2): 471–482.
Brynjolfsson, Erik, and Andrew McAfee. 2014. *The Second Machine Age*. Kulmbach: Plassen Verlag.
Chesbrough, Henry W. 2003. *Open Innovation. The New Imperative for Creating and Profiting from Technology*. Boston: Harvard Business Review Press.
Chesbrough, Henry W., and Melissa M. Appleyard. 2007. Open Innovation and Strategy. *California Management Review* 50 (1): 57–76.
Cooke, Philip. 2001. Regional Innovation Systems, Clusters, and the Knowledge Economy. *Industrial and Corporate Change* 10 (4): 945–974.
Dahlander, Linus, and David M. Gann. 2010. How Open Is Innovation? *Research Policy* 39 (6): 699–709.
David, Paul A. 1985. Clio and the Economics of QWERTY. *American Economic Review* 75 (2): 332–337.
Doz, Yves L., and Mikko Kosonen. 2007. *Fast Strategy: How Strategic Agility Will Help You Stay Ahead of the Game*. Pearson: Pearson Prentice Hall.
Eisenhardt, Kathleen M. 1989. Building Theories from Case Study Research. *Academy of Management Review* 14 (4): 532–550.
Feldman, Martha, and Wanda J. Orlikowski. 2011. Theorizing Practice and Practicing Theory. *Organization Science* 22 (5): 1240–1253.
Fitzgerald, Michael, Nina Kruschwitz, Didier Bonnet, and Michael Welch. 2014. Embracing Digital Technology: A New Strategic Imperative. *MIT Sloan Management Review* 55 (2): 1–12.

Glaser, Barney G., and Anselm L. Strauss. 1967. *The Discovery of Grounded Theory: Strategies for Qualitative Research*. New York: Aldine Publishing.
Hayashi, Shuji. 1988. *Culture and Management in Japan*. Tokyo: University of Tokyo Press.
Hernes, Tor. 2014. *A Process Theory of Organization*. Oxford: Oxford University Press.
Hussenot, Anthony, and Stéphanie Missonier. 2016. Encompassing Stability and Novelty in Organization Studies: An Events-Based Approach. *Organization Studies* 37 (4): 523–546.
Jacobs, Jane. 1985. *Cities and the Wealth of Nations*. New York: Vintage.
Kirk, Jerome, and Marc L. Miller. 1986. *Reliability and Validity in Qualitative Research*. Newbury Park: Sage.
Koch, Jochen, Hannes Krämer, Andreas Reckwitz, and Matthias Wenzel. 2016. Zum Umgang mit Zukunft in Organisationen – eine praxistheoretische Perspektive. *Managementforschung* 26 (1): 161–184.
Lange, Knut, Jörg Sydow, Gordon Müller-Seitz, and Arnold Windeler. 2013. Financing Innovations in Uncertain Networks – Roadmap Gap Filling in the Semiconductor Industry. *Research Policy* 42 (39): 647–661.
Langley, Ann. 2007. Process Thinking in Strategic Organization. *Strategic Organization* 5 (3): 271–282.
Langley, Ann, Clive Smallman, Haridimos Tsoukas, and Andrew H. Van de Ven. 2013. Process Studies of Change in Organization and Management: Unveiling Temporality, Activity and Flow. *Academy of Management Journal* 56 (1): 1–13.
Mahoney, James. 2000. Path Dependence in Historical Sociology. *Theory and Society* 29 (4): 507–548.
March, James G. 1995. The Future, Disposable Organizations and the Rigidities of Imagination. *Organization* 2 (3/4): 427–440.
Miles, Matthew B., and A. Michael Huberman. 1994. *Qualitative Data Analysis: An Expanded Sourcebook*. Thousand Oaks: Sage.
Müller-Seitz, Gordon, Mischa Seiter, and Patrick Wenz. 2016. *Was ist eine Smart City?* Wiesbaden: Gabler.
Neal, Zachary P. 2013. *The Connected City: How Networks Are Shaping the Modern Metropolis*. New York/London: Routledge.
Nonaka, Iikujiro. 1995. A Dynamic Theory of Organizational Knowledge Creation. *Organization Science* 5 (1): 14–37.
Pohl, Christian. 2008. From Science to Policy Through Transdisciplinary Research. *Environmental Science and Policy* 11 (1): 46–53.

Simard, Caroline, and Joel West. 2008. Knowledge Networks and the Geographic Locus of Innovation. In *Open Innovation. Researching a New Paradigm*, ed. Henry W. Chesbrough, Wim Vanhaverbeke, and Joel West, 220–240. Oxford: Oxford University Press.
Sydow, Jörg, Elke Schüßler, and Gordon Müller-Seitz. 2016. *Managing Interorganizational Relations – Debates and Cases*. London: Palgrave.
van de Ven, Andrew H., and Marshall S. Poole. 1990. Methods for Studying Innovation Development in the Minnesota Innovation Research Program. *Organization Science* 1 (3): 313–335.
Vanhaverbeke, Wim, and Myriam Cloodt. 2006. Open Innovation in Value Networks. In Open Innovation. Researching a New Paradigm, edited by Henry W. Chesbrough, Wim Vanhaverbeke, and Joel West, 258–281. Oxford: Oxford University Press.
von Hippel, Eric. 2005. *Democratizing Innovation*. Boston: MIT Press.
Yin, Robert K. 2013. *Case Study Research: Design and Methods*. Thousand Oaks: Sage.
Yoo, Youngjin. 2010. Computing in Everyday Life: A Call for Research on Experiential Computing. *MIS Quarterly* 34 (2): 213–231.
Yoo, Youngjin, R.J. Boland, K. Lyytinen, and A. Majchrzak. 2012. Organizing for Innovation in the Digitized World. *Organization Science* 23 (5): 1398–1408.

13

Creating Collective Futures: How Roadmaps and Conferences Reconfigure the Institutional Field of Semiconductor Manufacturing

Uli Meyer, Cornelius Schubert, and Arnold Windeler

Introduction

As a collectively created future, technical progress is at once organized and organizing. This duality becomes especially apparent in fields dominated by the pursuits of forging technical advancements and shaping the future. This chapter elaborates on practices of collectively creating social and technical futures by drawing on an empirical study we conducted in the semiconductor industry[1]—a field in which progress, prediction and promise have weighed heavily on many different levels since its emergence in the 1950s.

U. Meyer (✉)
Munich Center for Technology in Society, Technical University Munich, Munich, Germany

C. Schubert
Department of Social Sciences, University of Siegen, Siegen, Germany

A. Windeler
Department of Sociology, Technical University Berlin, Berlin, Germany

© The Author(s) 2018
H. Krämer, M. Wenzel (eds.), *How Organizations Manage the Future*,
https://doi.org/10.1007/978-3-319-74506-0_13

Central to our understanding of the semiconductor industry as an organizational field are the processes of institutionalization which take place within the field. They are part of what DiMaggio and Powell (1983) call the 'institutional life' of a field. Yet, this institutional life does not simply emerge and persist. In most cases, actors have put a great deal of effort into configuring and maintaining the field's institutional life. We also find the concept of 'institutional work' (Lawrence and Suddaby 2006) useful to understand how actors actively attempt to shape a field's institutional structure and its future development. More often than not, the institutional work within an organizational field draws on regularly occurring events, like conferences or trade fairs. Such events facilitate the creation and maintenance of the institutional order and we refer to them in the following as 'field-configuring events' or FCEs (Lampel and Meyer 2008).

In this chapter, we use technology development in the semiconductor industry as a case in point to illustrate how FCEs form locales of institutional work that shape the institutional life and hence the future of organizations, technologies and organizational fields. Research and development (R&D) in the semiconductor industry has emerged as a global, very explicitly organized organizational field in the past few decades. This can be attributed to the high investment costs and short innovation cycles that present extremely demanding challenges for the coordination of technology development in the industry. Due to the sheer impossibility of exploring all feasible options based solely on technical criteria, collective coordination is required on a field level. Creating new technologies therefore also depends on moulding and reshaping suitable institutions.

We will focus on two specific FCEs and the practices related to their organization: organizing roadmaps and organizing conferences. Both practices have emerged as central means of coordination within the field over the past 20 years (Schubert et al. 2013). Thus, they are central institutionalized practices for innovating semiconductor manufacturing technology (for conferences, see also Möllering 2010), not least because more direct forms of organizing are not available in the field. No single organization or other actor is able to take direct control over events in the field or to dictate the industry's next steps. We consider how these practices of organizing roadmaps and conferences create the necessary institutional certainties to transfer initially fictitious beliefs or 'anticipative structures' (van Lente and Rip 1998) into shared expectations which then become requirements and, finally, material arrangements used for the high-volume manufacturing of computer chips.

In addition to the illustration provided by the two empirical FCE cases, this chapter contributes to an understanding of institutional work in terms of the collective practices of creating and managing organizational futures: first, because collective institutional work is crucial for the creation and maintenance of shared expectations at the level of a field's institutional life[2]; second, because it can be fruitfully integrated into a broader practice theory approach that allows us to trace and analyse the collective creation of futures in the field as the medium and result of social practice; third, because institutional work always holds the potential for future institutional change, since it aims not only to maintain but also to disrupt and create institutions.

Theoretical Perspective

As indicated, three core concepts from neo-institutional theory are particularly relevant for this study: organizational fields, FCEs and institutional work. The concept of organizational fields emphasizes the interrelations, interactions and mutual influences of organizations as they engage with a shared issue and thereby constitute an area of institutional life (DiMaggio and Powell 1983; Hoffman 1999; Wooten and Hoffman 2008). Organizational fields constitute an important arena for the general activity of technological development, since they provide specific impulses regarding the pace and alignment of processes as well as the commitment of the involved actors.

FCEs are a specific form of 'temporary social organizations' (Lampel and Meyer 2008, p. 1026). They are specifically designed to influence organizational fields as they 'assemble in one location actors from diverse professional, organizational, and geographical backgrounds', as their 'duration is limited' and as they 'are occasions for information exchange' (Lampel and Meyer 2008, p. 1027). In addition, they 'include ceremonial and dramaturgical activities' and 'generate social and reputational resources' (ibid.).

In order to better understand how actors create and maintain FCEs, a third concept is necessary. Institutional work (DiMaggio 1988; Lawrence and Suddaby 2006) addresses 'the purposive action of individuals and organizations aimed at creating, maintaining and disrupting institutions' (Lawrence and Suddaby 2006, p. 216). Creating institutions involves political work, reconfiguring belief systems and altering the boundaries of meaning systems (ibid., p. 220). Maintaining institutions is defined as adhering to rule systems, and reproducing systems of norms and beliefs (ibid., p. 229). Disrupting institutions aims at ending institutions and includes processes of disconnecting rewards and sanctions from existing rule systems, procedures and technologies, as well as disconnecting the moral foundations of particular norms, and undermining taken-for-granted assumptions (ibid., p. 234). These three aspects resonate well with the generation, continuation and termination of technological paths, which we have discussed elsewhere (Meyer and Schubert 2007). In addition, they fundamentally endeavour to transform and extend institutions into the future.

However, the concept of institutional work needs some refinement. We use a practice theoretical approach informed by structuration theory (Giddens 1984) to clarify how FCEs and institutional work can contribute to the development and maintenance of a field's institutional life. From a practice perspective, institutional work is a process of structuration, reflexively and recursively produced and reproduced by knowledgeable agents in time–space, who, in their interactions, refer to the more enduring aspects of the social—structures and institutions in particular—and, thereby, reproduce or transform them at the same time (Giddens 1979, 1984). We view organizing roadmaps and organizing conferences as collective strategic practices of gathering, storing and disseminating information concerning future developments and practices of 'selective "information filtering"' (Giddens 1979, p. 78; 1984, p. 27) within the field.

Actors in the field align their institutional work with the field's rules of signification and legitimation as well as its resources of domination (Giddens 1984, p. 25). Institutional work thus addresses the reproduction and transformation of (analytically distinguishable):

- *practices of communication* and rules of *signification*, that is, meaning systems and general procedures and technologies of communication;
- *practices of exercising power*, that is, applying material artefacts as well as knowledge or sets of relations as resources of *domination*;
- *practices of sanctioning* and rules of *legitimation*, recursively applied to (e)valuate new ways of acting in the field or reinforce approved strategies.

Since institutional work often is future-oriented work that *intends* to shape institutions, agents (be they the state, state-like agents or networks of collaborating agents) will not always achieve their intended objectives. There will always be unintended consequences of purposeful action as well as conditions that actors do not understand. In addition, agents are bound by social as well as material constraints. Thus, even if agents do succeed in mobilizing the necessary resources to engage in institutional work, the outcome may be mainly unintended or even undesired.

Summing up, we comprehend and observe institutional work in the semiconductor industry as a set of collective practices aimed at creating and maintaining techno-organizational futures. In the quest for a novel dominant design in the semiconductor industry, uncertainty is pervasive with regard to not only the technological outcomes and the choices at stake but also the economic implications and future changes in the semiconductor industry landscape. Roadmapping and conferencing are two of the main practices employed to deal with this uncertainty and to create collective futures.

Research Setting and Methods

For decades, 'Moore's Law' has set the pace for innovation cycles in the industry. First formulated in 1965, Moore's Law predicts a steady doubling in the density of electronic circuits every 18–24 months

(Moore 1965). Today, however, the prevailing manufacturing technology—lithography—has exhausted its possibilities with regard to Moore's Law. This has led the industry to pursue alternative options for a next-generation lithography (NGL), starting in the mid-1990s. As semiconductor manufacturing is already a multi-billion-dollar collective effort, even the development and commercialization of one single NGL option cannot be accomplished by an individual company (Browning and Shetler 2000).

Thus, the search for a novel production technology is a case that is particularly well-suited for the examination of FCEs and the institutional work of creating collective futures in organizational fields. First, this organizational field is currently characterized by a variety of actors collectively involved in the joint production of future technological options for semiconductor manufacturing. Different actors in North America, Asia and Europe work to coordinate their efforts with the objective of continuing, extending or redirecting this highly dynamic development. Second, the selection, development and introduction of a new manufacturing technology for computer chips serve as an excellent opportunity for the analysis of institutional work in FCEs. Various companies try to influence, even dominate, the industry by shaping institutions and ultimately implementing their preferred options. Third, this industry constitutes an intriguing object of study due to its economic importance for highly industrialized societies and its inherent focus on the future in terms of technical progress.

Based on the assumption that we can adequately interpret strategic practices and institutional work only through the perspective of the actors involved, we decided to adopt an interpretative research methodology (Lincoln and Guba 1985). This methodology allows us to understand how expectations regarding future technologies are transformed into viable manufacturing solutions through the work of institution builders, many of whom are scientists and engineers. We chose to conduct a longitudinal case study (Yin 2009), as this approach enables us to generate novel insights as to the development of technologies, how actors engage in institutional work and how they create collective futures.

Data Sources and Data Collection

Aside from an initial survey of secondary sources (e.g. scholarly and non-scholarly publications), three main data sources were used to analyse the role of institutional work for FCEs. This allowed us to compare our sources as well as to prevent post hoc rationalizations (Lincoln and Guba 1985). In addition, the chosen approach—in particular the comparison of multiple sources and our prolonged engagement in the field—assisted us in avoiding misinterpretations of such complex social and technical dynamics.

Our main data source is over 100 semi-structured interviews related to the pursuit of NGL technologies, conducted with semiconductor industry experts and senior executives. We used snowball sampling with our interview partners in order to identify potential respondents involved in coordinating industry activities and in the practices of organizing roadmaps and conferences, as these emerged as significant practices as our research evolved. This enabled us to identify the relevant actors from within the field and to map their strategic positions in companies as well as in the organizational field. We conducted the interviews during on-site visits or by telephone, and recorded and transcribed them verbatim for subsequent analysis. In addition, we conducted follow-up interviews and corresponded with key respondents by e-mail as a form of member validation (Seale 1999). This inside perspective allowed us to follow the delicate manoeuvrings and activities within the field as sets of developing practices which are recursively and reflexively reproduced by the actors.

The second source of data was an annual panel with selected interview partners. Central actors were interviewed on current affairs within the field to enable us to stay up-to-date with rapid, ongoing developments.

As a third source, we used material from observations made during on-site visits and in particular from conferences. We collected this data through direct attendance at relevant events from 2001 to 2011, as well as from an analysis of archival data such as conference presentations, slides and public announcements related to NGL developments. Moreover, our presence at a number of different conference venues sensitized us to how institutional work was unfolding over time and space.

In addition to these main sources, industry respondents were asked to comment on prior drafts of this study in order to enhance internal validity. We report only those results that were consistently validated by a large cross-section of interviewees and research experts.

Organizing Roadmaps and Conferences as Forms of Institutional Work

Organizing roadmaps and conferences are two concrete examples of collective institutional work, which have four distinct properties regarding the collective creation of futures. They are performed by a collectivity of actors, they are materialized in FCEs, they are intended to impact the level of the organizational field and they represent continuous efforts to create, maintain and adjust an existing techno-organizational order in the present and for the future. We mainly focus on the ongoing activities of maintaining an existing order and show how such activities always include aspects of institutional creation and disruption.

Organizing Roadmaps

Roadmaps have frequently been studied in terms of their predictive content or their accuracy in displaying future technological challenges, that is, more in terms of their products than in terms of their production (e.g. Galvin 1998; Lee et al. 2012). We will concentrate on the institutional production of a roadmap by showing how field participants proceed to select a technologically feasible and economically viable successor technology by influencing how other actors perceive and evaluate technological options.

Until recently, the International Technology Roadmap for Semiconductors (ITRS) was considered by far the most important roadmap in the semiconductor industry.[3] Moreover, it is frequently cited as a role model for other industries and even as the 'mother' of all roadmaps (Probert and Radnor 2003; Borodovsky 2006).

We can trace the origins of this industry-wide roadmap to the National Technology Roadmap for Semiconductors (NTRS), which US semiconductor companies introduced in 1992 due to rapidly growing costs for R&D. In 1999, the participant base was broadened and the NTRS subsequently reformulated by additional members from Europe and Southeast Asia, the outcome being the ITRS. This international expansion mirrors the global coordinating efforts in the industry that can also be observed in its most important R&D consortium, SEMATECH (Semiconductor Manufacturing Technology), which started as a national effort in 1987 and became an international venture in 1999 (Sydow et al. 2012). SEMATECH is closely involved in the organization of the roadmap procedure. As a written artefact, the ITRS was (re)produced on a yearly basis, published in even-numbered years as an update and in odd-numbered years as a full revision. The ITRS essentially displayed and debated future technological milestones.

Triannual workshops ensured the (re)production of the annual ITRS report. Their frequency was less an organizational requirement than a political decision—each of the three workshops being held in one of the relevant regions: North America, Asia and Europe. These workshops entailed a detailed and multi-level process of information collation and a clear division of labour. Technology working groups (TWGs), bringing together delegates from the field to identify specific aspects of current and future states, are figured as crucial elements. Each TWG was formally responsible for the production of a specific chapter of the ITRS. Chapters addressed topics such as lithography, process integration, metrology or emerging research devices. Participation in these TWGs was voluntary and formally open to all interested parties.[4] During the research and drafting process, relevant agents discussed key challenges, which were subsequently transformed into measurable output. The ITRS's executive committee, the so-called International Roadmap Committee (IRC), continuously reviewed the cooperative efforts emerging from the TWGs: 'IRC members decide policy and set guidelines for the ITRS' (ITRS 2009).

The ITRS as an FCE was crucial for the creation of an industry-wide consensus on future technologies, the shaping of views and for the activities of multiple and heterogeneous actors in the field. It entailed a formally organized procedure for gathering, storing and disseminating information on technological progress as well as on challenges, and was used for strategically controlling this information. As a social practice, roadmapping reflexively and recursively tied the actors in the field to a collective effort, which in turn shaped the institutional setup of the field. This is not only true for the various participants involved in the process of ITRS production, but also for the manifold firms involved in the process of technology development along the value chain. Manufacturers and suppliers used the ITRS to guide their activities and to act in accordance with its predictions and requirements. Besides the firms directly involved in the process of technology development, other actors, for example venture capitalists, also utilized the ITRS to coordinate their activities: 'The background here at [our venture capital organization] is that we make investments that also have a strategic purpose […] The SEMATECH roadmap is, of course, important and it is important that we stand behind it, otherwise we would invest in the wrong companies.' (I-63)

The positive evaluation of a technological option on the ITRS was an important aspect in the decision to fund a specific company. The institutional work found here happens, first, when actors start to modify the rules of signification and legitimation, turning the ITRS into a central artefact within the field. Second, after field participants acknowledge the ITRS as a significant and legitimate locale for technology development, they can transform it into a resource of domination by adding or removing technological options. Further, in the course of meetings, participants recursively and reflexively created and maintained the ITRS as an institution. This made it a central part of the field's (re)production, a status which was explicitly acknowledged in the ITRS:

> The overall objective of the ITRS is to present industry-wide consensus on the 'best current estimate' of the industry's research and development needs out to a 15-year horizon. As such, it provides a guide to the efforts of companies, universities, governments, and other research providers or funders. The ITRS has improved the quality of R&D investment decisions made at all levels and has helped channel research efforts to areas that most need research breakthroughs. (ITRS 2009, p. 1)

This self-description mentions two very different aspects. On one hand, the ITRS is supposed to present an industry-wide consensus. On the other hand, it 'guides' and 'channels' research efforts. The ITRS not only involves sense-making and the constitution of meaning (Weick 1995), it is also an inherently political instrument. 'Guiding' and 'channelling' help to maintain the field's conditions of reproduction.

At an ITRS meeting in spring 2011, one TWG member told us that he and his fellow TWG members repeatedly see themselves faced with a choice, that is, whether to communicate results in line with what they expect or with what they would prefer for the future:

> We always have this discussion about the roadmap: Is this only a projection of how we expect the future to be or do we use the roadmap to shape the future? [...] And, of course, different interests collide here—personal ones, company interests, the environment, group dynamics, everything at the same time. [...] This time we have decided to define a direction. (I-31)

Though the ITRS might *prima facie* seem to present a neutral showcase of options, the highly institutionalized process of roadmapping was also actively influenced by major players in the field, especially by large organizations such as Intel. For example, major players took part in all working groups relevant to their interests and were also key actors in the IRC.

One example of how the ITRS was used to 'guide' and 'channel' can be seen in the additional section of the 2009 ITRS which deals exclusively with carbon-based technologies. However, carbon electronics fail to satisfy the requirements normally applied to ITRS candidates. One of the TWG's members described this process:

> So we looked at all [options] and, actually, the overall consensus was that none of them looked that promising. No one said, look, we really want to put it in the ITRS. [...] But we also felt, it's not like we don't have preferences here. [...] Well, the best thing is to put up the carbon electronics, because they seem to offer a lot of good possibilities. [...] We realized that we have all these devices we've been looking at—for five or six years now—and none of them is fully ready to be part of the normal TWGs, but we get pressure from the main ITRS to say, well, we understand that you're not ready, but we would still like some guidance. (I-34)

Thus, this explicit sponsoring of carbon-based devices was intended to set the wheels in motion for a self-fulfilling prophecy—making the ITRS an FCE par excellence. This assertion of influence still ultimately maintained the field's overall direction and future development, even if it generated increased certainty and marginalized other options.[5]

The creation of the ITRS through FCEs was itself an elaborate form of institutional work in a highly institutionalized setting in which actors tried to align the importance assigned to different technological options on the roadmap with their own strategic interests in order to contribute to the reflexive coordination of the field. Most actors in the field were aware of these strategic ITRS properties. Nevertheless, once the roadmap was published, it was widely perceived as at least partially binding and, moreover, communicated as being an allegedly 'objective' definition of the situation and thus a powerful FCE in terms of selective information filtering.

Organizing Conferences

Conferences are by far the largest gatherings of the industry's key actors. As institutionalized events, they have an important signalling effect for the field as a whole. Compared to ITRS workshops, conferences are generally open to everyone and primarily an end in themselves. Although their formal programmes feature many of the latest topics, conferences also provide 'unstructured opportunities for face-to-face social interaction' and 'occasions for information exchange' (Lampel and Meyer 2008, p. 1027).

Research on conferences (e.g. Zilber 2007), particularly studies that examine them as FCEs, tends to concentrate on the events themselves (e.g. Oliver and Montgomery 2008), often applying quantitative database analyses involving unconnected events (e.g. Zollo 2009). In contrast, we address the repeated engagement of actors in the organization of conferences as an ongoing practice of 'doing' FCEs.

There are several crucial conference series in the semiconductor industry. Some target a broad audience, for example, the NGL community as a whole; others cover a specific technological value chain like that of extreme ultraviolet lithography (EUVL). For NGL activities, one important venue is the annual conference of the Society of Photo-optical Instrumentation Engineers (SPIE), which all major players in the semiconductor industry attend. Another key conference series is the Workshops on Next Generation Lithography, which was specifically organized by the SEMATECH consortium to accelerate the decision-making process for NGL.

The construction of FCEs is by no means driven by consensus, but—like roadmapping—is a highly political process. In their meaning and relevance, these events are actively constituted as such; they do not simply exist (Munir 2005; Hoffman and Ocasio 2001). As with intraorganizational meetings (Jarzabkowski and Seidl 2008), we perceive conference organizing as a strategic practice for the creation of FCEs. Thus, conferences are fine-grained, highly institutionalized organizational locales and practices. Their composition ultimately influences how they impact the NGL community.

Conference organizing in the semiconductor industry follows an overarching score, which—by using institutionalized practices—involves the creation and preservation of shared views and the abandonment of others. For this composition, we identified the following seven elements.

First, conference organizing is characterized by meticulous reflexive planning before, during and after a conference. As for the conferences described in this paper, SEMATECH usually set the respective agenda. Industry consortia such as SEMATECH play an important role in the configuring of the semiconductor industry as an organizational field, maintaining its institutional life and focusing institutional work.[6] Conference organizers exert significant influence through the allocation of time slots. For instance, SEMATECH has explicitly favoured EUVL. The consortium regularly allotted more time to this option at the beginning of conferences when attendance is usually at its peak. Also, key time slots often go hand in hand with larger, more attractive physical spaces. At one important conference venue, representatives of EUVL were scheduled to present and discuss their results for a total of four hours, whereas representatives advocating alternative technologies like Electron Projection Lithography (EPL) received 75 minutes

(Möllering 2009). Similar patterns could be observed at other conferences. Some participants presented their research results in keynotes before hundreds of attendees; others were part of a poster presentation together with dozens of other posters in a small room.

Second, and closely related to these more implicit ways of ascribing significance to selected technological options and the representatives involved, actors also explicitly and literally received different labels. For example, actors representing favoured technological options were referred to as 'technology champions', or they wore different name tags (e.g. 'keynote' vs. 'speaker'), as was the case at the SEMATECH Litho Forum conference.

Third, organizing actors attempt to create an explicit consensus by polling conference attendees about their opinions on the specific technological options. Polling is used as a legitimizing technique; all actors are asked to voice their opinion, as it is widely assumed, objectively and without bias, based on the presentations and discussions at the event.

Fourth, the survey results are distributed during the event and evaluated at its conclusion. It is noteworthy that organizing committee members present and interpret the survey results. For instance, high-ranking members of SEMATECH gave speeches at the end of conferences and presented a conference summary. In this setting, as the polling results were announced, the field's preferences were presented as obvious facts and EUVL summarily declared the field's preferred technological option.

Fifth, as a follow-up to the conferences, media coverage and the documentation of the results corresponded with the survey results and the information and interpretations provided by the keynotes or technology champions. For example, extensive online archives document the conference events, materials, surveys and presentations.[7] SEMATECH documents the results of the conference, specifically the votes and related commentary, and makes them publicly available (SEMATECH 2010).

Sixth, and closely related to the previous element of this form of institutional work, actors referred to previous conferences and survey results in subsequent activities and statements. Referring to prior conferences is important insofar as it permits (re)interpretations of past results and the establishment of a seemingly coherent line of reasoning.

Finally, every conference is part of a series of conferences and embedded in the larger set of conferences taking place within the field. The institutional impact of conferences is constituted by the interplay of these sets of interrelated gatherings, which are used by strategically positioned actors to filter and store information as previously described.

In effect, the described score enacts the strategic guidance and orientation that the semiconductor industry generates in the pursuit of NGL. Even more than the ITRS, conferences are social and material locales of institutional work, where the allotment of time, space and visibility are elements of larger strategic manoeuvrings. Thus, conferences have the capacity to influence the cognitive landscape of the field: 'In addition to technical exchange, conferences are also important when it comes to creating a positive "push". There's excitement about breakthroughs demonstrated in different areas [...] simply some positive press.' (I-03)

To use Giddens' concepts, conferences are locales for the exchange and control of information. The internal circulation of information is heavily imbued with the strategic intentions of influential actors (e.g. sponsoring organizations) trying to rally others to support specific technological options. Interviewees described, for example, actors who promoted EUVL as the best NGL, as follows:

> They [the key actors] use all means at their disposal. They make sure that there are prominent keynote speakers at conferences who are pushing for EUV[L] and they have no qualms about standing up and saying that all major issues have been resolved, that the industry just needs to implement the solutions. This makes people think: 'Great, we just need to do it and it will work.' But that is not true. (I-01)

Conference organizers especially present conference summaries and final statements as a reliable overview of viable futures within the field. Then, participants, as well as others, use them as guidelines for subsequent activities within the field. As a major aspect of the field's institutional life, conferences have long been a part of its rules of signification and legitimation as well as resources of domination. Venues like SPIE simultaneously represent a locale in and a practice by which evaluation criteria for technological options are shaped on an industry-wide level, where interested actors reflexively disseminate information about activities and ascribe relevance to the specific technological options under discussion.

Field-Level Impacts of Organizing Roadmaps and Conferences

Even if described separately, roadmaps and conferences are deeply intertwined. The ITRS influences conferences, their structure, their content and the evaluation of their results. And the ITRS is influenced by conferences and the presentations given at them. Both are also tied to R&D consortia such as SEMATECH. In their combination, the different institutionalized practices are responsible for the development of shared perspectives on technology and the practices through which these perspectives are evaluated and disseminated. By drafting and circulating texts and documents—information collation, storage and dissemination—in an institutionalized way, roadmapping in particular contributes to the creation and maintenance of shared perspectives on technological and organizational futures.

The selective information filtering enabled by such practices reflexively regulates the field, reduces uncertainty and permits collective institutionalized action. This becomes obvious in formal decision processes such as conference votes, which are often conducted after informed decisions have been made. Expectations about the future in general, and the future development of certain technologies in particular, induce specific activities concerning the realization of promising technologies, which in return influence expectations about future developments. In this way, expectations and activities become self-reinforcing, which leads actors to view their own participation in certain activities as necessary, and even mandatory. Yet, it is these very same activities which mandate their own execution, for instance, by being 'compulsory'. The described usages of institutionalized practices are powerful forms of enactment (Weick 1995). By influencing expectations and actions, or by contributing to a technological bandwagon, groups of actors influence their environment by constructing a specific perspective and acting collectively towards it. Similar to a 'scientific bandwagon' (Fujimura 1988), after a period of time actors tend to rally around a specific development option because others have done the same (Abrahamson and Rosenkopf 1993). When support for one development option reaches a certain level, the overall tendency is for it to stabilize and gain even greater momentum. Hence, visions and fictitious descriptions of future technological milestones are first transformed into requirements, then realities and finally attain the status of inevitabilities (van Lente and Rip 1998). By putting descriptions of possible futures in writing, they become objectified. These documents and the 'facts' they describe confront actors in the field as objectified realities. Part of this objectification involves the transmission of meaning and shared beliefs to parties who played no role in their construction, both inside the field and out. Actors create and distribute documents and proofs that seem to neutrally demonstrate the superiority of a certain technological option. The processes of cultural and cognitive institutionalization are not only intertwined with processes of normative institutionalization and the institutionalization of domination, but also recursively (re-)produced by knowledgeable agents in time–space.

As with self-fulfilling prophecies, at some point the expectation that certain developments will materialize in the future becomes rational, regardless of how rational it first seemed. Competently organized roadmaps and conferences, and the practices that contribute to that perception, increase the momentum of a specific technological option. These activities lie at the heart of the described FCEs and shape the overall conditions of technology development by anchoring particular technology options and their evaluation within the organizational field. Actors attempt to implement future predictions and visions because they expect others to do the same and fear that they might fall behind if they do not concentrate their efforts on developing what are perceived as strong technological options.

The irony of this process is not lost on its participants. One interviewee, a leading research consortium member, succinctly formulated his view of roadmapping as follows: 'Look, I think, by and large when you look at it, I think it's a pretty successful process, apart from the fact that it's completely unable to predict anything' (I-32). Even though these processes may well be unable to make accurate predictions—and, indeed, how could they?—they do enable collective coordination and action, and, therefore, are crucial in terms of reflexive self-regulation within the semiconductor field. Practices like organizing roadmaps and conferences do not reduce uncertainty on a technological level. The technical options and obstacles stay the same. But they change perceptions of these options and increase commitment for some while reducing it for others. The reduction of uncertainty happens primarily on a social level, but because people act on their perceptions, it also influences the technological developments. As mentioned in the beginning, 'anticipative structures' (van Lente and Rip 1998) are transformed into expectations which will likely lead to the realization of new technological options.

Conclusion

FCEs are essential forms of (re)producing technology development in the field of semiconductor manufacturing. They are crucial for the institutionalization of the field and best understood through an analysis of the institutional work they require. The ITRS and conferences in the semiconductor industry are specifically used for the creation and institutionalization of shared beliefs and for the creation of collective futures. We have emphasized the fact that institutionalization is not merely a mental process, but one of collectively and strategically creating documents such as the ITRS and venues like the SPIE conference that lead to coordinated activities in the field. These two practices in particular support selective information collation and control, and highlight the strategic aspect of reflexive field regulation as emphasized by Giddens (1984). When working collaboratively, strategically positioned actors can reflexively coordinate the transnational field to some extent through these two practices and shape the technical and organizational future of the semiconductor manufacturing industry.

Our central argument is that FCEs are based on institutional work in order to coordinate actions and relationships between actors in an organizational field that lacks more direct forms of regulation for creating collective futures. Therefore, both practices are strategic forms of reflexive coordination, aimed not at setting formal rules, but at influencing cognitive and normative institutionalization and ways of using concrete artefacts and settings as facilities. They are the medium and result of collective institutional work by groups of actors representing different organizations. The ongoing organization of conference series and meetings to produce roadmaps, as well as of the conferences and roadmaps as concrete entities, is key to the constitution of institutional life in the semiconductor industry. Thus, the practices of organizing roadmaps and organizing conferences are to be understood as institutionalized as well as central practices of institutional work.

However, it is not useful to continuously add new forms of institutional work, such as conferencing and roadmapping, to the very long list collected by Lawrence and Suddaby (2006), which already subsumes quite different forms of activities under that label. Adding more categories does not clarify the properties and requirements of institutional work. Instead, we suggest a more theoretical analysis of institutional work based on a practice theory perspective and in the context of the organized creation of collective futures. Then we can grasp that the reflexive organization of conferences and roadmaps—by creating events, and especially through more fine-grained activities such as defining 'hot topics', keynote speakers and so on—contributes to the creation and maintenance of a shared perspective of the industry's situation and certain future options, while also disrupting others. This strategic filtering and control of information is elemental for the reflexive coordination of the field.

At the field level, aspects of maintaining expectations are expressed, for example, in the continuation of Moore's Law. This 'meta-narrative' (Zilber 2009), which is never subject to serious scrutiny, provides an important institutional basis for the reflexive coordination of the field. Actors only consider and modify its implementation in concrete activities. Forms of institutional work like conferencing and roadmapping change the field and its institutional structure to enable the continuation of technology development in accordance with the dominant business models. When the continuous improvement of a manufacturing technology is no longer seen as viable, the whole supply chain is likely to be overhauled to maintain the basic industry dynamic. Conferencing and roadmapping are central practices for maintaining and creating, and sometimes disrupting, the institutional rules of signification and legitimation in the field.

With both practices of institutional work, it is apparent that any one aspect—be it institutional creation, maintenance or disruption—is always based on and interwoven with the other two. Nevertheless, this distinction is useful for the analysis of collective future-making in at least two ways. First, one can analyse interrelations between maintenance, creation and disruption in varying forms of institutional work with respect to organizing collective futures. And second, even if all three forms are present in all instances of institutional work, different forms can be distinguished depending on whether and to what degree each of the three aspects is present. When creation and disruption dominate, their presence would seem to have stronger implications for collective future-making, but maintenance also always needs to take future uncertainties into account.

The search for future technological paths is an inherently political process: technology options are not chosen solely based on technological criteria. They are also evaluated in terms of their influence on a field's structure, for example, how a certain technology might influence the supply chain or shift the geography of relevant competencies. Issues of domination can be observed on at least two levels: strategically placed actors, those who are able to generate the necessary resources, influence the field and the concrete usages of institutionalized packages of actor–action relations, thus further stabilizing their own position(s). In other words, even in the past, actors have refused and abandoned technologies because of duelling competencies—located within other companies in other regions. Our study shows that technical and organizational futures likewise emerge from contested expectations and that they are carefully managed through institutional practices like roadmaps and conferences in often highly contested yet strategically organized fields.

Notes

1. This chapter is based on the research project 'Path-Creating Networks: Innovating Next Generation Lithography in Germany and the U.S.', which was funded by the Volkswagen Foundation from 2004 to 2009.
2. Another important institutionalized practice is the increasing use of consortia to push the technology from laboratory to factory, as we have discussed elsewhere (Sydow et al. 2012).
3. In 2016, a final version of the ITRS was published and an initiative was founded to create a new roadmap procedure (the ITRS 2.0) adjusted to the new challenges facing the industry. This shift shows how instruments like roadmaps are continuously adapted to requirements in the field. Our discussion, however, focuses on the original ITRS.
4. However, the TWG heads had the right to refuse interested parties who they believed lacked the skills or resources to make an adequate contribution to the TWG.
5. However, simply putting a technological option onto the ITRS will not necessarily make it happen. In current semiconductor technology development, extreme technical and financial challenges still have to be resolved before promises can go into production.
6. We have discussed the importance of consortia in the semiconductor industry elsewhere (Sydow et al. 2012).
7. www.sematech.org/meetings/archives/litho/ngl/20010829, accessed 2011-05-05.

References

Abrahamson, Eric, and Lori Rosenkopf. 1993. Institutional and Competitive Bandwagons: Using Mathematical Modeling as a Tool to Explore Innovation Diffusion. *The Academy of Management Review* 18: 487–517.

Borodovsky, Yan. 2006. Marching to the Beat of Moore's Law. Proceedings SPIE 6153, Advances in Resist Technology and Processing XXIII, 615301.

Browning, Larry D., and Judy C. Shetler. 2000. *SEMATECH. Saving the U.S. Semiconductor Industry*. College Station: A&M University Press.

DiMaggio, Paul J. 1988. Interest and Agency in Institutional Theory. In *Institutional Patterns and Organizations. Culture and Environment*, ed. Lynne G. Zucker, 3–22. Cambridge: Ballinger.

DiMaggio, Paul J., and Walter W. Powell. 1983. The Iron Cage Revisited. Institutional Isomorphism and Collective Rationality in Organizational Fields. *American Sociological Review* 48: 147–160.
Fujimura, Joan H. 1988. The Molecular Biological Bandwagon in Cancer Research. Where Social Worlds Meet. *Social Problems* 35 (3): 261–283.
Galvin, Robert. 1998. Science Roadmaps. *Science* 280 (5365): 803–805.
Giddens, Anthony. 1979. *Central Problems in Social Theory. Action, Structure and Contradictions in Social Analysis*. London: Macmillan.
———. 1984. *The Constitution of Society: Outline of the Theory of Structuration*. Cambridge: Polity Press.
Hoffman, Andrew J. 1999. Institutional Evolution and Change: Environmentalism and the U.S. Chemical Industry. *Academy of Management Journal* 42 (4): 351–371.
Hoffman, Andrew J., and William Ocasio. 2001. Not All Events Are Attended Equally: Toward a Middle-Range Theory of Industry Attention to External Events. *Organization Science* 12: 414–434.
ITRS. 2009. International Technology Roadmap for Semiconductors. 2009 Edition. Executive Summary. http://www.itrs.net/Links/2009ITRS/2009Chapters_2009Tables/2009_ExecSum.pdf. Accessed 18 Jan 2010.
Jarzabkowski, Paula, and David Seidl. 2008. The Role of Meetings in the Social Practice of Strategy. *Organization Studies* 29 (11): 1391–1426.
Lampel, Joseph, and Alan D. Meyer. 2008. Field-Configuring Events as Structuring Mechanisms. How Conferences, Ceremonies, and Trade Shows Constitute New Technologies, Industries, and Markets. *Journal of Management Studies* 45 (6): 1025–1035.
Lawrence, Thomas B., and Roy Suddaby. 2006. Institutions and Institutional Work. In *The SAGE Handbook of Organization Studies*, ed. Stewart R. Clegg, Cynthia Hardy, Tom Lawrence, and Walter R. Nord, 215–254. London: Sage.
Lee, Jung H., Hyung-Il Kim, and Robert Phaal. 2012. An Analysis of Factors Improving Technology Roadmap Credibility: A Communications Theory Assessment of Roadmapping Processes. *Technological Forecasting and Social Change* 79 (2): 263–280.
Lincoln, Yvonna S., and Egon G. Guba. 1985. *Naturalistic Inquiry*. Beverly Hills: Sage.
Meyer, Uli, and Cornelius Schubert. 2007. Integrating Path Dependency and Path Creation in a General Understanding of Path Constitution. The Role of Agency and Institutions in the Shaping of Technological Innovations. *Science, Technology & Innovation Studies* 3 (1): 23–44.

Möllering, Guido. 2009. Market Constitution Analysis. A New Framework Applied to Solar Power Technology Markets. *Max-Planck-Institut für Gesellschaftsforschung Working Paper*, 09/7: Köln.

———. 2010. Collective Market-Making Efforts at an Engineering Conference. *MPIfG Discussion Paper*, 10/2.

Moore, Gordon E. 1965. Cramming More Components Onto Integrated Circuits. *Electronics* 38 (8): 114–117.

Munir, Kamal A. 2005. The Social Construction of Events: A Study of Institutional Change in the Photographic Field. *Organization Studies* 26 (1): 93–112.

Oliver, Amalya L., and Kathleen Montgomery. 2008. Using Field-Configuring Events for Sense-Making: A Cognitive Network Approach. *Journal of Management Studies* 45 (6): 1147–1167.

Probert, David R., and Michael Radnor. 2003. Frontier Experiences from Industry-Academia Consortia. *Research-Technology Management* 42 (2): 27–30.

Schubert, Cornelius, Jörg Sydow, and Arnold Windeler. 2013. The Means of Managing Momentum. Bridging Technological Paths and Organisational Fields. *Research Policy* 42 (8): 1389–1405.

Seale, Clive. 1999. *The Quality of Qualitative Research*. London: Sage.

SEMATECH. 2010. Proceedings Archives. http://www.sematech.org/meetings/archives.htm. Accessed 22 Sept 2010.

Sydow, Jörg, Arnold Windeler, Cornelius Schubert, and Guido Möllering. 2012. Organizing R&D Consortia for Path Creation and Extension. The Case of Semiconductor Manufacturing Technologies. *Organization Studies* 33 (7): 907–936.

van Lente, Harro, and Arie Rip. 1998. Expectations in Technological Developments: An Example of Prospective Structures to be Filled in by Agency. In *Getting New Technologies Together. Studies in Making Sociotechnical Order*, eds. Cornelis Disco and Barend J. R. van der Meulen, 203–229. Berlin: De Gruyter.

Weick, Karl E. 1995. *Sensemaking in Organizations*. Thousand Oaks: Sage.

Wooten, Melissa, and Andrew J. Hoffman. 2008. Organizational Fields: Past, Present and Future. In *The SAGE Handbook of Organizational Institutionalism*, ed. Royston Greenwood, Christine Oliver, Kerstin Sahlin, and Roy Suddaby, 130–147. Los Angeles: Sage.

Yin, Robert K. 2009. *Case Study Research*. Thousand Oaks: Sage.

Zilber, Tammar B. 2007. Stories and the Discursive Dynamics of Institutional Entrepreneurship: The Case of Israeli High-Tech After the Bubble. *Organization Studies* 28 (7): 1035–1054.

———. 2009. Institutional Maintenance as Narrative Acts. In *Institutional Work: Actors and Agency in Institutional Studies of Organization*, ed. Thomas Lawrence, Bernard Leca, and Roy Suddaby, 205–235. Cambridge: Cambridge University Press.

Zollo, Maurizio. 2009. Superstitious Learning with Rare Strategic Decisions: Theory and Evidence from Corporate Acquisitions. *Organization Science* 20 (5): 894–908.

14

Organizational Artifacts as Pre-presentations of Things to Come: The Case of Menu Development in Haute Cuisine

Jochen Koch, Ninja Natalie Senf, and Wasko Rothmann

Introduction

The idea of focusing on artifacts in order to analyze the processual unfolding of organizations in time is a common one, rather than groundbreaking. Artifacts play an important role in very different fields of organization studies, including, for instance, those that consider organizational technology, change, culture or routines (Woodward 1958; Perrow 1973; Orlikowski 1992; Schultze and Orlikowski 2004; Martin 1992; Schein 1990; D'Adderio 2011). In all these streams, artifacts may be considered as the somehow materialized part of organizations, something that endures over time, providing an essential supplement to the ongoing flux of events and the fundamental processuality of organizations (Tsoukas and Chia 2002). Even if it is true that we never jump twice into the same river, there is, nonetheless, a form, shape or pattern known as 'river bed' and there are materials called 'water', 'sand', 'mud' and so on. And even if we know that this simple 'there is' already entraps

---

J. Koch (✉) • N. N. Senf • W. Rothmann
European University Viadrina, Frankfurt (Oder), Germany

© The Author(s) 2018
H. Krämer, M. Wenzel (eds.), *How Organizations Manage the Future*,
https://doi.org/10.1007/978-3-319-74506-0_14

us by reifying language (Vaara et al. 2005), we nevertheless refer continuously to these reifications and, so to say, materialize them (Scott and Orlikowski 2012). This holds true not only for the temporal modes of the past and present but also for the future of an organization. However, there is a fundamental difference between the temporal modes of the past and present and that of the future with regard to their relation to the material realm of organizations (Koch et al. 2016). Whereas the past and present of organizations relate to material representations, the future is not yet materialized as a representation of occurred or occurring organizational processes, but—as we argue in this chapter—the organizational materiality does not re- but pre-present the future. Consequently, the organizational becoming not only is a language category based on communication but also materializes as the body of an organization or, in other words, as inscriptions into the organizational body (Koch 2011). From this background, we focus on the following research question: How does an organization's future relate to the organization's artifact(s) constituted in the past and present?

Artifacts in Time: Inscription and *Agencement* in a Processual Perspective

If we ask how an organization's future relates to its artifacts, we need first to understand the organizational materiality in a process perspective that also includes the temporal modes of the past and the present. Therefore, it is necessary to embrace a dynamic perspective on organizational artifacts. One of the research streams in which the relation between organizational artifacts and processes has most recently prominently gained momentum is that of routine dynamics (Pentland and Feldman 2005; Feldman et al. 2016). This development is based on at least two different insights. First, it became apparent that the representation of routines in the form of the ostensive part of a routine is inherently connected to the socio-material realm. Whereas materiality had already played a role in earlier discussions (e.g. Cohen et al. 1996), it had been more or less lost from sight (D'Adderio 2011). Second, it is increasingly acknowledged that the mode of action unfolding the routine performance in particular cannot be grasped comprehensively without allusion to a 'material place' to condense or, as we will elaborate on later, to inscribe to.

Against this background, D'Adderio (2008, 2011) has suggested placing artifacts center stage in a generative model of routines. Such an understanding of artifacts within the context of routine dynamics essentially refers to the Actor-Network-Theory (ANT) and the idea that materiality (and thus artifacts) can be considered as actors (Latour 2007). This implies that artifacts are more than just inanimate materials and should be regarded as actors in their own right. Even if the idea of artifacts as actors might be considered as too extreme in all its consequences, it seems to be helpful to overcome the assumption of artifacts as dead material.

In addition, artifacts are not just things per se, but get realized in and through performance. The concept of performativity highlights the fact that artifacts get actualized within the process of actual performances and that, in turn, the performance is also related to and shaped by artifacts (D'Adderio and Pollock 2014). At the same time, performativity emphasizes the fact that organizational dynamics can be explained neither solely based on cognitive models of the actors nor solely based on the artifacts themselves. The key lies, rather, in the ongoing and continuous interaction between artifacts, actors and performances.

In this regard, the concept of the *organizational body* has become a fruitful perspective for further understanding the recursiveness of these dynamics (Koch 2011). Consequently, to address how performance is inscribed into the organizational body requires a specific understanding of the materiality and the absorbability of artifacts in organizations. The concept of inscription (Koch 2011) stands for how the performance of organizations resonates in its material body.

If we assume that already-occurred and occurring organizational processes get inscribed into the artifact through their performance, the concept of inscription offers different implications for grasping the functioning of organizational artifacts as a performative body in relation to things to come and, hence, the future. With reference to ANT, D'Adderio (2011), for instance, puts socio-technical relations and therefore technical artifacts (such as software) at center stage. In this chapter, we intend to propose a broader understanding of artifacts. This includes addressing organizational artifacts as being beyond a distinct and technical materiality (as it is the case, for instance, in many of the early technology studies, e.g. Woodward 1958), but rather as a *universal body*, in which performance can be comprehensively inscribed (instead of just partially). Such an understanding has the advantage that different forms of inscription are not merely limited to explicit and intentional aspects ('programmes'), but can include implicit and non-intentional aspects of performance as well. This also opens up room to consider co-lateral and side effects, such as processes of path dependence (Sydow et al. 2009), for instance.

The second concept to be introduced here in order to understand the relation between organizational artifacts and things to come concerns the relations between the ostensive part, the artifact and the performative part of the routine. Thus, it points to the influences of (a) the ostensive part on the artifact (and vice versa), (b) the ostensive part on the performative and (c) the artifact on the actual performance. MacKenzie (2003, 2006, see also D'Adderio 2011) distinguishes between four different forms of relation or influence. Those are located along a continuum, reaching from 'deterministic influence' to 'no influence', and prove quite fruitful when questioning the relation between model and reality. As the discussions of the last two decades have shown, the process of routine accomplishment cannot be regarded as entirely deterministic from design to action (Pentland and Feldman 2008). In this vein, it is very helpful to assume the artifact *as agencement* (Deleuze and Guattari 1987), which is more and less than the mere representation of the ostensive part of the routine. It is more because it reflects the actual performance; and it is less because the ostensive part is not totally represented in the performance, but only partly. Hence, the concept of *agencement* enables us to better understand the relation between the ostensive part of an organization and what is actually performed as an organizational process. Therefore, and this is crucial, we propose to differentiate between actuality and potentiality (Luhmann 1995, pp. 65–66). Actuality refers to the composition and the accomplishment of the organizational process with regard to what is actualized, that is, realized in practice. Potentiality refers to other potential options of *agencements*, not actually realized but nevertheless possible and therefore also included in the artifact.

The concept of *agencement* (Deleuze and Guattari 1987) refers to the idea of arrangement or assemblage, entailing the idea that something (for instance, a body) is made up of different parts and these parts interact with each other. Accordingly, *agencement* refers not only to the result of that arrangement (the *agencement*) but also to the process of arranging things together, hence the *process of agencement*. And furthermore, the notion refers to the idea that the arrangement of the different parts is fixed and fitting at the same time, hence the interplay between the different parts adds up to a functioning whole of a body.

In this vein, the accomplishment of an *agencement* is determined by the degree to which the elements included in the assemblage manage 'to put into motion a world in which it can function' (D'Adderio 2011, p. 217). D'Adderio in that regard emphasizes the role of the self-fulfilling or even self-reinforcing nature of such processes. The basic idea is that the functioning of the *agencement* can be understood by referring to the relationship between the different parts of a body and its context ('a world') that is put into motion.

Taking these perspectives into consideration, we can now summarize them in the form of a working model for our empirical study to explore the relation between artifacts and organizational futures (see Fig. 14.1).

The model distinguishes between the three different temporal modes of an organization (past, present and future) and induces a processual perspective in which the processes of inscription and *agencement* unfold in time. Given that our goal is to explore the relation between artifacts and an organization's future, we also need to understand the underlying processes of inscription into past and present artifacts in order to grasp their actual and potential impact on things to come. From an empirical point of view, *agencement*—understood as a process that leads to a performative texture of heterogeneous but interrelated elements—requires an exploration of the elements at stake and their interrelations. As *agencement* basically refers to an ongoing process of 'assemblage' of elements, we will explore the different types of elements in an attempt to understand their performative texture with regard to a continuum reaching from *replication* to *reformation*. This offers us the opportunity to grasp continuity and change in a process perspective. In the extreme case of total replication, all the elements are recombined in an identical way,

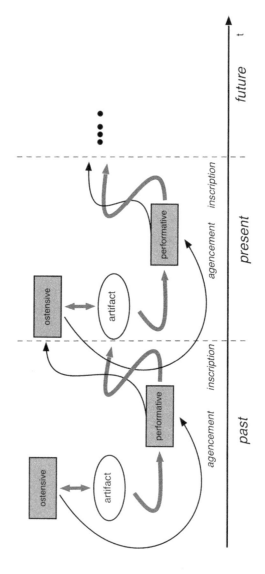

Fig. 14.1 Organizational artifacts in time

leading to an identical performance in terms of reproduction; in the extreme case of reformation, an entirely new arrangement is chosen with a disruptive impact on performance that is guided by the structural aspects of the artifact. The underlying assumption is that the artifact itself is a body of heterogeneous elements containing information, assumptions, structural elements and so on with the ability to inform and shape the things to come. *Agencement*, then, is the act of actualizing these elements and their relations either through replication or through reformation.

Inscription, on the other hand, is the performative effect of these actualizations on the past, present and then future artifacts. Hence, inscription refers to concrete performance and how it intentionally or unintentionally condenses in an artifact. To operationalize these effects, we propose to distinguish between *confirmation* and *overwriting*, which can also vary on a bipolar scale between an extreme case of total confirmation on the one hand and an extreme case of total overwriting on the other. When the performance confirms the existing structure of the artifact, it produces identical starting points of *agencement* for the subsequent performance cycle. Should changes occur and be inscribed into the artifact, the artifact may be overwritten, thereby altering the base of operation. Processes of overwriting also include the inscription of any additional element into the artifact. Given this conceptualization of our key elements, we need to identify a research setting where differences in *agencement* as well as inscription are observable in a process perspective.

Method

Case Selection

The case selected focuses on a very special artifact: menu development in the field of haute cuisine. This field is characterized by high dynamism on the one hand and perfectionism on the other. Unlike earlier times, when success depended solely on achieving and maintaining technical excellence and gastronomic quality, certainly since the early 2000s, more importance has been attached to the creativity and innovativeness of the offering (Bouty and Gomez 2010, 2013). Organizations in the field are obliged to develop high-performance routines, ensuring the daily accomplishment of perfectionism, while at the same time continually enabling creativity, innovation and, thus, change and renewal. This constant need for change accompanied by the requirement to continually reproduce equally excellent results renders this research field in particular relevant to our research question.

Creativity, innovation and renewal in haute cuisine are most regularly expressed through the introduction of new dishes on the menu. For our analysis, we have therefore selected the artifact of the menu as one of the most relevant and pivotal elements in haute cuisine. Focusing on the innovation process in haute cuisine over time provides us with an opportunity to observe the complex interaction between organizational processes and the menu, and how this interaction is driven by the artifact itself, thereby allowing us to understand its impact on things to come.

Our study is part of a larger research project on the haute cuisine sector that examines the strategic development of restaurants in that field (Koch et al. forthcoming). In this chapter, our case design involves an embedded single case study (Yin 2014), with the artifact as the case and multiple restaurants (with their own menus and menu development processes) as embedded units. The study focused on a specific region (Berlin) to keep the units comparable—as the innovation-related demands might differ in specific contexts. Nonetheless, Berlin is one of the most dynamic regions within the German haute cuisine sector, with, at the time of writing, 7 two-star restaurants and 14 one-star restaurants (*Guide Michelin*) but also a large number of ambitious restaurants below the star level. As a result, we could observe the interplay of organization and future in a very competitive context, and have been able to select our embedded units from a wide range of restaurants. In our final setting, we have included 11 restaurants with one or two Michelin stars and we have focused particularly on six restaurants with regard to menu development process.

Data Collection

Referring back to our research question and theoretical working model, it is necessary to use multiple sources of evidence to grasp the richness of the scrutinized object (Yin 2014). At the center of our data collection (see Fig. 14.2) is an in-depth analysis of the menu development of the selected haute cuisine restaurants, as this represents the ongoing interaction between artifact and performance over time in terms of what gets performed and actualized from the menu (*agencement*) and what gets inscribed into the menu.

The data collection process involved multiple interviews with the chefs of the six focal restaurants, exploring the concept of each restaurant, its culinary development process, the structure of the menu, changes and strategic decisions undertaken in the past and the present and those envisioned for the future, and the interaction between the restaurants and their environment. The interviews were recorded and subsequently transcribed for further analysis. In order to understand the culinary development process in detail, we also observed team meetings aimed at developing new ideas for the menu, which were then tested, revised and finalized over the course of a few weeks. This process was also recorded using film, photo and audio. Evidence gathering also involved informal interviews with the chefs as well as members of the kitchen team and staff during visits to the kitchen. Furthermore, we had dinner at all the restaurants in the study at least twice, which gave us a deeper insight into the

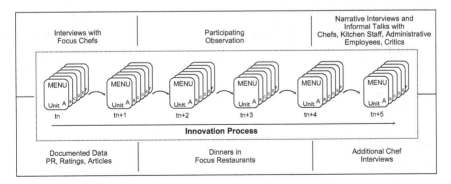

Fig. 14.2 Data sources in relation to menu evolution

'menu at work'. After those visits, we spoke informally to the chefs about the dining experience and the changes undertaken in between our visits. Changes to the menus and the culinary development process were observed not only in real time but also retrospectively. In addition, we verified our results in follow-up interviews with our focus cases once data analysis was completed.

As well as the direct observation and investigation of the innovation processes of the selected cases, our database was supplemented by further data sources: interviews with critics, interviews with other chefs and extensive secondary data. The interviews with critics were aimed at identifying the key determinants of the context, the most important players, general expectations and the evaluation criteria of the gourmet guides and the environment. This not only gave us a good overview of the setting and improved our access to the field, but it also confirmed the crucial importance of progression and the role of the menu as a picturization of it. Additionally, we asked for the critics' expert estimations of innovative menu concepts and the advantages and disadvantages of them. The interviews with other chefs beyond the selected units of analysis were used to confirm our understanding of innovation processes in haute cuisine in general and the role of the menu as artifact; significantly, these interviews were also very helpful in obtaining a critical review of the work of their colleagues. Secondary data collection involved other gourmet guide critiques of the selected units of analysis, as well as press releases and newspaper articles on haute cuisine in general and the chefs in particular. These data sources improved our retrospective understanding of the evolution of the sector and revealed the critics' reaction to change and their general evaluation of the restaurants. Table 14.1 provides an overview of our database.

Data Analysis

Our data analysis consisted of a multi-step iterative process (Eisenhardt 1989). We started by coding our data into two broad categories as suggested by the literature and the nature of our research question: the 'menu as artifact' (i.e. the artifact) and the 'menu development process' (i.e. the performance), which lead to sequenced changes in the menu. This

Table 14.1 Data

	Overall material
Primary	
Interviews with chefs (n|t)	35|40.90 h
Participating observations (n|t)	8|16.25 h
Informal talks with staff and chefs (n)	20
Product experience: Dinners (n|t)	8|36 h
Documented data, e.g. menus (n)	Anzahl
Secondary	
Interviews with critics (n|t)	24|20.85 h
Documented data, e.g. ratings, articles (n)	590

included all references to the menu and the process used to alter it and was done with the help of qualitative data analysis software (Atlas.ti). This first step aimed at gaining a general understanding of the characteristics of the menu, and properties of the menu development process. As a result of this first step, we were able to identify the distinct functions that a menu fulfills, which serve as important reference points in the development process.

Next, we reconstructed the evolution of the menus over time using the six units of analysis we selected for the case. This step was aimed at gaining a detailed understanding of the interaction between artifact and performance over time. In order to do so, we first collected all codes from step one with reference to a specific unit of analysis and ordered them chronologically as well as thematically (artifact, process).

In the third step, we used our two theoretical concepts of *agencement* and *inscription* as interpretative codes. In this process, we coded the data in a two-stage process: first we coded the data by distinguishing between potentiality and actuality, coding as '*agencement*' anything actors described as potentialities (Luhmann 1995, pp. 65–66), given the current properties of the artifact, as well as what they selected (actualized) from those potentialities and why. Any references to those aspects of the artifact that were changed and which remained stable over time as a consequence of performance were coded as '*inscription*'. In the second stage, we distinguished between different types of *agencement* and inscription by applying the two dimensions (replication vs. reformation, confirmation vs. overwriting) to the data. As a result, we were able to identify overarching patterns (textures and inscription into the textures) resulting from differences in *agencement* and their impact on ongoing performance, as well as different forms of inscription into the artifact (menu). In sum, our understanding of that process provided a platform for understanding how artifacts pre-present things to come.

Findings

Our findings follow closely the selected units of analysis and move from general to specific. In order to illustrate the central role that the artifact 'menu' plays in the context of haute cuisine, we first briefly describe the artifact. In this context, we reveal the characteristics and functions of the menu in haute cuisine restaurants that we identified and relate them to its inherent elements and structural properties. Since innovativeness and creativity within the context of haute cuisine are mostly expressed through changes of the dishes on the menu (Ottenbacher and Harrington 2006, 2007; Harrington and Ottenbacher 2013), we move on to show the close linkage between the underlying routinized menu development process and the artifact 'menu'. This is done by providing a generalized description of the 'traditional' innovation process, in which we show what role the menu plays in the development and selection of new dishes and thus in the evolution of the menu over time. This first step does not go into detail on the different subunits we included in the study, but rather shows the overall flow of events, which could be identified as identical in the subunits analyzed. Based on this understanding, we analyze the respective forms of *agencement* in order to understand how a given artifact may pre-present things to come.

Menu as Artifact

When analyzing the menu as artifact, as already mentioned above, it becomes apparent that the artifact is understood in the field in the application (consciously but also unconsciously) of a clear distinction between two elements of the menu. On the one hand, the menu consists of a sort of outer frame—that we have called the menu *concept*. This concept finds expression in the name given to the menu, the style of the kitchen and the overall structure—for example, 'À la carte', '12-course menu' and so on—and mostly serves to build up an identity and profile and becomes or remains recognizable. It also includes rather fixed *rules,* including specifications of the order of the courses of the menu (such as appetizer, soup, fish course, meal course, cheese course, dessert), as well as compositional elements ('no repetition of components between the courses', 'seasonality', etc.). The concept itself can be either concrete or more abstract.

On the other hand, the inner part of the menu, that we have called the menu *content,* contains the actual dishes that are offered to the guests. Those choices can either be very broad or very narrow, referring to both the number of dishes offered and the variance in the selection and number of components and elements in each of the courses (see Fig. 14.3).

As it is generally subject to different degrees of regular and ongoing change, the menu content gives expression to innovativeness and creativity. As we will show later on in the chapter, the inherent structure of the artifact (concept and content) steers the menu development process to a great extent through its influence on *agencement,* and is subject to different degrees of inscription. Accordingly, both parts of the artifact can have a differentiated influence on both inscription and *agencement* and therefore different forms of impact on things to come.

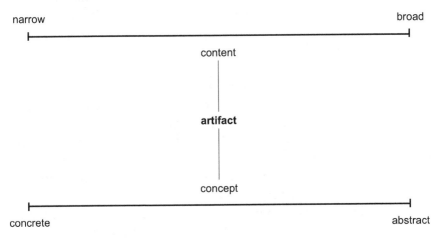

Fig. 14.3 Artifact dimensions

The central role of the menu relates to the functions the menu fulfills in the context of haute cuisine restaurants that not only render it the most visible and central artifact for the multiplicity of actors involved, but also necessitates consideration in the initial set-up as it is subject to diverging forces. Overall, the menu is the carrier and expression of four distinct functions, which are not only continually referred to by the chefs and their teams, but which also link all relevant processes within the restaurant and between the restaurant and its environment. The first most obvious function is directed to the environment, more particularly, the guest, and can be described as the 'communication function' (*face to the customer*). In this regard, the menu first of all serves as an advertisement for what is offered and thus can influence whether a specific restaurant is chosen for a visit or not. When at the restaurant, the menu provides orientation for the guest as to what to expect and what might be ordered. Along the same lines, it also determines the nature of the visit, as it structures the order in which the courses are served and the duration of the visit to the restaurant.

Closely related to this first function is the use of the menu as an expression of the identity of a restaurant and the profile of the kitchen. Generally, starred restaurants are expected and strive to develop a personal 'handprint' that makes them unique and identifiable. This 'signature' finds expression in the menu, which needs to reflect the individual style of the restaurant and to represent a coherent story. In this vein, the menu also serves as a narrative and a 'profile description', triggering and incorporating specific expectations on the part of both guests and critics (*profile*).

Aside from these externally oriented functions, the menu also has a great impact on the internal organization. Firstly, it opens and restrains the potential space for creative and innovative dish development (*innovation*). The new dishes that can be developed are restricted by the concept chosen, as well as the current content of the menu, and thus choices are actualized. This will become more obvious when we describe the menu development process later in the chapter.

Closely linked to this 'innovation function' are the two external functions as well as the second internal function: the 'value creation' function. Not only does the menu determine which supplies need to be in stock, which component suppliers need to be chosen or to be developed and which technologies should be applied, it also structures the production process, the 'distribution' logistics (as in timing the sequence of the dishes to be produced) and the service. That is, the menu reflects and influences the whole value chain of an haute cuisine restaurant (*value creation*).

Each of those functions reflects one or more of the typical dimensions of artifacts; in sum, giving the menu its instrumental, symbolic as well as aesthetic, artificial character (Rafaeli and Vilnai-Yavetz 2004). The menu plays, of course, an instrumental role in all four functions, as it leads the restaurant-guest interaction, plays a crucial role in the restaurant's profile development process, impacts on value creation from procurement to sales and frames the innovation potentialities. But it is also symbolic in nature, as it expresses the profile of a restaurant not only to the guests and critics but also reflexively for the organization itself. The aesthetic character is also reflected in all the four functions of the menu, because the narrative quality of communicating the emotional side of the menu is not only relevant to customers, but also to the internal processes of value creation, to innovation and to the restaurant's profile. In this vein, the menu also entails elements of all the different functions to tell a compelling story that 'explains' why the actual chosen appearance of the menu is the most appealing one.

The Menu Development Process

Looking at the evolution of the menu over time reveals two different processes: a regular menu development process within a given menu concept and structure, and a frame-breaking innovation process, which results in a revised concept and/or structure of the menu. The regular innovation process can be triggered from various sources: change of season, change in product availability, feedback from customers, motivation of the chef and team or inspiration from the environment. The starting point of the culinary development process is the existing menu of the restaurant. The first decision to be made by the chef concerns the degree of change to be made. The options are to innovate incrementally, that is, to only change certain parts of the menu content, or to innovate radically, that is, to change the whole menu and develop new content. Once this is decided upon, the team moves into the *idea generation phase,* which aims to identify a starting point for making changes. There are multiple options: either the chef has a concrete idea in mind (a product, a taste, an image) and assigns tasks to his team to work on in order to find ways to realize it; or the process gets initiated by brainstorming sessions with the entire team where possible ideas and alternatives are discussed and next steps are decided upon; or every team member is expected to come up with a potential new creation within his/her scope of action. This phase is to a large extent moderated by the current menu, wherein two aspects of the artifact play a key role: the menu concept and its content. Depending on the current menu concept (e.g. vegetarian, Austrian, local, classical, French and fish), only certain ideas or products can be actualized, which places a limit on available options. This is also true of the inherent structure rules, which provide specific requirements relating to the composition of the menu (e.g. à la carte, 10-course menu and lunch menu), to dish sizes and specifications (e.g. starter, main course and dessert), as well as to the inherent logic of the menu. The latter refers to the way in which the dishes on the menu 'fit together' to provide a coherent and comprehensive portrayal of the chef's oeuvre, while complementing but not repeating each other so that they offer an appropriate offering. As becomes obvious, these rules apply to both incremental and radical changes and concern either the fit between current and new dishes (incremental change) or the composition of new and significantly different dishes (radical change). With all of this in mind, the restaurant team then starts a *trial phase,* where newly developed ideas are gradually tested, presented to the chef, altered according to his feedback, retried and retested until they fit the ambitions. This phase usually takes place over a timespan of two to four weeks. Once the individual components are agreed upon, they are written down in a revised menu, which is the starting point for the final *test phase.* During this phase, the altered menu is tested with the service team and the sommelier, who work on the correct presentation of the new dishes and the story behind them. Once this step has been completed and no further alterations need to be made, the new or revised menu is put into action. This is the point at which new items get inscribed onto the menu. Whether they are only temporarily inscribed onto the menu or remain there longer or even permanently varies according to the subunit analyzed and depends on the menu concept and its structure rules as well as different timings for menu renewal. The new menu stays 'live' until a new cycle of innovation starts, triggered by any of the reasons listed above. When this happens, new processes of *agencement* are set into motion that might differ from the previous ones. This can occur when not only temporal content changes but also a higher degree of inscription into the outer or inner frame of the menu has taken place. While all of the steps described above take place within a given concept and structure, the latter can also be subject to alteration. The reasons for this rather radical step lie either within the culinary development process itself, or in any of the other functions the menu fulfills—namely *value creation, profiling* and *face to the customer*. If any one of those functions is seriously hampered by the current structure of the menu, the process of *agencement* does not lead to a setting that 'puts into motion a world in which it can function' (D'Adderio 2011, p. 217) and consequently changes have to be made in order to return to a situation where the assemblage of elements can properly function.

Discussion and Concluding Remarks

As we have seen in the findings, the menu as an artifact could be understood as a complex combination of different elements which are continuously put into a relation while being performed. This process of *agencement* refers to different underlying organizational processes which are orchestrated by the different dimensions and functions of the menu. Therefore, the menu can be understood as a moderator of the process of *agencement*, framing what kind of actualized assemblages are generally possible. The degree of variety depends on the two different dimensions of the menu (concept and content) and varies between abstract and concrete and broad and narrow. According to this perspective, the artifact has a direct impact on the potentiality of what is coming next and therefore describes a 'space of possibilities' in which possible forms of assemblages may be actualized. However, there is no direct impact on what is ultimately actualized in a concrete process of *agencement*, because what is actualized as a functioning assemblage of different elements depends in turn on the functions of the menu and hence the artifact. These functions are inscribed into the artifact by actual and past performances and therefore also reflect the interaction between the organization and its focal environment. Consequently, we can now understand that there are two different forms of impact the artifact has on things to come: the first impact is on the range of possibilities and hence on the potentiality of things to come, the second impact is that on the concrete functioning of an actualized assemblage.

This kind of differentiation offers a more nuanced and better understanding of the general question of the impact of organizational artifacts on organizational processes and on things to come. While MacKenzie (2003, 2006) suggests a continuum from 'deterministic' to 'no influence', we can now see that this determination has two different forms of impact. The first form refers to the potentiality of possible things to come, whereas the second refers to the functioning of an actualized assemblage. It is important to note that neither the first nor the second form of impact can be understood as a literal determination in the sense of a contingency. In comparison to a broad and abstract artifact, a narrow and concrete artifact reduces the potentiality of things to come, but it does not determine them. On the other hand, the functioning of an actualized assemblage of different kind of elements is a possible outcome but is not automatically the only possible actualization. Figure 14.4 summarizes these insights.

As a consequence, the idea of determination as applied to artifacts must be addressed using a more differentiated approach. The simple

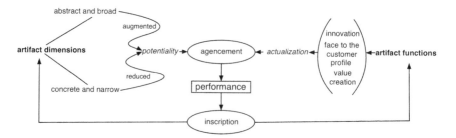

Fig. 14.4 Artifact dimensions and functions: potentiality and actualization

question of what comes next depends on both forms of impact and the crucial question is, how do both forms of impact relate to each other? On the basis of the background of our study and our findings, we are able to identify a possible relation between the two forms of impact: an abstract concept and broad range of content elements provide space for a wider spectrum of new things to come and hence for innovation, whereas a concrete concept and narrow range of content elements create a higher recognizability and understandability but a lower level of innovation. The latter effect might be caused by a direct link to, for example, specific iconographic products (in our case, certain 'signature dishes', or a specific culinary style which also finds expression in the name of the menu) and that automatically creates a restriction on possible choices. Thus, there might be an underlying strategic vector (Burgelman 2002) to narrower and more concrete artifacts if the functioning of the actualized performances might be more responsive to recognizability and understandability rather than newness and innovation. However, there is no indication as to why this should be the case in a general perspective. Consequently, it seems of much more interest to address the relation between artifacts and things to come beyond the dimension of 'determination versus no influence'. The question of the impact of artifacts on things to come is not that of 'if' and 'how much', but rather that of 'what kind' of ongoing process is occurring. Hence, the organizational artifacts which are produced and reproduced by a process of *agencement* and inscription do not already re-present the future as a concrete materialized form but pre-present the future as a range of variety of forms which might diminish or increase over time. Differentiating between an impact on potentiality and an impact on actualization and examining the interplay between them might be considered a first step toward a more nuanced and deeper understanding of such processes.

References

Bouty, Isabelle, and Marie-Léandre Gomez. 2010. Dishing Up Individual and Collective Dimensions in Organizational Knowing. *Management Learning* 41 (5): 545–559.

———. 2013. Creativity in Haute Cuisine: Strategic Knowledge and Practice in Gourmet Kitchens. *Journal of Culinary Science & Technology* 11 (1): 80–95.

Burgelman, Robert A. 2002. Strategy as Vector and the Inertia of Coevolutionary Lock-In. *Administrative Science Quarterly* 47: 325–357.

Cohen, Michael D., Roger Burkhart, Giovanni Dosi, Massimo Egidi, Luigi Marengo, Massimo Warglien, and Sidney Winter. 1996. Routines and Other Recurring Action Patterns of Organisations: Contemporary Research Issues. *Industrial and Corporate Change* 5: 653–698.

D'Adderio, Luciana. 2008. The Performativity of Routines: Theorising the Influence of Artefacts and Distributed Agencies on Routines Dynamics. *Research Policy* 37 (5): 769–789.

———. 2011. Artifacts at the Centre of Routines: Performing the Material Turn in Routines Theory. *Journal of Institutional Economics* 7 (2): 197–230.

D'Adderio, Luciana, and Neil Pollock. 2014. Performing Modularity: Competing Rules, Performative Struggles and the Effect of Organizational Theories on the Organization. *Organization Studies* 35 (12): 1813–1843.

Deleuze, Gilles, and Félix Guattari. 1987. *A Thousand Plateaus. Capitalism and Schizophrenia*. London: Continuum International Publishing Group.

Eisenhardt, Kathleen M. 1989. Building Theories from Case Study Research. *Academy of Management Review* 14 (4): 532–550.

Feldman, Martha S., Brian T. Pentland, Luciana D'Adderio, and Nathalie Lazaric. 2016. Beyond Routines as Things: Introduction to the Special Issue on Routine Dynamics. *Organization Science* 27 (3): 505–513.

Harrington, Robert J., and Michael C. Ottenbacher. 2013. Managing the Culinary Innovation Process: The Case of New Product Development. *Journal of Culinary Science & Technology* 11 (1): 4–18.

Koch, Jochen. 2011. Inscribed Strategies: Exploring the Organizational Nature of Strategic Lock-In. *Organization Studies* 32 (3): 337–363.

Koch, Jochen, Hannes Krämer, Andreas Reckwitz, and Matthias Wenzel. 2016. Zum Umgang mit Zukunft in Organisationen – eine praxistheoretische Perspektive. *Managementforschung* 26: 161–184.

Koch, Jochen, Matthias Wenzel, Ninja Natalie Senf, and Corinna Maibier. forthcoming. Organizational Creativity as an Attributional Process: The Case of Haute Cuisine. *Organization Studies*.

Latour, Bruno. 2007. *Reassembling the Social: An Introduction to Actor-Network-Theory*. New York: Oxford University Press.

Luhmann, Niklas. 1995. *Social Systems*. Stanford: Stanford University Press.

MacKenzie, Donald. 2003. An Equation and Its Worlds: Bricolage, Exemplars, Disunity and Performativity in Financial Economics. *Social Studies of Science* 33: 831–868.

———. 2006. Is Economics Performative? Option Theory and the Construction of Derivatives Markets. *Journal of the History of Economic Thought* 28: 29–55.

Martin, Joanne. 1992. *Cultures in Organizations: Three Perspectives*. New York: Oxford University Press.

Orlikowski, Wanda J. 1992. The Duality of Technology: Rethinking the Concept of Technology in Organizations. *Organization Science* 3 (3): 398–427.

Ottenbacher, Michael, and Robert J. Harrington. 2006. The Culinary Innovation Process: A Study of Michelin-Starred Chefs. *Journal of Culinary Science & Technology* 5 (4): 9–35.

———. 2007. The Innovation Development Process of Michelin-Starred Chefs. *International Journal of Contemporary Hospitality Management* 19 (6/7): 444–460.

Pentland, Brian T., and Martha S. Feldman. 2005. Organizational Routines as a Unit of Analysis. *Industrial and Corporate Change* 14 (5): 793–815.

———. 2008. Designing Routines: On the Folly of Designing Artifacts, While Hoping for Patterns of Action. *Information & Organization* 18 (4): 235–250.

Perrow, Charles. 1973. Some Reflections on Technology and Organizational Analysis. In *Modern Organizational Theory – Contextual, Environmental, and Socio-Cultural Variables*, ed. A.R. Negandhi, 47–57. Kent: Kent State University Press.

Rafaeli, Anat, and Iris Vilnai-Yavetz. 2004. Emotion as a Connection of Physical Artifacts and Organizations. *Organization Science* 15 (6): 671–686.

Schein, Edgar H. 1990. Organizational Culture. *American Psychologist* 45 (2): 109–119.

Schultze, Ulrike, and Wanda J. Orlikowski. 2004. A Practice Perspective on Technology-Mediated Network Relations: The Use of Internet-Based Self-Serve Technologies. *Information Systems Research* 15 (1): 87–106.

Scott, Susan V., and Wanda J. Orlikowski. 2012. Reconfiguring Relations of Accountability: Materialization of Social Media in the Travel Sector. *Accounting, Organizations & Society* 37 (1): 26–40.

Sydow, Jörg, Georg Schreyögg, and Jochen Koch. 2009. Organizational Path Dependence: Opening the Black Box. *Academy of Management Review* 34 (4): 689–709.

Tsoukas, Haridimos, and Robert Chia. 2002. On Organizational Becoming: Rethinking Organizational Change. *Organization Science* 13 (5): 567–582.

Vaara, Eero, Janne Tienari, Rebecca Piekkari, and Risto Säntti. 2005. Language and the Circuits of Power in a Merging Multinational Corporation. *Journal of Management Studies* 42 (3): 595–623.

Woodward, Joan. 1958. *Management and Technology*. London: Oxford University Press.

Yin, Robert K. 2014. *Case Study Research: Design and Methods*. 5th ed. Thousand Oaks: Sage.

15

Solid Futures: Office Architecture and the Labour Imaginary

David Adler

Introduction

In recent years, there has been an increasing level of interest in the relevance of future for economic and political practices. This has important consequences for the understanding of organizations. The financial crisis that has shaken the world economy since 2007 has sensitized both the public and science's perception of the unpredictability of economic developments. Of course, economic calamities are not unfamiliar to the twentieth century. However, while modern organizations tended to deal with external imponderabilities through internal rationalization and structuration, even the most complex forms of dealing with the future in a calculative way seem to fail today. The technological means to 'defuturize' the future—that is, to transform the open uncertainty of the things to come into a manageable risk—fall short of their promise (Esposito 2010; Opitz and Tellmann 2015; Luhmann 1976). In this context, the rationalist and

---

D. Adler (✉)
Carl von Ossietzky University of Oldenburg, Oldenburg, Germany

Ruhr-University Bochum, Bochum, Germany

© The Author(s) 2018
H. Krämer, M. Wenzel (eds.), *How Organizations Manage the Future*,
https://doi.org/10.1007/978-3-319-74506-0_15

functionalist image of organizations seems more and more problematic. Accordingly, Jens Beckert (2016) has, in his recent account of the temporality of capitalist dynamics, stressed the importance of the imaginary for dealing with the future. This chapter explicitly addresses this interest in the imaginary dimension. However, I see two shortcomings in recent debates. While there has been extensive work on the role of money for economic temporality and the handling of the future, labour and materiality are largely absent from the analysis. Beckert and others assert the general importance of the imaginary. However, the organization of work seems to chiefly remain the domain of an instrumentalist perspective.

In contrast, I want to argue that the imaginary also plays a fundamental role not only in financial projections or in organizational decision-making but also in the organization's everyday dealing with and performing of work. For this, I want to turn to office architecture. Contrary to the predominant instrumentalist perspective on office space, I argue that it takes effect as a *materialized imaginary*. And it is precisely the temporality of economic practices and the openness of future which render this dimension significant for an understanding of organizations and the material culture of capitalism.

Of course, this chapter cannot claim to sufficiently remedy the shortcomings mentioned above. Also, with the organization's 'futures' developed here, I do not raise a claim to completeness. I do not doubt the enduring significance of calculative modes of dealing with organizational futures, and such modes can clearly be found in the professional discourses on office architecture as well as the organizational processing of architecture and space. However, it can be problematic to ignore that these calculative practices are accompanied, supported or subverted by culturally sedimented and practically incorporated imaginaries.

Office Space and the Labour Relation

The main currents in organization studies have traditionally seen organizations as parcels of a process of rationalization. Organizations are defined by more or less explicit goals, which are pursued with an ever more efficient deployment of resources (cf. Thompson and McHugh 2009, pp. 6–13). In this perspective, organizational architecture must first of all be conceived within an instrumentalist paradigm. In *work organizations*, human labour becomes the focal point of this instrumental endeavour. The appearance of the office as a specific building type is closely linked to the most prominent way of 'governing' work activities: Taylorism. By minimizing the individual workspace and preventing unnecessary movement and communication, the office building was expected to increase the overall efficiency of administrative work (cf. Galloway 1922). Even though the design of offices has a long history, it is only since the beginning of the twentieth century that the construction and design of office spaces have become objects of a systematic interest, a means of production of its own, which have to be deployed thriftily and efficiently (cf. Fritz 1982). This vision was gladly taken up by modernist architects, who sought to rationally organize social life based on the ideal of a smoothly running machine, abandoning the dissipation of traditional buildings along with their ornamentation. In his seminal textbook *Bauentwurfslehre*, first edited in 1936, the Bauhaus-educated architect Ernst Neufert symptomatically bases guidelines for offices and many other spaces on the 'smallest possible dimensions' of railway carriages and buses (Neufert 1936, pp. 26–27; see also Le Corbusier 2007, pp. 145–192).

Of course, today's work life has changed dramatically. Individualizing and mechanistic models have been substituted by concepts of organizational culture and human resource management. Office design is increasingly meant to foster productivity rather than just to overcome inefficiency. Communication and creativity have become central objectives in contemporary management (Bröckling 2016; Reckwitz 2017). Despite all these changes, and despite the fact that these categories are arguably much more difficult to put into numbers, even today, the dominant perspective on office architecture is an instrumentalist one. Interestingly, this holds just as true for management consultancy and applied research as it does for 'critical' approaches. While one side admires the increased productivity brought about by new spatial models and technologies, the other side decries a process of a progressing subtlety and efficiency of control based on the refinement of governmental knowledge (Fritz 1982; Remmers 2011; Parker 2016).

To move beyond such an instrumentalist understanding of office architecture, it is helpful to remember that in capitalism the labour relation is temporally structured. Despite work being treated as a commodity in capitalism, the entrepreneur acquires no clearly defined good. On the contrary, labour as a 'fictitious commodity' (Polanyi) is constitutively a mere potentiality: only as such does it allow for organizational adaption to the unforeseeable new and, ultimately, the appropriation of surplus value. The tension between labour as commodity and labour as potentiality means that organizations must deal with labour as something *which has yet to be realized*. The organization is dependent on the creativity and adaptability of labour; its realization cannot be guaranteed by a labour contract fixed in advance. This trait of the labour relation has been discussed extensively under the label of the 'transformation problem' (cf. Braverman 1998; Deutschmann 2011).

But how do we know about the absent potentiality of labour? Historical studies have pointed out that neither modernism nor Taylorism were just historical givens, but rather counterfactual ideals that helped to structure and direct economic and architectural discourses as well as practices (cf. Gartman 2009). In this sense, organizational technologies themselves seem to imply constructions of the 'future' of labour, making it practically relevant for present activities, providing meaning and orientation.

My argument is, in short, that work organizations have to establish an imaginary relation to the potentiality of labour. In this respect, office architecture plays an important role not only as an instrument moulding work practices but also as a materialized imaginary.

Architecture Beyond Instrumentalism

Traditionally, architecture has been seen as an expression of the social or economic structures and the knowledge and intentions of its time. In this vein, architecture is either a more or less passive 'expression' of existing social conditions, or it is explained by given functional needs (cf. Delitz 2009). Alternatively, architectural sociology can help to stress the active, imaginary and temporal dimension of the built environment.

In contrast to a representationalist approach to architecture, recent debates have stressed the active quality of architecture (Müller and Reichmann 2015). For instance, science and technology studies and

Actor Network Theory specifically point out the constitutive role of material artefacts for social practices, thus levelling the difference between human and non-human 'participants' and decentring the origin of action (Latour and Yaneva 2008; Johnson 1988). While this approach points to important blind spots of social theory, it entails on the other hand a danger of succumbing to an instrumentalist perspective once again. This becomes most evident when Bruno Latour highlights the importance of the design process, inscribing constraining scripts into artefacts while at the same time minimizing the contingencies and the recalcitrance of human practices in favour of a 'symmetrical' approach (cf. Latour 1994).

An interesting effort to integrate the symbolic and the constitutive dimensions of architecture has been put forward by Heike Delitz. Drawing among others on Henry Bergson and Cornelius Castoriadis, Delitz understands architecture as a 'media' of the social. In this perspective, society is not a positive 'fact'. Rather, society comes into existence only when it is made perceivable in images and symbols. Society is thus constituted by an imaginary projection, which is based on an ongoing process of 'becoming', rather than being premised on self-identity (Delitz 2009, especially pp. 111–126). This implies a temporal dimension of architecture as the imaginary constitutively transcends the self-sufficient present of the social. There is, however, another cultural theorist who has made the relationship between built space and time much more prominent: Walter Benjamin.

In an ambitious project, Benjamin studied the emergence and transformation of the Paris arcades—iron and glass-covered interstices between buildings which became central scenes of commerce in the nineteenth century—as well as department stores and the world exhibition structures (Fig. 15.1). Despite Benjamin understanding architecture, with its material 'persistence', as a 'witness' of the past (Benjamin 1983, 2002b, D°, 7; cf. Morton 2006), I want to argue that he delivers important tools for grasping the future-relatedness of architecture.

First, architecture cannot be understood as a simple representation of the past, because it is the product of an *active* engagement with its social preconditions. Architects are not just passive puppets of, say, the economic status quo, but they try to handle, use, change it; they follow ideologies and technological promises. Accordingly, architecture includes

Fig. 15.1 Passage de l'Opéra, Paris. (Photography by Charles Marville, ca. 1866)

imaginaries of what is to come. This aspect is most succinctly expressed in the historian Jules Michelet's motto, which Benjamin includes in his exposé for the arcades project: 'Each époque dreams the one to follow' (Benjamin 2002a, p. 4).

Second, Benjamin is interested in the 'afterlife of buildings' (Morton 2006). He dissociates the objects from the intentions of their creators, and asks how their meaning changes over time and maintains an urgency for the present by forming a constellation with other objects, ideas and so on. Benjamin emphasizes the active and constructive character of this constellation, in which an interpretation is produced. Talking specifically of architecture, he points out that the main form of its reception consists of its *usage*, not its visual contemplation (Benjamin 2008, 40f.).

Finally, according to Benjamin, the commodities exposed in the arcades not only contain an exchange value and a use value, as traditional Marxist analysis has pointed out, but also a 'spiritual value'. This value 'endows the things of the everyday with an illusory glitter, an *aureole*: a weak remnant of the sacred' (Markus 2001, 16f.). The arcades do not only harbour this spiritual value neutrally, they embody it in themselves, in their construction and their atmosphere (Benjamin 2002a, pp. 3–5). With this insistence on the mythical dimension of capitalism, Benjamin contradicts the Weberian conception of modernity as a process of ever-growing rationalization (Steiner 2011). Taking up these thoughts from Benjamin means thus to problematize one of the core assumptions of classical organization studies. For Benjamin, the 'phantasmagoric' character of architecture primarily supports the dream-like reality of capitalism.

It would, of course, be fruitful to further pursue the context of Benjamin's writing and to delineate his philosophical and historiographic endeavours more faithfully. However, I want to quarry out these thoughts from Benjamin and to position them in another constellation: that of contemporary office architecture and the organization of labour. Taking up Benjamin's interest in the dreamy and anticipatory dimension of architecture, I will address contemporary discourses on office architecture, in order to examine its promises and threats. Subsequently, I will tie the architectural discourse back in with the practical context of its usage in processes of planning and with the performative effects of its material manifestations. I thereby try to extend Benjamin's interest in the 'afterlife' of buildings to an interest in the 'life' of buildings. Finally, I want to propose that contemporary office architecture provides a stage for the organizational exposition of labour.

Discourse, Materiality, Praxis: A Brief Remark on Methodology

The following reflections on the interplay of space and time in work organizations are based on ongoing empirical research on the role of office architecture in contemporary capitalism. My methodological outline strives to grasp the imaginary dimension of architecture without lapsing into a purely hermeneutic attitude, interpreting architecture's forms and symbols from a detached position. I therefore assume a reflexivity of knowledge, materiality and praxis. In this perspective, practical effects of architecture are symbolically mediated, as much as architectural discourses have to be related back to practices. Accordingly, for my analysis, I employ a mixed methods approach, mainly drawing on discourse analysis and ethnography.

My discourse analytical empirical material consists of textbooks, professional and popular journals, newspaper articles, texts from leading architects and scientific articles. The documents are assembled into an open thematic corpus, with the main focus being on German publications since the turn of the twenty-first century. These documents are supplemented by ethnographic protocols, tape recordings, field documents and interviews from a three-month ethnographic study carried out in a midsize PR agency. The material was collected in a participant observation with daily presence from March to June 2015. The ethnography is influenced by my own strong participation as a trainee, working on several projects. At the same time, my established presence as a scientific observer allowed me to participate in additional meetings, to ask questions extensively and to sporadically conduct additional interviews. Even though further ethnographic investigation into the process of designing, planning and implementing office spaces would have been desirable, I limited myself to additional interviews with architects, to get some access to the strategies and negotiating practices which mediate conceptual knowledge of office architecture with the specific building at hand.

The Future(s) of Office Architecture

This section presents four dimensions in which office architecture is related to the future. First, I address how the future is dealt with in contemporary architectural discourses on the office. Second, I want to ask how, in the process of planning office space, the colluding and contradicting temporalities of organization and architecture are dealt with. Third, I point to a specific practical temporality that is grounded in the performativity of office spaces. Finally, I want to argue that office space discursively, practically and materially supports a confidence in the fundamental future-ability of the organization at hand and, by extension, in capitalist labour relation's capacities to set free the potential of labour.

The Promise of Office Architecture

The discourse on office architecture is strongly marked by a temporal logic. The proclaimed aim is not an adaption to a current state of affairs, but, to use a common formula, the 'office of the future'[1] (Rief 2014). The general temporal orientation becomes evident at the semantic level in a vast amount of future-related expressions, such as 'fit for future', 'dreams of the future', 'potential for the future', 'guaranteeing the future', to mention but a few of the phrases from one seminal textbook (Staniek 2005). The temporal infrastructure narratively constitutes the office discourse and infuses it with urgency, thereby normatively motivating it. This becomes evident in an article on the 'quality of encounters'. The article starts with two scenes, which are described as occurring simultaneously in different corporations: one employee sits secluded in a grey cellular office, attached to a gloomy corridor with an unattractive staff kitchen; the other works without a fixed desk, is in permanent exchange with his colleagues and has access to an espresso bar with an inviting ambience. The author concludes his micro-narrative by stating: 'Two-thirds of the office workers are still placed in traditional offices similar to the first example. The second example, in contrast, describes the typical workday in a corporation which has already chosen an office concept headed towards the future' (Muschiol 2005, p. 201). In a similar vein, Wolfgang

D. Prix, co-founder of Coop Himmelb(l)au and architect of the new European Central Bank in Frankfurt, explains that an architect has to think ahead for 'at least 10–20 years' (Prix 2013, p. 3). What is at stake in both cases is not only an anticipation of what the present will look like once the building is realized and what is sought is not only a future present, but also a future that will still be a future tomorrow.[2] The aim is for the building to be permanently ahead of its time. On the symbolical surface, this ambition can easily be observed in the 'futuristic' allusions of current IT and social media corporations. For instance, the new Apple headquarters, a giant circular structure designed by the high-tech architect Norman Foster, is generally compared to an unidentified flying object (cf. for instance Wadewitz 2015, 80f.) (Fig. 15.2).

The future is, however, not only inscribed into the façade of contemporary office designs. In fact, organizations are faced with a complementary discourse of promises and threats. While the rhetoric is largely scientific, the 'office of the future' is promoted using truly miraculous

Fig. 15.2 Has the 'mothership' landed? The new Apple headquarters in Cupertino is constantly compared to a spaceship

forecasts, such as decreasing process costs by 40 per cent and workplace costs by 30 per cent (cf. Muschiol 2005, p. 207). On the other hand, corporations which do not cater to the dynamics of present futures—explicitly eluding easy calculations—'run the risk of losing their position to competitors on the global market place' (Messedat 2005, p. 15).

Strong promises made for the new technologies of work are certainly not new. Frederick W. Taylor emphasized that his method 'would readily in the future double the productivity of the average man' (Taylor 1913, p. 142). There is an important difference though. Taylor's future is primarily an overcoming of the past—eliminating wrong attitudes, conflicting relations, bad habits, which prevent the human machines from whirring smoothly. Ultimately, this future is grounded in a mechanistic optimum. This changes with the transformation of office work and the increasing importance of communication and creativity (Allen 1984; Reckwitz 2017; Krämer 2014, pp. 30–58), which opens up a new potentiality of the future. Office spaces are now expected to become 'generative' on their own, producing communication and creativity (Kornberger and Clegg 2004; Klauck 2002). This situation produces a certain ambivalence: in stressing the openness and unimaginable potentiality of future, it becomes more and more unforeseeable—and that means also less claimable by architecture. This directly points to the next aspect of the intersecting temporalities of architecture and organization in the process of planning.

Planning (for) the Future

The particular temporality of office buildings means that they cannot be understood as purely functional for present circumstances. Architecture plans for a future present, the time of completion, *and* a present future, which cannot be exhausted by technical procedures. The persistence of built space confronts the organization with a need to construe a proper future.

While architects need to 'fix' a future at some point, to be able to execute and complete a building, economic organizations incessantly alter their future according to given and anticipated events. This can produce a conflict between clients and architects, in which architectural work is repeatedly subverted. With changing market situations, changes in public discourses or impending scandals, assessments of the future needs of the organization can change drastically. However, in order to 'go on' without ending in chaos, at one point a 'design freeze' becomes essential, as one architect pointed out in an interview on an office project for a large international corporation. By 'freezing' the future, however, it is cut off from the horizon of possibilities and thus risks becoming outdated. For example, the number of workstations can be too few, once the building is completed.[3] Architects and organizations react to this risk with the inclusion of a certain amount of leeway in the project. Wolfgang D. Prix (2013, p. 3) proposes an 'intelligent Himmelblau meter' in this context, consisting of 1 m × 1.05. The unforeseeable future of market developments and innovations is thus complemented by the generalized assumption of moderate but continual growth.

A second way of handling the future can be seen in efforts to include openness and flexibility in office spaces. As '[a]nything which lasts into the future lasts into uncertainty' (Duffy et al. 1976, p. 5), architects will have to *avoid* strong architectural programmes. This has led to an internal temporal differentiation of the office. 'Shell design is for (say) 40 years; scenery design for seven years; set design for three months' (Duffy et al. 1976, p. 5). Although adaptability has always been of interest for office buildings (Galloway 1922, pp. 43–44; Neufert 1936, p. 171), reversibility has become an ever more pressing requirement since the 1990s, due to the demands of sustainability and flexibility, as well as the diversification of work forms. And, how could it be otherwise, reversibility is marked as a sine qua non for future success: 'Adaptability is therefore for sure a fundamental constituent of the future viability of buildings' (Voss et al. 2006, p. I). The extensive promises generally found in architectural discourse are thus confronted with the recommendation to avoid rigid architectural determinations in planning.[4] Architecture tries to handle the contingencies of the organization's future by increasing the contingencies of built space. This implies a redistribution of the decision-making and the responsibility for the office design from architects to interior designers, management and, finally, employees.

Performing Office Architecture

Office architecture promises to foster creativity, stimulate communication and, not least, increase productivity. If we look at local practices within the organization, the virtues attributed to architectural concepts appear less to be given facts guaranteed by the spatial arrangements but rather something which must be actively produced in organizational practices and work activities. Microsociologists have pointed out that technology does not 'work' on its own, but has to be performed (Law and Singleton 2000). This leads us to recognize the active engagement with and transformation of office spaces, rather than assuming an instrumental effectivity of office layouts. If architecture 'acts' in the organizational context, it is quite often as a problem, not a solution. During my field work, a recurrent question—and likely the first one to be discussed—would be *where* to carry out a specific activity. In the multi-option office, the employees are responsible for finding the best spot for their work, taking into account potential disturbances to co-present colleagues, access to technological resources as well as aesthetically and semiotically marked territories, such as the 'informal' and 'cosy' kitchen versus the 'official' conference room.

The prospect of a wilful spatial creation of creativity is in itself paradoxical. Even though the social aspect of creativity can be stressed in relation to its heroic attribution to lonely geniuses or venturous entrepreneurs (cf. Krämer 2014, pp. 160–168; Deutschmann 2011, p. 95), the architectural production of creativity claims a technological grasp of something which is quintessentially valued for being non-technological.

Set against this background, organizational space does not only present an everyday problem for situating work practices, it is also problematized itself. In my case study, the employees perceived the tension between the aspirations built into their work environment and the mundane reality of their work activities. There was the shared feeling that (a) work in the agency was not as creative as it should be, and (b) the creativity of the employees and their work was not sufficiently reflected in the agency's spatio-material appearance. This feeling resulted in an extensive effort to revamp the office space, initiated neither by the head of department nor the CEO, but by a group of senior and junior consultants.[5] This transformation of the office will not, in all likelihood, be the last. It should be considered to be one attempt among many to practically bring about that which was already promised in office discourses, thereby keeping alive the imaginary of office architecture. Other than simply *producing* a future, office architecture thus constitutes a perpetual practical occasion and need for *performing* the future.

Staging the Potentiality of Labour

I have argued that architecture's promises have to be practically performed, but this also includes a scenical aspect. Architecture is not only construed as a machine to produce creativity, communication and ultimately productivity, it also *stages* the general capacity of the organization to access the potential of human activity and put it to its use. In my ethnographical case study, the CEO would regularly take potential clients for a tour around the agency, telling them: 'This is where we do our PR work'. He was referring to current projects based more on free association than on any detailed knowledge of the everyday activities of the department—sometimes even mentioning projects that were never realized. It was thus less the actual work that was (re-)presented here, but the capacities that can and will be activated for the benefit of the client. These capacities are, however, hardly tangible by the mere glance at everyday work practices. As an intern, I was regularly confronted with the problem of the surprising *intransparency* of the bodily practices of my colleagues, not knowing when it would be best to approach them. A presentation of the organization's potential cannot rely on the display of work alone. This is where office architecture comes into play again. In providing an imaginary charged frame, the material work environment permits this 'presentation'—the making-present of the constitutively absent—in a particularly palpable manner.

In his ethnography of creative work, Hannes Krämer points out that there is a blending of organizational 'backstage' and 'frontstage', understood as spaces of production and spaces of representation (Krämer 2014, pp. 137–147). In keeping with the argument put forward here, it is even more apparent that the space of work and production has in itself become a central representational space of the organization. In times when network economics prevail, the interpenetration of organizations increases and self-marketing becomes an ongoing necessity. This implies that organizational 'impression management' (Goffman) is relocated from the official façade to the depth of the organizational space. Accordingly, staging work seems to become more and more important for the public display of a corporation's economic potency, and work moves from the back room of the organization to its showroom (cf. Warhurst et al. 2000; Castells 2010). For the organization, this exhibition of labour is essential, because it gives a sensory impression of the organization's own human 'assets' delivering the necessary services or goods to potential clients.

Furthermore, office architecture has become the object of newspaper articles, business magazines as well as documentary films, some of which I have mentioned above. Office architecture thus becomes relevant for a societal imaginary of labour, moving beyond the professional circles immediately concerned with its construction and utilization. This public dimension of the office architecture's imaginary becomes manifest in the structure of new buildings. The monolithic block of modernism is dissolved into more or less complex layers, blurring the inside world and the outside world. Atria, passages and even parks make the office building partly accessible to the public. The Unilever headquarters for Germany, Austria and Switzerland in Hamburg is one of many examples of this. The building, designed by Behnisch Architects, splits into two parts connected by an atrium, with bridges and balconies providing shared spaces for informal meetings. At the same time, the atrium invites the public into the building, providing a café and a small shop (Fitz 2012, p. 39) (Fig. 15.3).

Interestingly, such interstitial spaces echo the semi-public spaces of the arcades, galleries and department stores with their characteristic iron and glass roofing as described by Benjamin. In his exposé to the Arcades Project, he remarks, in respect of the World Exhibitions of the nineteenth century, that the objects on display gain an auratic value, which exceeds both exchange value and use value (Benjamin 2002a, p. 7). Perhaps office architecture, in its imaginary dimension, provides something similar for the realm of labour. Architectural promises, the building's practical problems, its effects on work performance, as well as organizational self-marketing, all of these form a

Fig. 15.3 Artrium and meeting points. The Unilever headquarters for Germany, Austria and Switzerland in Hamburg by Behnisch Architekten

constellation in which office architecture represents the quasi inexhaustible communicative, creative and productive potential of labour, while at the same time promising managerial access to it.

In presenting the 'commodity of labour power' (Marx), the 'arcades' of contemporary office architecture and their amplification in journals and magazines add up to a societal understanding of the productive prospects of work organization(s), which is probably not only fostering confidence in the future-ability of a specific corporation, but, beyond that, in the capitalist labour relation itself.

Conclusion

This chapter attempts to show how office space is generated by and generates an anticipation of the future. It therefore cannot simply be understood in terms of its functionality or instrumentality for given social or economic structures. In the perspective proposed here, instrumentality and functionality must rather be understood based on concrete practices of knowledge generation and usage, which are themselves part of complex organizational procedures and dynamics. Office architecture is impregnated with specific concepts and imaginaries of rationality and efficiency, creativity and productivity. Building on recent theories about the future in economic sociology, I have tried to 'materialize' the discussion by putting labour and its built environment at the centre of my argument, pointing out that both are essentially constituted by relating to a future. This change of perspective allows for a wider reflection on the importance of the future for work organization. I have tried to show how the materiality of the contemporary office, in performing and staging access to the absent potential of labour, moulds actual working practices as well as infusing them with a subjective meaning. Instead of simply assuring objective technological progress, which either makes the office more and more rational and efficient or subjects the employees to more and more subtle and effective modes of power and control, office architecture *produces* an imaginary of an ever more successful utilization and activation of labour—an imaginary, which consolidates societal confidence in both work organizations and the labour relation.

Acknowledgements I want to thank David Waldecker, Jens Maeße, Thomas Alkemeyer, Thomas Scheffer, Johannes Angermuller, the editors and the anonymous reviewer for critical remarks and helpful suggestions. Furthermore, I am grateful to Annika Raapke for proofreading the article.

Notes

1. Quotes from German texts are the author's own translations.
2. I make use of the terminology proposed by Niklas Luhmann in 'The future cannot begin' (1976). Drawing on Edmund Husserl's phenomenology of time, Luhmann distinguishes between a future present, a date in the future we will once call now, and the future as a horizon of the present, which is marked by a constitutive openness and as such, can never be reached. While Luhmann opposes technology and utopia as two distinct modes of dealing with the future, my analysis would rather suggest the entanglement of both.
3. The first non-territorial open space office in Germany is said to have been born from this problem. The number of employees had outnumbered the number of workstations by the start of construction. The new office form allowed for the accommodation of more employees than desks (Staniek 2005, p. 59), thereby loosening the strict coupling of staff and surface.
4. Paradoxically, this is determining the architectural creative leeway quite a bit. For instance, the building's depth is bound to be between 14 and 15 metres in order to provide sufficient lighting for different office concepts (cf. Staniek and Staniek 2013, p. 39).
5. This case is analysed in detail in Adler (2017).

References

Adler, David. 2017. Die Entstehung einer Lounge. Ästhetisierung als praktischer Vollzug. In *Ästhetisierung der Arbeit*, ed. Ove Sutter and Valeska Flor, 33–49. Münster: Waxmann.

Allen, Thomas J. 1984. *Managing the Flow of Technology. Technology Transfer and the Dissemination of Technological Information Within the R&D Organization.* Cambridge/London: The MIT Press.

Beckert, Jens. 2016. *Imagined Futures. Fictional Expectations and Capitalist Dynamics.* Cambridge/London: Harvard University Press.
Benjamin, Walter. 1983. In *Das Passagen-Werk*, ed. Rolf Tiedemann. Frankfurt a. M: Suhrkamp.
———. 2002a. Paris, the Capital of the Nineteenth Century <Exposé of 1935>. In *The Arcades Project*, 3–13. Cambridge/London: The Belknap Press of Harvard University Press.
———. 2002b. *The Arcades Project.* Cambridge, MA/London: The Belknap Press of Harvard University Press.
———. 2008. The Work of Art in the Age of Its Technological Reproducibility: Second Version. In *The Work of Art in the Age of Its Technological Reproducibility and Other Writings on Media*, ed. Michael W. Jennings, Brigid Doherty, and Thomas Y. Levin. Cambridge/London: The Belknap Press of Harvard University Press.
Braverman, Harry. 1998. *Labor and Monopoly Capital: The Degradation of Work in the Twentieth Century.* New York: Monthly Review Press.
Bröckling, Ulrich. 2016. *The Entrepreneurial Self: Fabricating a New Type of Subject.* Los Angeles: SAGE.
Castells, Manuel. 2010. *The Rise of the Network Society.* 2nd ed. Chichester: Wiley-Blackwell.
Delitz, Heike. 2009. *Gebaute Gesellschaft. Architektur als Medium des Sozialen.* Frankfurt a. M./New York: Campus.
Deutschmann, Christoph. 2011. A Pragmatist Theory of Capitalism. *Socio-Economic Review* 9 (1): 83–106.
Duffy, Francis, Colin Cave, and John Worthington. 1976. The Principles of Office Design. In *Planning Office Space*, ed. Francis Duffy, Colin Cave, and John Worthington, 3–7. London: The Architectural Press.
Esposito, Elena. 2010. *Die Zukunft der Futures. Die Zeit des Geldes in Finanzwelt und Gesellschaft.* Heidelberg: Carl-Auer.
Fitz, Angelika. 2012. Arbeiten an der Identität. In *Arbeitende Orte. Büros mit Wert und Mehrwert*, ed. Angelika Fitz and kadawittfeldarchitektur, 11–39. Wien/New York: Springer.
Fritz, Hans-Joachim. 1982. *Menschen in Büroarbeitsräumen. Über langfristige Strukturwandlungen büroräumlicher Arbeitsbedingungen mit einem Vergleich von Klein- und Großraumbüros.* München: Heinz Moos Verlag.
Galloway, Lee. 1922. *Office Management. Its Principles and Practice.* New York: The Ronald Press Company. https://archive.org/details/officemanagement00gall.
Gartman, David. 2009. *From Autos to Architecture. Fordism and Architectural Aesthetics in the Twentieth Century.* New York: Princeton Architectural Press.

Johnson, Jim [Bruno Latour]. 1988. Mixing Humans and Nonhumans Together: The Sociology of a Door-Closer. *Social Problems* 35 (3): 298–310.
Klauck, Birgit. 2002. Vorwort. In *Entwurfsatlas Bürobau*, ed. Rainer Hascher, Simone Jeska, and Birgit Klauck, 8–9. Basel/Berlin: Birkhäuser.
Kornberger, Martin, and Stewart R. Clegg. 2004. Bringing Space Back in: Organizing the Generative Building. *Organization Studies* 25 (7): 1095–1114.
Krämer, Hannes. 2014. *Die Praxis der Kreativität. Eine Ethnografie kreativer Arbeit*. Bielefeld: transcript.
Latour, Bruno. 1994. On Technical Mediation – Philosophy, Sociology, Genealogy. *Common Knowledge* 3 (2): 29–64.
Latour, Bruno, and Albena Yaneva. 2008. 'Give Me a Gun and I Will Make All Buildings Move': An ANT's View of Architecture. In *Explorations in Architecture: Teaching, Design, Research*, ed. Reto Geiser, 80–89. Basel: Birkhäuser.
Law, John, and Vicky Singleton. 2000. Performing Technology's Stories. On Social Constructivism, Performance, and Performativity. *Technology and Culture* 41 (4): 765–775.
Corbusier, Le. 2007. *Towards an Architecture*. Los Angeles: Getty Publications.
Luhmann, Niklas. 1976. The Future Cannot Begin: Temporal Structures in Modern Society. *Social Research* 43 (1): 130–150.
Markus, Gyorgy. 2001. Walter Benjamin or The Commodity as Phantasmagoria. *New German Critique* 83: 3–42.
Messedat, Jons. 2005. *Corporate Architecture. Development, Concepts, Strategies*. Stuttgart: Avedition.
Morton, Patricia A. 2006. The Afterlife of Buildings: Architecture and Walter Benjamin's Theory of History. In *Rethinking Architectural Historiography*, ed. Dana Arnold, Elvan Alta Ergut, and Belgin Turan Özkaya, 215–228. London/New York: Routledge.
Müller, Anna-Lisa, and Werner Reichmann. 2015. The Actions of Architecture: Constituting a New Sociology of Architecture. In *Architecture, Materiality and Society. Connecting Sociology of Architecture with Science and Technology Studies*, ed. Anna-Lisa Müller and Werner Reichmann, 215–246. Houndmills/New York: Palgrave Macmillan.
Muschiol, Roman. 2005. Begegnungsqualität. In *BürobauAtlas. Grundlagen, Planung, Technologie, Arbeitsplatzqualität*, ed. Johann Eisele and Bettina Staniek, 200–207. München: Callwey.
Neufert, Ernst. 1936. *Bauentwurfslehre*. 2nd ed. Berlin: Bauwelt Verlag.
Opitz, Sven, and Ute Tellmann. 2015. Future Emergencies: Temporal Politics in Law and Economy. *Theory, Culture & Society* 32 (2): 107–129.

Parker, Lee D. 2016. From Scientific to Activity Based Office Management. *Journal of Accounting & Organizational Change* 12 (2): 177–202.
Prix, Wolfgang D. 2013. Homland Utopia. Presented at the KunstFestspiele Herrenhausen. Hannover, June 1. http://www.coophimmelblau.at/architecture/news/heimat-utopie-speech-by-wolf-d-prix/
Reckwitz, Andreas. 2017. *The Invention of Creativity Modern Society and the Culture of the New*. Cambridge/Malden: Polity.
Remmers, Burkhard. 2011. Office Design and Knowledge Economy. In *DETAIL Work Environments*, ed. Christian Schittich, 27–34. Basel: Birkhäuser.
Rief, Stefan. 2014. Das Büro der Zukunft ist Erlebnisorientiert [Interviewed by Myrta Köhler]. *Competition* 7: 65.
Staniek, Bettina. 2005. Büroorganisationsformen. In *BürobauAtlas. Grundlagen, Planung, Technologie, Arbeitsplatzqualität*, ed. Johann Eisele and Bettina Staniek, 54–67. München: Callwey.
Staniek, Bettina, and Claus Staniek. 2013. A Typology of Office Forms. In *DETAIL Best of Office*, ed. Christian Schittich, 32–43. München: Edition DETAIL.
Steiner, Uwe. 2011. Kapitalismus als Religion. In *Benjamin Handbuch: Leben – Werk – Wirkung*, ed. Burkhardt Lindner, 167–174. Stuttgart/Weimar: J. B. Metzler.
Taylor, Frederick Winslow. 1913. *The Principles of Scientific Management*. New York/London: Harper & Brothers.
Thompson, Paul, and David McHugh. 2009. *Work Organizations. A Critical Approach*. 4th ed. Houndsmills/New York: Palgrave Macmillan.
Voss, Karsten, Günter Löhnert, Sebastian Herkel, Andreas Wagner, and Mathias Wambsganß. 2006. *Bürogebäude mit Zukunft*. 2nd ed. Berlin: Solarpraxis.
Wadewitz, Felix. 2015. Büro der Zukunft. *Impulse*, no. 03/15: 81–87.
Warhurst, Chris, Dennis Nickson, Anne Witz, and Anne Marie Cullen. 2000. Aesthetic Labour in Interactive Service Work: Some Case Study Evidence from 'New' Glasgow. *The Service Industries Journal* 20 (3): 1–18.

Index[1]

A

Activity, 3, 6–8, 46–53, 55, 58–62, 136, 137, 147, 156, 174, 179–181, 226, 227, 234, 236, 245, 255, 256, 259–262, 265–271, 301, 302, 311, 312
Actor-Network-Theory (ANT), 12, 279, 303
Actuality, 280, 287
Administration, 1, 239
Adorno, Theodor W., 69
Agencement, 278–283, 285, 287–289, 293, 295
Amabile, Theresa M., 60, 71, 80
Antenarrative, 133–148
Anticipation, 2, 37, 45, 49, 68, 70, 74, 98, 100, 102, 118, 140, 173, 179, 186, 255, 270, 305, 308, 309, 315
Architecture, 7, 11, 299–315, 316n4
Arrow, Kenneth, 75
Artefact, 11–13, 175, 261, 262, 271, 303
Autopoiesis, 27, 29, 30, 127n1, 225, 227

B

Bauhaus, 301
Beckert, Jens, 1, 74, 95, 113, 117, 118, 133, 154, 231–233, 245, 246, 300
Benjamin, Walter, 303–305, 313
Bergson, Henri, 47, 69, 91, 303
Bertalanffy, Ludwig von, 115
Boje, David M., 133–137, 140, 142, 144, 147, 148

---

[1] Note: Page numbers followed by 'n' refer to notes.

322　Index

C

Capitalism, 300–302, 305–307, 315
Change, 8, 9, 26, 27, 32–34, 36, 37, 39, 40, 46, 47, 50, 51, 54, 57, 59, 61, 68, 70, 75, 76, 78, 80, 91, 95, 99, 121, 124, 133–148, 158, 161, 166, 173, 176, 179, 181, 184–186, 232, 248, 255, 257, 270, 271, 277, 281, 283–289, 291–293, 301, 303, 305, 309, 310, 315
City, 10, 11, 231–248
Coherence, 135, 138, 140, 143, 145, 163, 168, 266, 290, 292
Communication, 27–30, 60, 121, 140, 174, 184, 185, 219, 221, 232, 235, 240, 245, 257, 278, 290, 301, 309, 311, 312
Complementarity, 69, 72–74
Connectivity, 27–30
Context, 3, 32, 47, 48, 57, 59, 62, 68, 78, 80, 82, 93, 101, 107, 107n2, 120, 134, 140, 154, 160–162, 175, 176, 182, 184–186, 196, 209, 210, 233, 236, 271, 279, 281, 284, 286, 288, 290, 299, 305, 310, 311
Contingency, 28, 30, 59, 68–72, 79–82, 90, 92–101, 103, 115, 116, 175, 294, 303, 310
Continuity, 115, 175, 224, 281
Corporate actorhood, 69, 83

Corporate incubating, 9, 114, 118–120, 125, 126
Corporation, 1, 83, 83n3, 120, 122, 124, 307–310, 313, 315
Creativity, 8, 26, 46–48, 51, 60, 61, 67–83, 284, 288, 289, 301, 302, 309, 311, 312, 315
Cross-Impact Balance Analysis (CIB), 156, 157, 159–168
Crowdsourcing, 9, 118–119, 125

D

Darwin, Charles, 50, 59
Dasein (Heidegger), 51, 52, 58, 101–104, 106, 107
Data analysis, 123, 237, 286–288
Database, 264, 286
Data source, 259–260, 285, 286
Decision, decision-making, 5, 7, 8, 12, 25–40, 68, 69, 74, 80, 101, 114, 116, 117, 122, 123, 125, 126, 154, 156, 158, 160, 174, 175, 178, 181, 183, 216, 218–221, 225, 245, 261, 262, 265, 268, 285, 291, 300, 310
Deconstruction, 153–169, 169n3
Defuturization, 25–40, 299
　See also Futurization
Derrida, Jaques, 70, 73, 74, 157
Destruction, 71
Digitalization, 11, 143–147, 232–234, 238, 240, 242, 243, 245, 248

Digital transformation, 10
Disaster, 10
Disclosure, 106, 123, 183
Discourse, 4, 12, 27, 32, 33,
    133–136, 138, 141, 143–145,
    148, 154, 157, 160, 167, 168,
    215, 217, 300, 302, 305–308,
    310, 312
Discourse analysis, 11, 33, 160, 306
Diversification, 147, 310
Durkheim, Émile, 25

E
Efficiency, 25, 26, 34, 116, 239,
    301, 315
Elster, Jon, 69, 78–82
Emergency, 4, 215, 216, 219, 222,
    223, 227
Emergency planning, 10, 216, 217,
    222–227
Empirics, 5, 7, 10–12, 27, 29, 32–34,
    47, 48, 100, 160, 217, 227n1,
    233, 253, 255, 281, 306
Enactment, 6, 75, 178–181, 186,
    223, 268
Entwurf (Schutz), 74
Environment, 3, 26, 35–38, 47, 50,
    51, 57, 62, 78, 93, 99, 115,
    143, 145, 146, 154, 158, 166,
    173, 178, 225, 247, 263, 269,
    285, 286, 290, 291, 294, 302,
    311, 312, 315
Event, 2, 5, 13, 27, 28, 47, 49–53,
    57–59, 61, 62, 93, 94, 98,
    100, 121, 123, 134, 135,
    138, 139, 146, 175–177,
    179, 182–185, 216, 220,
    221, 233, 237, 254, 259,
    264–266, 271, 277,
    288, 309
Experience, 3, 25, 26, 34, 46–51,
    54–59, 91, 94, 95, 97, 99,
    135, 138, 140, 147, 176,
    182, 223, 235, 241,
    286, 287

F
Fictional expectations (Beckert), 154
Fidelity, 135, 138, 140, 142,
    143, 145
Field-configuring events (FCE),
    11, 254–256, 258–261, 264,
    265, 269, 270
Flexibility, 35, 181, 310
For-profit organization, 238, 240,
    246, 247
Foucault, Michel,
    157, 169n1
Future, 1–13, 25, 45, 67, 90,
    113–127, 133–148, 153–168,
    173–187, 215, 231–248, 253,
    278, 299–315
    collective, 253–272
    imagined, 12, 74, 75, 154, 232,
    233, 245, 246
Future-perfect thinking, 90, 96–98,
    100, 101, 187
Futurity, 12, 101–104, 106
Futurization, 25–40
    See also Defuturization

Giddens, Anthony, 68, 73, 79, 82, 116, 117, 256, 257, 267, 270
Globalization, 72, 158, 162
Global Outbreak Alert and Response Network (GOARN), 219, 220

Haute cuisine, 11, 277–295
Hayek, Friedrich von, 116
Heidegger, Martin, 47, 51, 59, 61, 77, 90, 102, 103, 106
Hernes, Tor, 3, 5, 26, 31, 90, 92, 97, 232, 245, 246
Hierarchy, 13, 83, 145, 221
High-hazard organization, 195, 196, 207, 209, 210
High-reliability organization, 195, 207
Historical methods, 9, 10, 12, 173–187
History, 2, 3, 39, 71, 92, 98, 160, 173–177, 183, 185, 186, 231, 237, 301
Hobbes, Thomas, 218
Human capital, 196
Human rights, 222

Impact(s), 51, 56, 160–161, 163–165, 173, 178, 180, 181, 184–186, 201, 204–206, 216, 219, 220, 260, 265, 267–270, 281, 283, 284, 288–291, 293–295
Innovation, 9, 60, 75, 76, 79, 80, 82, 114, 117–120, 125–127, 174, 233, 238, 239, 245–247, 254, 257, 284, 286, 288, 290, 291, 293, 295, 310

Innovation network, 11, 13, 78, 233, 235–237, 242–248
Inscription, 11, 49, 278–283, 287–289, 293, 295
Institution, 139, 175, 176, 215, 219, 254–258, 262
Institutional creation, maintenance and disruption, 260, 272
Institutionalization, 254, 269–271
Institutionalized practices, 8, 254, 265, 268
Institutional life, 254–256, 265, 267, 271
Institutional theory, 11, 255
Institutional work, 11, 254–267, 270–272
Intelligibility, 53, 104–107
Interorganizational network, 233, 246, 247
Interpretative research methodology, 258
Intervention, 10, 73, 215–217, 219–222, 225, 226, 241
Intuitive Logics, 161–163, 167, 169n4

Kierkegaard, Søren, 79
Knight, Frank H., 7, 78, 95
Kontingenzbewältigung (Lübbe), 70
Koselleck, Reinhart, 25, 32, 33, 93–95, 100–102

Labour, 77, 261, 299–315
Lakoff, Andrew, 216, 221, 222, 224, 225
Leadership, 126, 178, 209

Learning, 34, 67–84, 115, 120, 174, 186, 195, 198–204, 209, 210, 242, 243
Legal person, 218
Legitimation, 6, 25, 26, 32, 69, 134, 145, 257, 262, 267, 272
Lübbe, Hermann, 70
Luhmann, Niklas, 1, 7, 25, 27–32, 35, 67, 71, 79, 80, 95, 127n1, 218, 227, 280, 287, 299, 316n2

M

Management, 3, 26, 71, 92, 114, 137, 173, 233, 301
Materiality, 278–280, 300, 306, 315
Mead, George Herbert, 8, 47–51, 57–62, 97
Media, 12, 122, 127, 145, 174, 176, 266, 303, 308
Meta-narrative, 271
Mexic City, 200, 205
Moore's Law, 257, 258, 271

N

Narrative, 9, 12, 80, 134–138, 140, 141, 143, 145, 154, 157, 158, 160, 177, 183, 216, 290, 291
Natural person, 218
Neo-institutional theory, 255
Network, 47, 72, 78, 169n4, 219–221, 223, 225, 233–239, 241–243, 245–247, 257, 313
Nietzsche, Friedrich, 69, 80–82
Novelty, 46–48, 50, 51, 56–62, 246

O

Object, 50, 55, 57, 77, 83, 115, 234, 258, 301, 304, 305, 313
Office, 7, 11, 55, 299–315
Ontology, 5, 8, 49–53, 58–62, 90, 91, 97, 102, 106, 154, 156, 157, 167
Open innovation, 9, 113–127, 247
Openness, 9, 12, 29, 74, 114–116, 122, 125–127, 232, 300, 309, 310, 316n2
Organism, 50, 51, 60, 62
Organizational artifacts, 277–295
Organizational change, 133–136, 147, 148
Organizational communication, 134
Organizational creativity, 82
Organizational culture, 79, 301
Organizational fields, 254, 255, 258–260, 265, 269, 270
Organizational futurity, 8, 89–107
Organizational knowing/knowledge, 8, 89, 90, 92–101, 103, 104, 107
Organizational network, 217, 219, 225
Organizational practice, 6, 26, 32, 40, 105, 114, 117, 125, 169n1, 311
 of openness, 114, 116–117, 127
Organizational resiliency, 223
Organizational storytelling, 134, 136
Organizational structure, 120
Organizational temporality, 89–92, 97, 102, 103, 105
Organization of work, 116, 300
Organization/organizing, 1, 25, 29–32, 45, 67–83, 89, 113, 133, 153–168, 173–187, 215–227, 231, 253, 299
Orlikowski, Wanda, 5, 6, 94, 95, 113, 117, 236, 277, 278

P

Pandemic, 7, 10, 215–228
Paradox, 4, 30, 31, 37, 40, 67–69, 72–74, 78–80, 96, 116, 125, 311, 316n4
Path dependence, 2, 68, 70, 71, 245, 280
Performance, 12, 53, 62n1, 70, 105, 279, 280, 283, 285–288, 294, 295, 313
Perrow, Charles, 78, 226, 277
Philosophy, 7, 8, 12, 46–51, 59, 62, 67–83, 97, 176, 305
Planning, 2–4, 6, 10, 26, 36–38, 69, 98, 99, 114, 116, 117, 167, 216, 217, 225, 265, 305–307, 309–310
  instruments, 26
  process, 223, 224
Plato, 75, 79
Polanyi, Michael, 79, 302
Popper, Karl, 115, 116
Positive adjustment, 195
(Post-)modernity, 1, 2, 25
Poststructuralism, 153–169
Potentiality, 280, 287, 291, 293–295, 302, 309, 312–315
Practice, 2, 26, 45–62, 69, 93, 113, 156, 179, 217, 232, 253, 280, 299
  collective, 255, 257
  digital, 245
  future-oriented, 113, 114, 117, 122, 125, 126
  strategic, 93, 256, 258, 265
  temporal, 113, 117
  theory, 8, 11, 12, 45–62, 255, 256, 271
Pragmatism, 8, 45–62

Prediction, 4, 93, 114, 117, 253, 262, 269, 270
Preparedness, 45, 216, 223–226
Present, 2, 28, 47–51, 67, 90, 114, 133, 153, 174, 222, 232, 254, 278, 302
Private organization, 223, 226
Process theory of organization (Hernes), 232, 245, 246
Productivity, 26, 101, 105, 159, 301, 309, 311, 312, 315
Prospective, 90, 92–101, 103, 133, 135, 137–138, 141, 143, 145–148
Public health, 215–219, 221–223, 227
Public-health organization, 219, 221, 226, 227
Public organization, 223, 224, 226, 238, 239, 247

R

Rationalization, 117, 259, 299, 300, 305
Rational planning, 26
Rational prognosis, 93, 95
Reconstruction, 33, 49, 50, 58, 62, 97, 158–160, 169n3, 227n1
Recursiveness, 69, 72–74, 116, 256, 257, 259, 262, 269, 279
Reflexive field regulation, 270
Reformation, 281, 283, 287
Renewal, 80, 104, 199, 207, 208, 210, 284, 293
Replication, 281, 283, 287
Resilience, 223, 226
Resilient organizing, 10, 193–210
Resolution, 195, 205, 209
Retrospective, 90, 96–101, 104, 135, 142, 239, 286

S

Scenario, 9, 36–38, 117, 153–168, 187, 223, 224, 226, 227
  See also Scenario planning
Scenario planning, 26, 33, 95, 100, 160, 185, 223
Schatzki, Theodore R., 6, 8, 47, 48, 51–53, 58–62
Schutz, Alfred, 69, 74, 97, 98, 100
Search paradox (Plato), 69, 75–78
Self-binding (Elster), 81
Semantics, 32–34, 36–40, 307
Semiconductor manufacturing, 11, 253–272
Semi-structured interview, 140, 235, 236, 259
Sense-making (theory), sensemaking, 3, 8, 34, 89, 90, 96–101, 104, 133–138, 141–143, 145–148, 154, 166, 174, 177–181, 184, 185, 263
Serendipity, 70, 76, 77
Signification, 257, 262, 267, 272
Simulation, 161, 223, 224
Situation, 29, 30, 32, 35, 52, 57, 60, 61, 69, 70, 93, 133, 134, 137, 138, 147, 153, 184, 221, 222, 236, 242, 264, 271, 293, 309, 310
Social action, 27, 60–62, 116
Social future, 45–47
Social order, 45, 47, 57, 59, 159, 224
Social system, 29, 31, 127n1, 218
Society of organizations (*Perrow*), 78, 224–227
Story Index (SIX), 133–148
Strategic planning, 3, 6, 26, 92–96, 98, 100, 101, 104, 114, 137, 142, 181

Strategizing
  inclusive, 9, 114, 121, 123–124, 126
  transparent, 114, 121–123
Strategy, 3, 26, 72, 92, 114, 133–148, 156, 181, 216, 232, 256, 284, 306
  blogging, 121, 122
  open, 9, 113–127
  as practice, 134
  theory, 89, 90, 93, 95, 96, 99, 100, 105
Structural coupling, 220
Structuration theory, 27, 31, 256, 299
Structure, 7, 27–32, 48, 52, 57, 73, 74, 79, 81, 117, 120, 126, 134, 135, 157, 167, 174, 179–181, 185, 218, 221, 225, 235, 240, 241, 247, 254–256, 268, 270–272, 283, 285, 289–293, 302, 303, 308, 313, 315
Subject, 25, 46, 48–50, 71, 73, 75, 81, 93, 135, 147, 175, 218, 239, 271, 289, 290, 293, 315
Supplementarity (Derrida), 69, 72, 73
Sustainability, 162, 179, 247, 248, 310
Synchronical emergence, 83
Systems theory, 7, 12

T

Taylor, Frederick W., 71, 309
Temporality, 26, 32, 39, 45–62, 68, 69, 73, 74, 89–92, 102–105, 117, 300, 307, 309

Time, 2, 6, 8, 10, 11, 26–29, 31–35, 37, 39, 40, 46–52, 54, 56–59, 61, 62, 62n1, 67–72, 77, 81, 83, 91, 94, 98, 101, 116–118, 120, 123, 127, 134, 139, 140, 142, 156, 160, 174–176, 178, 179, 181–185, 218, 221, 222, 225, 232, 234, 239, 246, 248, 256, 259, 263, 265, 267, 269, 277–288, 291, 295, 302, 303, 305, 306, 308, 309, 313, 315, 316n2
Transformation, 10, 35, 40, 46, 78, 141, 146, 231–248, 257, 302, 303, 309, 311, 312
Triangulation, 182–184

Uncertainty, 2, 30, 35, 37, 38, 68, 69, 71, 72, 75–78, 95, 98, 113–127, 137, 158, 161–163, 166–168, 173, 174, 231, 232, 257, 268, 270, 272, 299, 310

Vaara, Eero, 6, 123, 126, 134–136, 138, 147, 148, 177, 180, 278

Waldenfels, Bernhard, 78, 80
Weber, Max, 26
Weick, Karl E., 84n4, 94–101, 134, 135, 263, 268
World Health Organization (WHO), 10, 216–223

CPSIA information can be obtained
at www.ICGtesting.com
Printed in the USA
LVHW02*0238050718
582681LV00013B/171/P